Theatre 73

OVERLEAF: *Sir Noël Coward, 1899-1973*

Theatre 73

Plays
Players
Playwrights
Theatres
Opera
Ballet

Edited by **Sheridan Morley**

HUTCHINSON OF LONDON

Hutchinson & Co. (Publishers) Ltd
3 Fitzroy Square, London W1

London Melbourne Sydney Auckland
Wellington Johannesburg Cape Town
and agencies throughout the world

First published 1973

*Set in Monotype Scotch Roman and
printed in Great Britain by
William Clowes & Sons, Limited
London, Beccles and Colchester*

ISBN 0 09 117920 3

Contents

Sheridan Morley
Prologue 9
Ralph Richardson
Home Movies: The Young Olivier 12
Harold Hobson
Daubeny and the World Theatre Seasons 20
Felix Barker
Vivat! Vivat Chichester! 27
Jeremy Kingston
Year of the Flash: the West End 37
Nicholas de Jongh
Notes from the Underground 46
Trevor Nunn/David Jones
Writing on Sand: the Royal Shakespeare Company 54
Peter Buckley
Top Banana? A Year in the life of the Old Vic 68
B. A. Young
Love-Song for the Young Vic 80
Michael Green
The World Coarse Acting Championships 85
Philip Hope-Wallace
Opera: Perilous Freight in International Waters 89
Peter Williams
Ballet: Moving from Centre 96

Eric Shorter
Repertory Round-up 105
Clive Barnes
On and Off Broadway 115
Michael Rudman
Edinburgh's Traverse Now and Then 123
Charles Spencer
The Stagestruck Cecil Beaton 132
Christopher Matthew
Tuning the Instruments 140
Michael York
Tennessee Williams in Rehearsal 154
Peter Bull
To the Playhouse in an Omnibus 163

Reference Section 171

Index 195

Illustrations

The numbers below refer to the chapters; the photographs are keyed by letters within each chapter.

Frontispiece
Sir Noël Coward, 1899–1973

Between pages 56 *and* 57

1 Laurence Olivier and Ralph Richardson in *Q Planes* (1939)
2 World Theatre Seasons at the Aldwych
3a John Clements
3b Keith Michell
3c–k Productions at Chichester

Between pages 88 *and* 89

4a Her Majesty's: *Applause*
4b Mermaid and Cambridge: *Journey's End*
4c Palace: *Jesus Christ, Superstar*
4d Royal Court: *Not I*
4e Hampstead Theatre Club: *Po' Miss Julie*
4f Savoy: *Lloyd George Knew My Father*
4g Queen's: *Private Lives*
5a Roundhouse: Red Buddha Theatre
5b Open Space: *An Othello*
6a–c RSC Stratford
6d–f RSC Aldwych

Between pages 120 *and* 121

7a–b Directors of the National Theatre: Laurence Olivier, Peter Hall
7c–e Productions at the National
8a–c The Young Vic
9a–d Some examples of the Art of Coarse Acting
11a Northern Dance Theatre: *Cinderella*
11b Ballet Rambert: *There Was A Time*
11c Royal Ballet: *Poème de l'Extase*
12a Prospect Productions: *Richard III*
12b Birmingham Repertory: *Macbeth*
12c Nottingham Playhouse: *The Tempest*
12d Actor's Company: *The Three Arrows*
13a–c Broadway 1972–73

Between pages 152 *and* 153

14 Traverse Theatre, Edinburgh: Traverse Tattoo
15a–i Designs by Cecil Beaton
16 (a) Flora Robson, (b) Charles Laughton, (c) Joan Greenwood, and (d) Kathleen Harrison as RADA alumni
17a Michael York and Tennessee Williams at work on *Out Cry*
17b In rehearsal: Peter Glenville with Michael York
17c Tennessee Williams

Sheridan Morley

Prologue

It has been a year of farewells and new appointments in the British theatre; not only at the National, where after ten years Sir Laurence Olivier handed over the artistic directorship to Peter Hall amid murmurs of a possible National/RSC amalgamation, but also at Chichester where Sir John Clements handed over to Keith Michell and at the Aldwych where, again at the end of a decade, Sir Peter Daubeny announced the last in his series of World Theatre Seasons. Elsewhere, Oscar Lewenstein took over the direction of the Royal Court, Robin Phillips went to Greenwich, Michael Rudman to the Hampstead Theatre Club, Michael Simpson to the Rep in Birmingham, John Harrison to the Playhouse in Leeds and Michael Comdon to the Theatre Royal in Norwich, while it was announced that Michael Blakemore, Jonathan Miller, Harold Pinter, John Schlesinger and John Russell Brown would be joining Hall and Olivier in the administration of the National.

In a year when directors seemed to transfer as frequently if not as expensively as footballers, the theatre in general found itself embattled on two fronts: the arrival of VAT forced up ticket prices while the continuing advance of the property men, most notably in London's Piccadilly and Covent Garden districts, threatened the Shaftesbury and other older and more strategically situated playhouses.

On the brighter side, London acquired one new theatre (the New

London to be precise), playhouses were saved at least temporarily in Portsmouth and Ayr and new ones were announced for Lincoln, Derby, Manchester, Plymouth, Kidderminster and Birmingham. On the other hand Scarborough and Bradford lost theatres, Blackpool and Notting Hill Gate had theirs severely threatened and fire badly damaged the Close in Glasgow, while serious money troubles beset Sadler's Wells, the Old Vic in Bristol and the Playhouse in Oxford where sadly a reduction of Arts Council support forced Frank Hauser to announce the end of Meadow Players, the company he has run there for the past sixteen years.

It has been a harsh year in other ways too; within three winter months the theatre lost an actor, Max Adrian, an impresario, Hugh Beaumont, and a master of all stage trades, Sir Noël Coward – three men who had in common little more than their irreplaceability.

Within the profession Equity, having successfully negotiated a new £30 minimum wage, found itself scarred by internal dissent and TUC suspension after its failure to deregister under the Industrial Relations Act; in less overtly political areas, Michael Croft's Youth Theatre found itself at risk through the withdrawal of *Daily Mail* support, the RSC found itself involved in a bitter confrontation with John Arden and Margaretta D'Arcy over the rights of a playwright once his or her work is in rehearsal, and the New Theatre found itself renamed the Albery in honour of its one-time owner and manager Sir Bronson. The Royal Shakespeare at Stratford, Wyndham's in London and the Festival Theatre at Chichester got actual or promised facelifts and the National, now rising as a three-auditorium complex on the South Bank at a reputed cost of some nine million pounds, was 'topped out' by its chairman Lord Cottesloe in May. In the West End it was a year of huge commercial success and consequently little activity, while in the regions a renewal of touring interest was marked by Ian McKellen's creation of the Actors' Company.

It has, as all that might suggest, been a somewhat mixed – not to say confusing – year for the theatre but, as is perhaps indicated by the chapters which follow, by no means an altogether despondent one. In this the third annual of its series the aim is again to provide a kind of international theatrical balance sheet, a picture of the theatre past, present and future as it appears to a widely assorted group of critics, playwrights, actors and directors in each passing year. For this purpose I have taken 'theatre' to include plays, operas and ballets both conventional and experimental, commercial and subsidised; and in the eighteen chapters of THEATRE 73, all incidentally making their first appearance in print, will again be found comment, criticism, idealism, despair, optimism, fear, ambition, admiration, distaste and nostalgia . . . in short most of the elements that have constituted the theatre in the past twelve months and indeed the past twelve centuries.

For their help in the preparation of this book my thanks must go first as always to the contributors themselves, many of whom gave up valuable time stolen from other projects; I am additionally grateful to Peter Williams and Tom Sutcliffe for providing the reference material in their fields of ballet and opera, and to Ronald Bryden for collating the Royal Shakespeare Company material. For other information contained in the reference section I owe thanks to *The Stage* and *Plays and Players* as well as to Craig Macdonald at the National, Peter Harlock at the RSC and David Fairweather at Chichester. For photographs, I am especially grateful to Sir Cecil Beaton and Sir Peter Daubeny who generously placed their files at our disposal; further thanks for photographs are due to Lord Olivier, *Plays and Players*, Roger Clifford, Joan Hirst, the Royal Academy of Dramatic Art, *Dance and Dancers*, Ray Mander and Joe Mitchenson, Patricia York, the press offices of innumerable theatres up and down the land, and of course to the following photographers: Sophie Baker, Beata Bergstrom, Jise Buhs, Anthony Crickmay, Alan Cunliffe, Dominic, Estudo Faixat, Mark Gudgeon, Willoughby Gullachsen, John Haynes, Allan Hurst, Philip Ingram, Douglas Jeffery, Patrick Morin, Jacques Pourchot, Diane Tammes, John Timbers, Reg Wilson and Rosemary Winckley.

Finally, an acknowledgement to Wendy Garcin for her help in typing parts of the manuscript, and to Harold Harris and the production staff at Hutchinson for the infinite care taken in the publication of these annuals. One last word of thanks: to you, whoever you are, for continuing or maybe just starting to support what I and a reassuring number of others believe to be a worthwhile project.

Home Movies

As Laurence Olivier retires from solo leadership of the National Theatre he founded just ten years ago, one of his oldest friends and colleagues unreels some early memories.

There is room in many places in our society for the inclusion of such a person as a lord: it is fine to have a lord about the place; such a presence can embellish, decorate and light up, and there is no place more suitable for such illumination than the theatre, and there is no one better suited than Laurence Olivier to shine there. Laurence is admirable as the first lord of the theatricality and I am happy to have been alive at the time of his creation.

Everyone in the world knows that as an actor Olivier's range and power give him a clear claim to the title, but not everyone has known him as a man for as long as I have, and I know nothing of him that diminishes my affection. I have in mind a collection of snapshots, slides of memory and soundtracks of Laurence; time has not faded them, and I might show him in a sort of home movie, with a commentary.

My earliest shot is from the brow of a hill, looking down on a country road; it is a warm summer's day. A car approaches and it comes to a halt at the top of the hill; the engine is switched off. Now you can see what year it is, because the car is a new 1925 open Morris Cowley with a domed brass radiator. Three young people are sitting along the front and only seat; they are three members of the Birmingham Repertory Theatre, and they are on their way to Bridlington to play for a week in '*The Barber and the Cow*'. At the wheel is Ralph Richardson, next to him is his first wife, an honoured member of the Repertory Company, 'Muriel Hewitt' on the programme, but called 'Kit' by her husband and friends in the theatre. Next to her is Laurence Olivier, who has just joined the company, and he has been asked along by the Richardsons for the fun of the ride. In those days it was rather fun to travel by car; we actors usually went on the Sunday 'fish and actors' train. It had been a proud event for me to acquire this car, but now I was gravely concerned by it. I have said that the day was warm, but while climbing the hill the thermometer on the radiator read 'boiling'. But it seemed that my concern was not shared by the others, the two were talking and laughing their heads off. Now we see Richardson rising from the wheel, squeezing past the others and getting out of the car by the one door that it possessed.

Richardson approaches the radiator and listens for rumbles of boiling, and sniffs for evidence of steam. He is worried. The two sitting in the car now are silent; then Olivier gets out and stands by Richardson, he whispers something to him. 'What?' says Richardson. 'I wanted to ask you something – come over here for a moment, will you.' He takes a few steps. 'What the devil is it, Larry?' 'I wanted to ask you, Ralph, if you would mind if I called Muriel, Kit.'

This little event reveals one or two characteristics of the young Olivier which remain with him today. First, his youthful gaiety – I have never ceased to laugh my head off with him; next, the absence of dull care for mundane difficulty; then note the tact, the consideration for others, and, last, his warm and ever affectionate nature.

I have a couple of other memories with cars in them, which also have a moral, but I shall allow that to speak for itself. Laurence is driving my car, we are going down to Brighton, just the two of us, we are on the Croydon bypass; after the aerodrome there is a steep hill with a wicked crossroad at the bottom. Now, of course, there are plenty of traffic lights there, then there were none. Laurence approaches this crossroad at about fifty m.p.h., which is almost as much as the car will do, and he goes bang over it. I am absolutely horrified and cannot speak for a time. When I can, I say, 'Laurence, never, never, as long as I do live will I forgive you for that.' Laurence is cheerful: 'It is a well-known thing, Ralphie,' he says, 'that when you get to a point of danger, get over it as quick as you can.'

A while later, Laurence goes to New York; he makes a success and he brings back with him a smashing American car. I meet him in the West End after the show – he has the new car with him. 'I want you to try this', he says. I get in and go down Piccadilly. As we get to the Ritz, I open up a bit, we do eighty-five before Apsley House – sheer madness – immediately, Laurence says, 'I thought you'd like it, Ralphie.'

I have said that I am older than Laurence, and there was a time during the War when I was senior to him in rank. We were both in the Fleet Air Arm. When he joined in May, 1941 he was posted as a pilot to Worthy Down; I was not any longer flying but was on the Admiral's staff at Lea-on-Solent. One of my jobs there was to look after the parachute maintenance on all the shore-based air stations. After Laurence had been a few months at Worthy Down I was partly instrumental in his being appointed parachute officer for that station. It is the happy practice in the Naval service to allot extra jobs to officers; these do not add to toil or hours, but can be a refreshment. There are some invisible perquisites that go with these jobs, too long to explain them now but 'invisible' is not a bad description. It is, without deception, not necessary for everyone, at all times, precisely to know one's whereabouts.

After Lieutenant Olivier had been doing this work for a while I thought I should go and see how he was getting on. So the 'Flags' of Lea-on-Solent sent a signal to the Captain of Worthy Down to say I would be coming: my Admiral would not think it polite to send one of his staff without due notice. When I arrived I paid my respects to the Captain. He said, 'Yes, we had the signal and are expecting you, will you go over to the parachute section?' When I got to the building Laurence was there to meet me. I had not seen him for a while, not since his recent promotion to Lieutenant. He looked fine, his natural perquisite of good looks went well with his uniform. The uniform was perfect: it looked as if it had been worn long on arduous service but had kept its cut. The gold and wings on his sleeve had no distasteful glitter; only the shoes shone. The hair under his cap had a touch of debonair cheek, being perhaps a quarter of an inch longer than the dead correct. His manner was Naval, it was quiet, alert, businesslike, with the air of there being a joke somewhere around. His salute to me touched the exact point in meeting and greeting the representative of the Admiral and a very old friend. He said he would show me round.

A parachute store and workroom is an interesting place: part of it has to be high and some of it must be long; from the outside it can look like a square-towered church, inside, it is always quiet and it should be clean. Parachutes need to be unpacked from time to time and hung up; the big white silk canopies with white silken cords hang limp and motionless from rafters in the tower, taking their air – they are strangely beautiful. Later, they are taken down and laid upon the long, narrow green-topped tables, where the workers, in overalls, fold them, with the help of wooden spatulas, into their packs. This work must be very carefully and precisely done; it could take me the best part of an hour to pack one, for I had to learn how it was done. They must so lie in a small space as to be ready, at an instant, to spring out into life-giving embrace. Parachute packs are not at all times a comfortable piece of equipment to be harnessed to; they are awkward to move with, and after a time villainously hard to sit upon; still, there are certain times when it could be more uncomfortable to be without one. Lieutenant Olivier's parachute section was clean as well as being quiet, I found no fault at all; it surprised me that he had, in so short a time, got such a hang of the work, but what surprised me more was the way he had with the workers; he seemed to know each one, not only by rank but by name as well.

I have never been very bright at getting hold of people's names; I have a lack of concentration in that respect. I can even get the fictitious names of characters in the play I am in wrong; I have, in '*The School for Scandal*', called Charles Surface, Joseph. That was bad. In Naval service I had further difficulty, because everyone had a different rank as well. The ranks were numerous and complicated; a seaman was a seaman, and a Wren a Wren, but each had a different species. They wore symbols of distinction, but these were complicated and confusing. They did not confuse Laurence. As we went round he spoke to Wrens and seamen and sometimes introduced me, he never made a mistake, and in this case most were in overalls with no distinction showing.

In the first few moments of my visit I had made some remark about the fresh white paint on the ceiling above the rafters where the canopies hung. 'Oh, I'm glad you noticed that', said Laurence cheerfully, 'would you mind if I tell Hamble what you said? He's just over there – Hamble! This is Chief Petty Officer Hamble, he is in charge of everything here,' said Laurence, 'and I think,' he continued, 'that it was Leading Seaman Ramsay who got up there and painted it. Ramsay,' said Laurence to me regretfully, 'is off on leave today.' And so it went on. 'Yes, that is a nasty nick, but I expect Second Officer Wren Ashby can save the panel.' They might have been his cousins and his aunts.

Our little tour went smoothly, there didn't seem to be any problems, and soon I felt that I could leave; I said goodbye to Laurence; the Petty Officer who was in charge was by the door, we shook hands; I said, 'Good-bye, er – um.' 'Sir, Chief Petty Officer Hamble, sir,' he said. I left. Outside, I walked a little way down the asphalt path; stopped, and looked back at the building: 'Larry did that very well indeed,' I said to myself; I walked on. Then a thought crossed my mind: 'I wonder if he rehearsed it?'

On a fine Spring morning in 1944 Laurence and I walked briskly up a street in Glasgow. It was lunchtime, and in 1944 the chance of a decent meal was worth tracking down; we did not loiter. We had been rehearsing all the morning, and when lunchtime came I reminded Laurence that we had been sent cards from the Glasgow Arts Club. I had known it in former times, it was attractive, the members talented, and before the war the food had been good. 'Should we not go there now?' I asked: he did not reply, he put on his hat and we were off.

We had been released from Naval service to work for the 'Old Vic' and it was to prepare for our first season there that we had been rehearsing. It had been a long time since we had performed and I was worried on this score; I wondered if I had lost the 'knack' or whatever it was that I had worked with. I didn't know how Laurence felt about this, because I had not asked him. I never mentioned it to anyone, except to Lord Castlerosse. I don't know how it came about that I told him; I hardly knew him, but once in the darkest middle of the war, over a drink, the subject cropped up, and to him I blurted out my fear. He was a large, avuncular figure who sat up very late in a brown checked suit, with a long cigar. 'Not a hope, old man,' he said, 'once a jockey lays off, he never rides again.' This had not encouraged me at the time, and I had not forgotten what he had said. But now, with the granite sparkling in the sun, we went up the steep street; the nip in the air we were inhaling was champagne; I was elated. After about half a mile, we reached the club, on our left. We mounted the few steps before the portico and then we were stopped.

The Scots are a generous and hospitable people in their land; they have much to be admired and it is thought that some Celts possess a mystic, extra-sensory cognisance. Now, a very fine-looking Celt came suddenly out of the door of the club and stood on the steps before us. 'Hey,' he said majestically. 'Morning,' I said. 'Hey?' he seemed to ask. 'Richardson,' I said; this failed to interest. He fixed his gaze upon Laurence. 'But that man,' he said, 'I tell you that that man has the eyes of a poet.' Then he went past us and out into his world. We entered the Club, hung up our hats, went down the picture-lined hall to the luncheon room. I looked at the menu. My appetite was not working. I am sorry to say, I must confess, that I was miffed; I felt that I had been passed over. I thought of Lord Castlerosse. I was envious, and Envy is a curious sin; it belongs, of course, to the group of the seven and deadly sins. It is said that it can turn people green. But, then, there is this about Envy; it soon wears off, it seldom lasts long. It is unlike Lechery, in the same deadly group, of course; Lechery can wear off too – but it takes its time. Sloth and Wrath are best avoided – they can become chronic. My Envy did not take away my appetite for long; another and very useful sin – Gluttony – came along and restored it. The lunch was worth the walk and I enjoyed Laurence's company as freely as ever. I have never been envious of him again, and I am always pleased when he is praised; what follows is a single example of why that is so.

We were playing '*Uncle Vanya*', and the most beautiful lyric performance I have seen was given in it by Laurence's 'Astroff'. He had a great scene with Helena:

'Look there! That is a map of our country as it was fifty years ago. The green tints both dark and light represent forests. Half the map as you see is covered with it. Where the green is striped with red, the forests were inhabited by elk and wild goats.'

With these words, Astroff commences to describe, with the help of his map, the Russia he loves to the woman he loves. Laurence did this beautifully:

'You see I have dotted down here and there the various settlements, farms, caves and water mills.'

We know that Astroff is unable to tell Helena what he feels. He seems only concerned with the map, but as he continues his exposition of it, he becomes overwhelmingly conscious of her. He stops; the pencil he has been holding falls from his hand; there is a ripple of sound as it rolls down the board. There is silence. Then, Astroff looks long at Helena, with the eyes of a poet. For me, that moment was a knockout.

I do not know if Laurence would agree with me if I were to say that he owes a part of his success as an actor to the fact that he never took my advice. I have said that I am older than Laurence Olivier, and it often happens that a difference in age, marked when one is young, closes in significance as one gets older. Years ago, partly, perhaps, because I was older, Laurence would seek my advice; I hope I gave him my best thoughts; he always listened carefully, but he never did what I told him. For example, he asked me if he should play Macbeth in 1937. I said, 'By no means play this part: nobody can play it; and, besides, you are much too young.' He played it: he was quite good, but this early preparation enabled him to play the part magnificently in 1955. I played the part just once. If anyone had a nightmare, it was me.

Another time he asked me if he should make a film of *Hamlet.* I said, 'By no means make such a film; you can have a silent film of Shakespeare, but not a talkie.' This film is walking and talking to this day. Although he never took my advice about what he should do, he may have been guided by me, at least once, on how something should be done.

In 1935, Laurence wrote to me in New York, where I was playing Mercutio, to ask me if I had any advice to give him about the part, as he was going to undertake it in London. I wrote back to tell him that there was one thing that must be watched: I reminded him that after his death scene he would have a long spell of waiting in his room, and that one must watch how one refreshed oneself in that time, because much of the beauty of a performance could be marred by falling on one's face at the curtain call.

I saw Laurence last week: a few days before our meeting a mutual acquaintance had told me that he had spoken of retiring. When I saw Laurence, I was on tenterhooks; there was a chance that he might revert to his old habit of asking my advice; had he done so, my thought would be to say, 'By no means retire, Larry, it is a dull thing to do and, besides, you are much too young.' What would he have done then? Happily, the age gap has closed and he never asked me.

Daubeny and the World Theatre Seasons

In a year which saw the tenth and last in the present series of WTS at the Aldwych, the drama critic of The Sunday Times *assesses the theatrical importance of the seasons and their founder whose knighthood was announced after this article was written.*

Few people in the theatre have ever come upon their hour with happier punctuality than Peter Daubeny. He brought the world to London in his World Theatre Seasons at the Aldwych at a time when London, after years of enforced isolation, was uniquely ready to receive the world. During the war years London was cut off from all external influences, and was compelled to live on the derivatives of its own culture. But the desire for communication with the Continent increased as peace drew near, and rumours reached the ears of the British public of what the French theatre had achieved under the German Occupation. This desire was strengthened when London was able to see on the screen *Les Enfants du Paradis*, and thereby gain some sense of the exceptional talents of Jean-Louis Barrault, Arletty, and Pierre Brasseur.

Almost as soon as the war was over Britain, with unusual speed and enterprise, began, not to bring the Continent to England, but to take England to the Continent. The resumption of cultural relations started with the export, not the import trade. In July 1945 Laurence Olivier appeared at the Comédie Française in, amongst other things, *Richard III*. Soon after that stories of the great accomplishments of the contemporary French theatre penetrated into even comparatively unsophisticated parts of Britain. The first time I heard any new French play mentioned was not in the theatrical milieu of central London, but at an amateur Any Questions programme (then called a Brains Trust) in the Church Hall in Woodford Green in Essex in the late summer of 1945. One of the questions asked was at what theatrical presentation would members of the panel most have liked to be present. A young schoolmaster replied, 'The first performance of Jean-Paul Sartre's *Huis Clos*'. This was the first time I had heard of Sartre or his plays, and even a year later I was not sufficiently interested in them to go and see *Huis Clos* itself given at the Arts Theatre under the title of *Vicious Circle,* even though the chief part was played by Alec Guinness. But in more alert parts of the theatre interest in the French continued to grow. Yet it still was more a matter of the French wanting to see us rather than of our wanting to see the French. In 1948 Noël Coward appeared at the Théâtre Edouard VII in his own play, *Joyeux Chagrins* (*Present Laughter*). It was not until 1951, when Peter Daubeny had already been actively engaged as a theatrical producer for six years, that London vividly realised how much the French (and if the French, why not other countries too?) had to offer us.

We owe this realisation to Laurence Olivier. Olivier and Vivien Leigh were then in the middle of their dazzling and doomed tenure of the St. James's Theatre. Jean-Jacques Gautier had told me that when he was in Paris Olivier had been so impressed by the Comédie-Française that if ever he were called on to direct a National Theatre in England he would base it on the French model. (When I mentioned this to him later Olivier seemed both astounded and horrified). Nevertheless Olivier must have been deeply impressed by the French stage, for he decided to present a series of French plays at St. James's. For this purpose he brought over the Madeleine Renaud-Jean-Louis Barrault company, which presented André Gide's *Oedipe* and Armand Salacrou's *Les Nuits de la Colère.* Salacrou's *Les Nuits de la Colère* was a remarkable play about France and the Resistance, and was expected to make the big sensation of the season. It made a good impression, but the big sensation came from another production, Paul Claudel's *Partage de Midi,* in which for the first time we saw the incomparable Edwige Feuillère, whom some of us, in her poise and beauty, in her laughter and the suggestion of a cankered loveliness, instantly recognised and greeted as the greatest actress we had ever seen. It was this production which made the British public realise the importance of the theatres beyond our shores.

By this time Peter Daubeny was well established in the West End. He had begun in 1945 at the Piccadilly with a production of William Lipscomb's *The Gay Pavilion*, and followed it with an intriguing presentation of Frederick Lonsdale's *But for the Grace of God*. In 1949 he put on a controversial production of Noël Coward's *Fallen Angels*, with Hermione Baddeley and Hermione Gingold. Then in 1951 he took a giant step forward towards his destiny (though the general public did not realise it at the time) by presenting *The Gay Invalid*, adapted from Molière's *Le Malade imaginaire*, with Elizabeth Bergner and A. E. Matthews. *The Gay Invalid* was in English, but it was in origin French, and it marked Peter Daubeny's first association with that theatrical work of foreign lands which has secured for him an enduring fame, and extensively widened the horizons of the British public.

The Gay Invalid occupies a large place in Peter Daubeny's affections. Several times he has spoken movingly of the particular pleasure he took in including in his tenth and most ambitious World Theatre Season the Comédie Française's *Le Malade imaginaire*, with its echoes of his first adventurous foray into those foreign lands in which he became the signed and sealed standard-bearer of British culture. Yet it was not an outstanding popular success, and this fact may have for some years delayed the great work for which Daubeny was manifestly destined, by turning him down into byways which, however attractive they may have been, were not the great throughway of his life.

The Gay Invalid turned Daubeny's attention to Continental entertainment, but its relative failure made him think of other Continental things than the drama. His mind became occupied with dance, and to such effect that, had not his subsequent achievements obscured what he did in this part of his career, he would be known as one of the greatest dance impresarios the western world has ever known. It was Daubeny who introduced us to the miraculous zapateados of Antonio and the seductive grace of his partner Rosario. He discovered a whole series of Spanish dancers – Carmen Amaya, Pilar Lopez, Teresa and Luisillo – of the highest accomplishments; he brought to London the remarkable Katherine Dunham, the State dancers of Yugoslavia, Roland Petit's Ballets de Paris, the Grand Ballet of the Marquis de Cuevas, Martha Graham, to say nothing of Bulbul and the Oriental Ballet. When in June

1953 at the old Winter Garden he presented Sacha Guitry in *Ecoutez Bien, Messieurs*, this venture into straight foreign drama seemed rather the pleasant relaxation of a man whose enduring fame, which was already certain, lay in the land of dance, rather than the real beginning of that illustrious career with which Daubeny's name will always be associated in the history of the British stage. It is wrong to restrict Daubeny's celebrity to his World Theatre Seasons, astonishing as they are. They are the peak of his achievement, but even without them he still would be a man to be long remembered. The time, as I have tried to show, now was ripe, and the man was ready.

Yet I do not recall that *Ecoutez Bien, Messieurs* was a wild success. The real triumph, the breaking of box office records, the cheers and stampings and shouts and applause came two years later with the actress whom Sir Laurence Olivier had introduced to us in 1951: Edwige Feuillère. Peter Daubeny presented her to us at the Duke of York's in Alexandre Dumas fils' memorable defence of humdrum married life against courtesans, *La Dame aux Camélias*. This performance, with its romance and tears and pathos, and its stern morality, created one of the greatest sensations the post-war British theatre has experienced, and it was followed in 1960 at the Savoy by a three-week season of the Compagnie Marie Bell which was scarcely less remarkable. In Madame Bell's repertoire were *Phèdre, Britannicus*, and *Bérénice*. This season was perhaps the biggest risk that even Peter Daubeny has ever taken. Racine is supposed to be unplayable in Britain, where his unique talent for containing burning passion within a rigid and frigid frame is not appreciated. In addition to this, *Bérénice*, because of its lack of conflict, is said to be unplayable anywhere. Yet *Bérénice* came as an extraordinary illumination of the stage, and for the first time the British public was shown that Racine is a very great dramatist, one of the greatest in the whole world's literature. Jacques Dacqmine made unforgettably brilliant and sad the conflict between Imperial duty and private affection, the necessity to sacrifice love in order to save a world. Against it Marie Bell, in those supreme verses of deserted, blasted, and resigned love, exquisitely demonstrated that the victory at last goes to those who do not resist, but who in quietness, dignity, and peace accept the betrayal of all that is due to them, wringing from us, on behalf of Bérénice, the words with which the worthless lover at last pays tribute to his meek, discarded mistress in the conclusion of Jules Renard's *Le Plaisir de rompre*: 'Il vous reste le beau rôle.'

It may be thought that I have dwelt at undue length and out of proportion with Madame Feuillère and Madame Bell, but this, in my opinion, is not so. They are the most glorious of the many treasures that Mr Daubeny has brought us. It might paradoxically be said, without any belittlement of what came later, that the highest achievements of the World Theatre Seasons were recorded before the World Theatre Seasons started.

But in themselves, as has often been recognised and said, with every possible accent of praise and gratitude, they have placed before us the theatrical splendors of the world, if not from China to Peru, at least from Belgium to Japan. Czechoslovakia, France, Germany, the United States, Greece, Ireland, Israel, Italy, Belgium, Japan, Spain, Poland, Russia, Sweden have sent us their best companies, in their best productions These exerted on our native stage a considerable influence. The German production of *The Captain of Kopenick* was extremely bad and lumbering, but it is generally thought (though not by Kenneth Tynan, who denied the suggestion in a letter written from the National Theatre to *Plays and Players* in May 1973) that it was the inspiration of the National Theatre's much finer presentation of the same play, with Paul Scofield in the principal part; and Ingmar Bergman's obstetrical *Hedda Gabler* undoubtedly led to Maggie Smith's stomach-pawing performance under the same director for the National, a performance which I thought worthy of far greater praise than it actually received. There can, I think, be no question that it was Jacques Charon's direction of Feydeau's *Un Fil à la patte* in the opening 1964 season which led to John Mortimer's *Une Puce à l'oreille*, one of the National's greatest successes.

There are three characteristics which mark Mr Daubeny out amongst theatre people. First he is a man of enormous courage, and tireless negotiating qualities. Dogged by ill-health that would have daunted even the stoutest heart, there is no discomfort he will not undertake, no task too hard for him to tackle. He is equally skilful at circumventing the endless obstacles placed as a matter of course in the way of foreign impresarios by the Russians, as he is at successfully flattering the preposterous pride of the Comédie

Française. In the ten or fifteen years during which he has brought foreign companies to London, Peter Daubeny has, at the cost of tremendous nervous and physical strain, overcome problems that would have broken many a man of stronger physique but lesser spirit.

The second characteristic is his loyalty. He is not the man to throw anyone over because he fails. The Germans and the Poles have grossly disappointed audiences, but Mr Daubeny has stood by them with a steadfastness which even those who think it mistaken cannot but admire.

Thirdly is his flair. Certain companies he has brought over, such as the Comédie Française, the Noh company from Japan, and Jean-Louis Barrault's Théâtre de France, which because of their reputation, their known skill, and the already established public interest in them, were sure of resounding and continuing triumph and popularity. To have brought them to London, is, because of their world-wide celebrity, one of Mr Daubeny's highest achievements. But to choose them did not test Mr Daubeny's personal taste. These were companies that in a sense chose themselves. They would have been put on even the most casual theatregoer's list of the things he wanted to see.

But there are five companies – two from Italy, one from Spain, and two from Czechoslovakia – that it is unlikely we should ever have heard of had not Peter Daubeny, relying on his own personal flair, put them into his World Theatre Seasons. In this he has widened our horizons, he has added to our comprehension of the wonders of the world. The first, from Italy, came in the opening 1964 Season, and was deservedly invited back for the tenth Season in 1973. It was an unpretentious show, none of your drum-beating, prestige-seeking spectaculars, but it had an ingratiating charm, a bubbling innocence that were entirely captivating. In the matter of sheer simplistic attractiveness Peppino de Filippo's Italian Theatre's *Metamorphoses of a Wandering Minstrel* has never been surpassed. The second Season gave us valuable things, such as the Théâtre de France's *Oh Les Beaux Jours*, and the Compagnia dei Giovanni's *La Bugiarda*, as well as a disastrous *Three Sisters* from the Actors' Theatre Studio; but nothing so memorable, so original as the Peppino de Filippo company.

The third and fourth Seasons kept up a high average, but so far as I could see they did not produce anything which we could take as evidence of Mr Daubeny's extraordinary flair in the realm of the foreign theatre. The fifth, however, in 1968 showed him in his very best form. Who before Mr Daubeny in this country had heard of the clown Fialka? Actually at the first night of this truly remarkable man the theatre was half empty. Very few critics had taken the trouble to see him. But those who did immediately recognised him as a clown of the first order. Then a fortnight later came one of Mr Daubeny's most astonishing revelations. This was the Rome Stabile Theatre's production of two short plays. The first, *Naples by Night*, was of little consequence. But the second, *Naples By Day*, was superb. The audience was comparatively sparse, and even those who were there hardly seemed to realise the enormous privilege they were enjoying. It was merely a melodrama; the anecdote is of no importance. What was striking, what stands out from everything else that Daubeny has done, was the poignancy of the silhouette of an orchestra of blind musicians on the terrace of a shabby Neapolitan cafè, backed by a radiant Neapolitan sky. This was unforgettable, and it was caviare to the general. Nevertheless it remains Daubeny's greatest achievement.

As a companion piece to Fialka we have had, in the sixth Season, also from Czechoslovakia, a very fine *Three Sisters*, in which the three sisters were, in Arnold's phrase, like great birds beating their luminous wings in the void in vain; and in the ninth the Nuria Espert company from Spain in Lorca's *Yerma*, an exhibition of controlled and passionate eroticism from which the English theatre, with its crude belief that a nude body is the summit of daring, surely has much to learn. But whether it is capable of learning a lesson so esoteric remains to be seen. If it proves incompetent to do this, we can hardly blame Mr Daubeny.

Vivat! Vivat Chichester!

As Keith Michell succeeds John Clements (who in turn succeeded Laurence Olivier) as director of the Festival, the drama critic of the London Evening News *looks back over a dozen years at the actors theatre in Sussex.*

Virtually the first words spoken from the stage at Chichester were delivered by the man who is now going to have the last word. Keith Michell, who played in *The Chances*, the opening production, has been appointed the theatre's Director. He returns to the theatre where twelve years ago he swaggered on ('by kind permission of the Rank Organisation') as Don John, a Spanish adventurer with black moustachios. It was a lively performance by an actor who, at thirty-four, was well established, but by no means a big international name.

As he has no administrative experience, Mr Michell must be keen to add another facet to his versatility as a performer. And, since he got the job over several more likely contenders, the board of the Chichester Festival Theatre obviously believe his personality is especially well fitted to his new role. A Director of Chichester has to combine ability and flair as a man of the theatre with plenty of social charm. Probably more important than dazzling experiment is good horse-sense in judging public taste.

Mr Michell has a lot to live up to. He succeeds John Clements who followed Laurence Olivier, and is taking over a theatre which is now very much part of the summer scene. It appears to be buoyantly successful, but no 'festival theatre', which positively has to draw people to plays scheduled for a set run, can afford to be anything but constantly interesting. If London yawns or Sussex is alienated, a rot could quickly set in.

As he plans his 1974 season, Mr Michell must be looking back over the last decade in an attempt to divine what has contributed to Chichester's success. Will he find in the plays, actors, and style of productions in the past a formula for the future? Will he dare to change that formula or even want to?

In retrospect, Chichester's success seems deceptively easy. How could it fail? You simply find a pleasant park on the edge of a fine old cathedral city sixty miles from London, and you build a theatre. You break away from tradition and get an edge on Stratford-on-Avon – and indeed all Europe – by making it hexagonal and by banishing the proscenium arch in favour of an open stage.

You have, do you not, a limitless choice of plays, ancient and modern? Actors of note beat a path to your stage door. With a unanimous shout of 'Wonderful!' the public fills every one of your seats for every performance. Initiative is rewarded by instant success.

But, of course, things aren't like that. Few projects could have been more hazardous than the undertaking pioneered in 1960 by Mr Leslie Evershed-Martin, a former mayor of Chichester. How a TV programme first gave him the idea, and how he brought it to fulfilment three and a half years later, is already part of theatre legend. There were so many set-backs, dire prophecies, and problems of raising money, that it makes one tired just to read about them in Mr Evershed-Martin's book, aptly titled *The Impossible Theatre*.

The next stage in the game of creating a theatre which no one knew was wanted until it was there involved finding the right architects. They had to have knowledge and imagination, and somehow work within a budget of £110,000. That is a small sum – less than the cost of a modest film – but it was still the very devil to raise from private subscriptions. The firm which answered the call, Powell, Moya and Stevens, got just about everything right except the acoustics, a technical problem that has always been a headache for theatre architects. But that, too, was put right after a time.

Coming on it suddenly for the first time twelve years ago, it seemed to me that the parentage of the Chichester Festival Theatre was not in doubt. After a robust liaison with Billy Smart's Circus, Shakespeare's Globe had pupped in Oaklands Park. In an expanse of green, and under a cluster of great elms, stood a white circular building the like of which none of us had seen anywhere in Europe up to that time.

Wide-eyed enchantment at the setting took a bit of a knock when we went inside. The auditorium looked so very severe, and, until the stage lights went up, unduly gloomy. The audience of nearly 1,400 were seated on rising tiers on three sides of the bare open stage. This was a stadium, not a theatre. On that first night, until a boy in shirtsleeves took down a surrounding rope, we were looking at a boxing ring. Neither baroque cupids nor goddesses of plenty carrying gilded cornucopia were above our heads. Instead, there was a lattice-work of thin steel cables, and they cracked with the ominous percussion of pistols as the modern concrete theatre expanded or contracted. But magic quickly reasserted itself as *The Chances*, a Restoration comedy, got away to a flounce of fine plumage, and by the evening's end my feeling was one of dazed elation.

Was Chichester well placed for such an enterprise? Certainly it is far enough away from London to make a visit a bit of an adventure, but not too distant to create isolation. The promoters must have been encouraged by the nearness of Southampton, Brighton, and Portsmouth, though they can hardly have visualised that before long not only royalty but American culture vultures would be landing by helicopter a few yards from the entrance. But basically, they reckoned, the new theatre would have to draw on the surrounding population of 45,000, a figure doubled in the summer by holiday-makers. All this seemed promising, but against this they had to set the stern reminder that England – and especially semi-rural England – is not exactly ravenous for drama. Unlike music, the theatre does not automatically command devotees of the kind who flock to Glyndebourne.

It didn't happen, but in the wrong hands or with mediocre direction, Chichester's phenomenally successful theatre could easily have been a white elephant, and now be used for Bingo or auctions of livestock. Even today, as I think Mr Michell will find out, a careful course has to be steered. During a particularly recondite passage in T. S. Eliot's *The Cocktail Party* (something about 'disillusion can in itself become illusion') I couldn't help wondering if there wouldn't be some local bewilderment. I had a sudden wild vision of the Cowdray polo set roaring up in the belief that anything to do with cocktails was just their sort of chukka. But fortunately the fate of Chichester has not been in the hands of thin-lipped advocates of the Higher Drama. In its first director, Laurence Olivier, the theatre had a combination of brilliant actor, inspired producer, and cunning showman. His successor, John Clements who ran the theatre with ever increasing success for eight years, is another shrewd man of the theatre with an understanding of public taste. For every *Cocktail Party* there has been a compensating *Farmer's Wife*. As a result, in the first ten years, thirty-six plays were performed by resident companies and to steadily increasing audiences. The seasons have become longer, the number of plays increased from three to four, and, advance bookings are five times what they once were.

From the start, all the plays were infused with the sort of excitement that Olivier gives to everything he touches. It was a particularly happy chance that the theatre was conceived at the exact moment when he was in a position to become its director. The even greater responsibility of the National Theatre lay a year or so ahead, and he needed just such a nursery as Chichester offered. He was also at a point in his career when he required this sort of challenge. As an actor, he had few peaks to scale; as a director, his touch was certain; but as an actor-manager, co-ordinator, planner, and artistic director of a municipal theatre he had something new to get his teeth into. 'It seemed to me exactly what the dear, kind doctor had ordered,' he said as he set about his first production on the kind of open stage of which his friend, Tyrone Guthrie, was so passionate an advocate.

With Olivier at the helm, the auspices were favourable. But between great expectations and their realisation lay one problem. The plays. What was wanted for this modern equivalent of Shakespeare's Globe? What would suit the multi-level stage without a proscenium or wings and surrounded on three sides by the audience? In his determination to avoid the obvious solution of one-Shakespeare-one-Restoration-one-Shaw, the new director did much ploughing through volumes of World Drama. Friends were canvassed. Dozens of ideas were toyed with and discarded before *The Chances*, was unearthed in the British Museum. But even while one applauded this capricious choice for an opening, with which Olivier enjoyed a director's field-day, there were misgivings. I carried away from the first night one particular worry that was not to be dispelled through the whole of the first season. The possibilities of the arena stage were obvious, but so were its disadvantages. An inordinate amount of movement seemed demanded of the actors. Two people in simple conversation would deliver their lines while taking a little circular walk. On their own, they tended to go off on short unnecessary jaunts to the limits of the stage. One was reminded of the cinema's efforts to fill the whole screen in the early days of Cinemascope.

To John Dexter must go the credit for solving this problem. He did so by ignoring it. In his coolly marshalled *St Joan* (1963), he put an end to excessive rushing about. Actors no longer roamed the plains simply because they felt they must enjoy their new freedom or make certain that the audience on all sides got a fair share of their full-face. People were grouped statically, yet the eye was never bored. The myth of movement was exploded, and has never had to be recalled at Chichester.

Another early trouble was the technical one of audibility. As soon as voices were raised above a certain pitch, speech became blurred. A turned back (inevitable with the audience on three sides of the stage) could mean virtual unintelligibility. Though fitted with acoustic reflectors and absorbents, the spider's web of overhead girders seems to have been the cause. Only with the insertion of 'ears' or slanted flats on either side of the stage was this particular trouble cured or, anyway, vastly lessened.

With the feeling that an open stage demanded movement and vocal projection went another natural idea that crowds and pageantry were also essential. But this myth was one that Olivier was determined to banish as soon as possible. He believed in the arena stage's versatility, and with *Uncle Vanya* set out to show that it was suitable for a play of an entirely different style, period and convention.

From our arena seats we looked down like gods on the fickle mortals – Chekhov's rural Russians at the turn of the century – as if on creatures from a different planet. These civilised yet tragicomedy figures of provincial life at first looked curiously remote. But a wonderfully sensitive production focussed attention on them so closely that soon we were sharing the emotions of Olivier's whimsical, very human Astrov, Michael Redgrave's nihilistic Uncle Vanya and the love-starved Sonya of Joan Plowright. Some impact may have been lost, some subtleties may have scurried away into dark corners; but the case was proved. Really well done, a small-scale naturalistic play was possible at Chichester. That triumph was all the more remarkable because, as we learnt long afterwards, the whole cast approached the first night in despair after a disastrous dress rehearsal. Never in his life, Olivier said, was he more certain of failure. So great was the play's success that it was revived at Chichester the following season, and then went into the repertory of the National at the Old Vic.

But this was not the scale of drama for which the theatre was best suited. Chichester cried out for intelligent pageantry, and nearly every season has provided a big spectacle. One of the greatest triumphs came with *The Royal Hunt of the Sun* (1964) in which Peter Shaffer presented a subtle, philosophical study of religious conflict within an elaborate framework. Chichester's Wooden-O had to hold the vasty fields of Peru and the snow-capped Andes for the story of how Pizarro's small company of Spaniards overcame a nation of ten millions. In the scene when the Incas crowd round their murdered god-king in masks of beaten gold, and exhort him to rise from the dead, Michael Annals, the designer, gave us one of the most visually exciting moments in the contemporary theatre.

A more unexpected success for the open stage was *Trelawny of the 'Wells'* (1965), a Victorian social comedy that might seem least suited to it. A big scene change – from the Telfers' lodgings in Clerkenwell to the splendour of the Gowers' house in Cavendish Square – had to be made without a drop curtain and in full view of the audience. Alan Tagg, the scenic designer, the producer Desmond O'Donovan, and Motley carved a virtue out of necessity. With the aid of shirt-sleeved Victorian footmen who moved with unhurried dignity, tables and chairs were removed, a carpet rolled up and another laid, a chandelier lowered, the scenery transformed. One group of actors was replaced by another, and the operation was carried out with a discipline that held the audience mesmerised. It was far more than a scenic stunt. The transformation had a psychological rightness. We were seeing in tangible form the transition which Rose had to make from her theatrical life to the stuffy conventions of high society.

John Arden provided two spectacles for the early years – *The Workhouse Donkey* (1963) and *Armstrong's Last Goodnight* (1965). The first was a colourful satire on local government corruption in Yorkshire with Frank Finlay and over sixty characters. But light-hearted pantomime slithered into incomprehensible sermon. With *Armstrong*, starring Albert Finney, we were plunged into even deeper waters. Here was a three and a half hour epic in broad Scots (with a little French and Latin for good measure) requiring detailed knowledge of clan warfare in the Lowlands during the early sixteenth century. There were forty faultless performances and the whole thing had a poetic grandeur. But when Mr Arden insisted that his play was really an allegory about the modern Congo, I, for one, refused to become further involved. A workhouse donkey of a critic can take on only so much!

When Danny Kaye disappointed Chichester by going to perform to troops in Israel instead of appearing in Goldoni's *A Servant of Two Masters*, the desperate dilemma of a replacement produced *An Italian Straw Hat* (1967). This old French farce lent itself to a tumultuous, highly flavoured production. Peter Coe, the director, also returned to put on three further pageants, *The Skin of Our Teeth* (1968) with Millicent Martin, Brecht's *The Caucasian Chalk Circle* (1969) with Topol (the only major foreign star who has been to Chichester), and *Peer Gynt* (1970). All were a success except Ibsen's untidy masterpiece which didn't come off despite an ingenious presentation.

Fortunately 1970 had a second pageant up its sleeve in the form of *Vivat! Vivat Regina!* Though not quite the towering play for which we had hoped from Robert Bolt after *A Man for All Seasons*, it proved to be the best account yet written of the conflict between Mary Queen of Scots and her English cousin. It was also the occasion for an outstanding performance by Eileen Atkins as Queen Elizabeth.

Chichester has given us so much pleasure each summer with varied plays and visiting stars that you hardly notice one thing which is missing – continuity. No particular *purpose* seems to govern the choice of programmes. There is no individual 'house-style' for productions. The companies differ every season, though there has been the recurring pleasure of seeing such excellent actors as Michael Aldridge, Bill Fraser, and Hubert Gregg over the years.

Perhaps what one misses most is a 'festival' dramatist, a writer to provide the kind of continuity that Shaw gave to the Malvern Festival before the war and T. S. Eliot supplied for Edinburgh. But of living British playwrights only three have had more than one play at Chichester – Arden, Ustinov, and Shaffer (whose second was that hilarious 'sport', *Black Comedy*). Any of these might have been ideal. So might Robert Bolt. Were they sufficiently encouraged, or did Olivier and Clements fear that, if they virtually commissioned plays, they might be under a moral obligation to produce something they didn't like? Will Keith Michell be more daring?

The most splendid possibility of all would have been Peter Ustinov. He always has half a dozen ideas for plays turning over in his volatile mind, and, if prodded into actually getting them down on paper, could be as prolific as Shaw. The sort of thing we could hope for was shown by *The Unknown Soldier and his Wife*, the outstanding new play of the 1968 season. A few months before, Ustinov, who said he wanted his writing to catch up with his acting, announced that in future he would not act in his own plays. It was, of course, quite in character that hardly was the ink dry on this self-denying ordinance, than he accepted the invitation to direct his play at Chichester – and appear in it as well. Curiously – and perhaps it is an inverted compliment to Chichester – this satiric anti-war pageant, presented with such whirlwind success on the open stage, proved far less effective when revived in London early in 1973.

If John Clements, apparently, did little to nurture playwrights, his other achievements were outstanding. When it became clear in 1966 that Olivier could no longer continue to ride the tandem of Chichester and the National Theatre, he resigned and hailed his successor 'as the best man in the country for the job'. It sounded a fulsome, extravagant compliment, but we very soon saw that it was true. Olivier's lustre had been necessary to get Chichester away to a flying start; it was Clement's task to consolidate, improve, and keep the spirit of excitement alive. This he did by being, as Olivier put it, 'more *shrewdly* adventurous than myself'. Where his predecessor would try to be too clever, and therefore have one box office failure out of three, Clements was more consistently successful in his eight years as director.

What was the key to his success? When the tenth season opened with *The Rivals* in 1971, I remember thinking that here was an example of a play that many directors would have turned down because Sheridan is – well, a bit obvious. Obvious, too, for Clements to choose it because he could play Sir Anthony Absolute, a part which he had acted well in the past. But occasionally it is a positive virtue to put on something good simply because it *is* good, rather than because it is audacious and original. Clements never scrambled after effect. His choice of plays was catholic – in his last season, for instance, plays by Chekhov, Pinero and Anouilh and a musical by Ustinov – but never way-out. You did not find him in breathless pursuit of the latest trend, or wooing the newest wonder boy with an Arts Council bursary for playwriting. His critics may have regarded him as too determined a middlebrow, and seen this as the reason why he did not put on any plays by Pinter, Osborne, Mercer, Wesker, Bond or other darlings of the Royal Court school. Lindsay Anderson was the only director from the same severely cerebral world to come to Chichester during the Clements regime – and that was eight years ago.

I think Clements's decision was governed by certain definite values, and a sound knowledge of what will and will not go at the theatre in Sussex. While he was not prepared to treat his Home Counties audience with excessive deference, he certainly had no inclination to regard their wishes with contempt. First and foremost, Clements is an actor, and was concerned with maintaining an actor's theatre. For *Dear Antoine* (1971) he assembled the most brilliant company that I can recall on any English stage outside an All-Star Matinée. Anouilh's dazzling (and not exactly simple) play offers at least eight superb parts and under Robin Phillips's direction, they were taken by Edith Evans, Joyce Redman, Renée Asherson, Jane Baxter, Michael Aldridge, Hubert Gregg, Clive Swift and Sir John Clements himself. Miss Redman gave the performance of her career, and every other member of the cast was perfect. This was the kind of acting feast only possible when famous players are prepared to give up better paid jobs to come to a theatre where they know they are going to enjoy themselves.

Actors will tell you that they find the atmosphere of Chichester irresistible. They take cottages and visit country pubs. They learn their lines on the beach and have early read-throughs on the grass behind the theatre. In their eyes are views of the Downs, the estuary at Bosham, the spire of the cathedral. In these tranquil surroundings have been created some of the really great performances of the decade. At random, I pick Irene Worth in *Heartbreak House*, Maggie Smith in *The Country Wife*, Joan Plowright in *St Joan*, Laurence Olivier in *Uncle Vanya*, Robert Stephens in *The Royal Hunt of the Sun*. There are many others.

As far as I know, Chichester has no formal policy, and this will give Mr Michell an opportunity to put his personal stamp on the theatre. There is no stern declaration of intentions. If anyone bothered to assess the reason for the benign, easy-going, yet always highly professional standards, it would probably be that a summer evening in Sussex calls for a special kind of entertainment. This is, after all, a *festival* theatre. The players should contrive to keep their audiences in holiday mood. When Margaret Rutherford arrived at her dressing room to put on her costume for *The Clandestine Marriage* a few years ago, she did so remembering that only recently she had taken off her bathing costume and come out of the sea at Littlehampton. Ustinov came into the theatre from the tennis courts, and Topol from a day's outing with his young family on the beach at West Wittering. They played to an audience who also felt the sand between their toes. This has nothing to do with the Art of the Theatre. It has everything to do with the Theatre of Enjoyment.

The Year of the Flash

The playwright and drama critic of Punch, *whose comedy* Signs of the Times *opened at the Vaudeville in June, surveys the West End.*

The period under review has been dominated by long-runners. There are thirty-four major London theatres; take away the four subsidised theatres (Aldwych, National, Royal Court, Mermaid) and of the remaining thirty there are fifteen where the show in occupation at the start of the period was still playing there twelve months later. As if this weren't enough, in five of the theatres that did witness a change it was a case of one long-runner finally coming to an end (with *The Secretary Bird* and *There's a Girl in my Soup* after runs of four and six years) and its replacement by a new play that has remained there ever since.

Although new plays in London are not yet forced to fit into the New York categories of Instant Smash Hit or Instant Dodo, plays that do become a commercial success tend nowadays to remain a success longer. London's theatres have become a major tourist attraction and the tourist season now extends from May to November. The Christmas outing season lasts through December and January. Given our now usual mild and fogless February and March, a show that might in former days have petered out by April – leaving the theatre available for a successor – will now just scrape on until May when it can gather up the tourists again, last a further six months and maybe repeat the circuit yet again.

Since 1895, when *Charley's Aunt* became the first play to complete 1,000 performances, 53 other shows have passed that magic number. Only 32 managed it in the first sixty years of this century: no fewer than 21 have done it in the twelve years since.

The year opened with Edward Albee's *All Over* at the Aldwych and Tom Stoppard's *Jumpers* at the National, a pair of intelligent, literate and witty plays it was good to welcome at a time when the Goths of the Fringe were thumping ever more insistently on the gates. Incredibly, these were the only new plays of the year to provide audiences with wit to enjoy during the performance and thought to provoke the mind afterwards. Revivals provided some satisfaction and so did – not here my province – the Fringe. Beckett's brief masterpiece *Not I* eventually supplied the thought, and new plays by E. A. Whitehead, Osborne and Arden claimed their adherents. It should be noted that none of these was presented by a 'commercial' management.

Whitehead's *Alpha Beta* at the Royal Court brought both Albert Finney and Rachel Roberts back to the London theatre after absences of several years. This harsh exposure of a hate-filled marriage fulfilled much of the promise of *The Foursome.* If it was marred by what seemed like excessive rancour and bone-headedness from the wife the author's prime target was the working-class morality that had brain-washed her to expect marriage to be an everlasting union between swine and martyr. Such domestic ferocity is a rare subject in English plays. The performances were powerful and intelligent and Anthony Page's direction showed the surging and ebbing crisis of the marriage and the tenderness of the brief truces. Albert Finney's production company Memorial Enterprises transferred the play to the West End for a twelve week run.

Meanwhile two curious plays had come and gone. David Ambrose's *Siege* (presented by Michael Codron) daydreamed about a London in which the love revolutionaries had taken over society. The setting was a St James's club with eighty-one year old Stanley Holloway bringing on the brandy. There were verbal felicities here and, dream or not, more credibility than in Thomas Muschamp's *The Beheading* (Julie Daugherty Prods) concerned with clerical hanky-panky on some Mediterranean isle. I couldn't believe in this one at all. The two plays provided not much more than confirmation that Alastair Sim makes an unflappable Prime Minister and John Moffatt an urbane bishop.

Against the prevailing trend of long-runners the Globe Theatre enjoyed, if that's the word, five First Nights in eight months. The first was *Notes on a Love Affair* (Marvin Liebman and David Fasken). I am favourably disposed towards plays about writing a play (or novels about writing a novel or a Steinberg drawing of a hand drawing a Steinberg drawing) but the style is tricky to work in and Frank Marcus did not provide the multitude of surprises needed to keep an audience intrigued during the creative author bits. The evening's delight was Julia Foster's gauche little victim, expressing uncertainty and pluck through quick, throwaway gestures and bright smiles arriving just too late to do their social trick.

After this came *Parent's Day* (presented by John Gale) which lasted a month. The musical *Popkiss* followed, of which more later.

John Gale brought two more plays to London in the same month. One is happy for one's colleagues when their business ventures succeed. (I should mention that at the time of writing a play of mine is being steered towards London under Mr Gale's wing.) But it is a disconcerting discovery that a sex comedy as thin as *The Mating Game* can pack audiences in for a year, and that the English theatregoer's fondness for plays concerning quaint behaviour among the gentry can give a long run to such an off-form William Douglas Home as *Lloyd George Knew My Father*. Of course the first enjoyed the star presence of Terry Scott and the second the presence of Dame Peggy Ashcroft and Sir Ralph Richardson. Some critics (a euphemism for Harold Hobson) saw in Mr Home's play a distillation of passion that fell short, one gathered, by only a small chalk from such masterworks as *Phèdre* and *Partage de Midi*. The last-minute decision of a stubborn old general's stubborn old wife not to 'do herself in' after all – because her husband would so miss her if she did – struck me as a fearful dramatic cheat. Mr Home might have devised a less banal explanation to advantage. But then, why should he bother if the coach parties nonetheless come rolling up and rolling up!

A play that ought to have failed and did was *I, Claudius* (Michael White plus Woodfall Ltd). David Warner's hunched and gentle emperor made one regret the play that might have been written around him; Tony Richardson's direction was dreadful.

Earlier in the year David Warner had made a welcome return to the stage (at the Hampstead Theatre Club) as a flashing MP in

The Great Exhibition. David Hare's comedy of manners – mostly bad manners – covered the familiar territory of ailing marriage, hopes grown sour and the Aldermaston marcher come to a last halt, but it showed a shrewd understanding of eccentric character and an alert ear for the fatuities of speech. Critics who had much admired *Slag* professed themselves disappointed; I was less impressed with Mr Hare's first play and enjoyed the second more.

I can discern no coherent policy behind the Hampstead Theatre's production: revivals of early David Mercer, wartime Rattigan, a loony (though Pulitzer Prize-winning) man-in-the-moony hunk of New York schmaltz, the first interesting Tennessee Williams for a decade, Herb Greer's unjustly scorned version of Strindberg, *Po' Miss Julie.* What possible pattern links such diverse offerings? Only the artistic director's decision that they were worth putting on – and four of the six I've mentioned were worth a visit – and his realisation that no West End theatre would risk them.

I suppose one can imagine one or two of them popping up at the Royal Court (another theatre where the artistic policy is sometimes hard to pin down) or the Mermaid (which never had one for us to pin). After a laboured attempt at a turgid Camus, Sir Bernard Miles's theatre revived *The Caretaker.* Leonard Rossiter's pathetically mean-minded tramp, whining with the accents of an ancient actor down on his luck, and Jeremy Kemp's placid, matter-of-fact Aston showed that Pinter's play remains, after twelve years, mysterious, alarming and enthralling. The terror conveyed in Aston's long hospital speech is still more heart-clutching than any of the callous, nose-rubbing demonstrations of *Lay-By*, *Blow Job* and their like.

After this admirable beginning the Mermaid brought down from Manchester's University Theatre (by arrangement with Eddie Kulukundis and Richard Pilbrow) a superb production of *Journey's End.* Eric Thompson – whose programme entry omitted any reference to magic roundabouts – proved himself at his first attempt an accomplished director. The evident care taken with the casting (Peter Egan as the gaunt, haunted Stanhope, James Maxwell's calming ex-schoolmaster Osborne), such details as sound-effects that followed the flight of shells across the trenches, all these contributed to the telling conviction of the production. It later went on to the Cambridge Theatre, hardly the best place for it. In the relative intimacy of the Mermaid the play's effect was shattering. Even radical old *Time Out* enthused.

As the unfitting cap to these achievements the Mermaid put on *Cowardy Custard*, a programme of songs and sketches by the late Sir Noël Coward, which was all very well if you like that kind of thing (and many obviously do) but frankly not what you expect from a subsidised theatre with a whacking big annual grant.

In the course of the year William Gaskill resigned as Artistic Director of the Royal Court and Oscar Lewenstein took over command. Most, if not all, of the year's productions had been planned in Gaskill's time – the familiar mixture of works by the Court's tried hands and some bold chances taken with new writers. The policy is a sensible one: the established dramatists are able to entice established players, and the names of John Gielgud and John Mills, Finney or Jill Bennett flickering above the theatre in red neon entices the public and helps the box office.

In John Osborne's adaptation of *Hedda Gabler* Jill Bennett perceptively conveyed discontent, artifice and thinly disguised cruelty. Anthony Page's direction projected an impressive sense of reality (though carrying more laughs than the play requires) and among a notable cast I recall with pleasure Denholm Elliott's slim, satanic Judge Brack and Barbara Ferris's Mrs Elvsted, a determined woman in place of the usual sweet-haired schoolgirl.

The play that won an award for the year's Best Comedy was Charles Wood's *Veterans*. Having set his previous plays either among soldiers or among actors, in *Veterans* he brought his two interests together by having his cast play actors playing soldiers – heroes of some Indian Mutiny epic being filmed on the burning Turkish plains. What plot there was concerned the troublesome compulsion of the John Mills character to flash himself at pretty girls. (1972 was the year of the flash.) But in effect the play was an account of life on location, where actors are pushed around by technicians whose jargon they barely comprehend, and a portrait of a much-loved and respected actor-knight pardonably interpreted as a portrait of the much-loved and respected actor-knight who played him. Sir John Gielgud's performance was funny yet touching where he and Ronald Eyre's fine production indicated the inner remoteness of a man whose attention was almost totally concentrated on his own self and work. Perhaps the play could have transferred to the West End (Michael Codron co-presented it) but after six weeks of capacity business at the Court Gielgud departed – to film an epic.

With Harald Mueller's *Big Wolf* Gaskill made a praiseworthy attempt to interest audiences in the new generation of German playwrights, a field that has otherwise been left entirely to the Fringe. The Court's other war play was *Crete and Sergeant Pepper*, John Antrobus's wild version of life in a German prison camp, absurd, nostalgic, anti-nostalgic, anarchic. It made me laugh a good deal.

A couple of discursive Irish plays appeared during the autumn, and out of a misplaced sense of loyalty the Court put on Wesker's *The Old Ones*. Osborne's *A Sense of Detachment* was acclaimed by some critics (another euphemism) as one of the treasures of English literature. This celebration of beauty and rage against its degradation revealed the author's accomplishment in the skills of interjection and juxtaposition; I disliked the tone of haughty contempt.

And so to the Court's major achievement of the year, an overwhelming experience in any year, the premiere of Beckett's *Not I*. Beckett has frequently written of man's need to communicate his sensations, foredoomed though the attempts are to be partial, misleading or impossible. There was a time when he seemed to be walling himself and his characters behind ever higher hindrances to communication. The works became briefer – ultimately, in *Breath*, a single breath inhaled and exhaled over a heap of miscellaneous rubbish. While the imagination remained at work the content was becoming trivial. In moving away from that minimal point he created in *Not I*, with that disembodied mouth pouring forth a frantic stream of words, a sublime image of man's scared longing to communicate sensation – within his (her) own mind as much as to another person. Billie Whitelaw gave a performance that unforgettably conveyed the racing thought, the tension of self-discovery desperate to be expressed and the panic self-control.

The new plays by David Storey, Edward Bond and Christopher Hampton fall outside the scope of this year's commentary but together with those of Osborne and Antrobus – and to a lesser extent Beckett and Wood – they are the fruits of trees that were nourished by William Gaskill and by George Devine before him. It has been Oscar Lewenstein's good fortune that in his first year so much rich fruit has fallen into his hands. The question mark hanging over the Court's future is his ability to nourish the other talents that must join them in the years to come.

Returning to the unsubsidised theatre, the autumn brought three competent, agreeable middlebrow plays from Michael Codron. None of them is likely to resound through the halls of posterity but Royce Ryton's *Crown Matrimonial* will secure itself a place by being the first play to include recently dead – and in two cases, still living – members of the Royal Family among its characters. *Time and Time Again* was an unusually unconvoluted Alan Ayckbourn with Tom Courtenay embracing his girl in a garden pool, but otherwise demonstrating the doubtful virtues of disengagement. And while Charles Laurence's first stage-comedy *My Fat Friend* may not have penetrated very deeply into why his heroine (Jennie Linden) was fat or how her ménage of mutely adoring Scot and camp Kenneth Williams survived together, nonetheless the predicament was novel and sufficiently plausible for one to feel slightly better disposed towards the commercial theatre.

Private Lives (Tennents) was a natural for success. Unexpectedly, for those who know the Noël Coward/Gertrude Lawrence records, Maggie Smith and Robert Stephens made Amanda and Elyot seem, at least for the first two acts, perfectly credible people reacting entirely naturally to a disconcerting situation. Maggie Smith made me laugh a lot; my only fear is that she might one day turn, her voice already turning, into Kenneth Williams.

My memories of the Deborah Kerr/Julia Foster weepie, *The Day After the Fair* (Frith Banbury), have almost totally faded from my mind but I see that at the time I described it as 'old-fashioned fare, not bad of its kind.'

A nod of thanks to Eddie Kulukundis for transferring the Royal Shakespeare's *London Assurance*, even though performances did deteriorate towards the end of the run. A shake of the head for another transfer, *The Unknown Soldier and His Wife*, revived by Bernard Delfont some years after its Chichester premiere to open his new London theatre – named, aptly but confusingly, the New London Theatre. The overlaps of time in Peter Ustinov's 'two acts of war separated by a truce for refreshments' remained ingenious but the pieces of message came across as artlessly flat.

Ustinov himself acted in his play as well as directing it, which suggests Delfont has a fondness for one-man trinities since he also produced Anthony Newley's direction of Anthony Newley in Anthony Newley's *The Good Old Bad Old Days*. Allegories in which devils are roguish are about my least favourite art-form; when they go on to sing sentimental ballads like 'The fool who dared to dream' I want to throw up.

Several other of the year's musicals were distinctly unenchanting. *Applause* (Bernard Delfont and Alexander Cohen) travestied the subtleties of a clever film to pay yet another act of homage to the American matron. Its unmemorable score and story bent in half by contradictions enjoyed greater box office success than the stylish *Company* (Harold Prince and Richard Pilbrow). Stephen Sondheim's critical view of marriage at least set out for something different and the catchy 'You could drive a person crazy' became my favourite musical number of the year.

Julian Slade's *Trelawny* (Bristol Old Vic), in which the late Max Adrian gave his last performance, was gently charming. *Popkiss* (Donald Albery and Ian Hunter) added little to the Ben Travers base but some accomplished dance and song routines for John Standing and Daniel Massey. Harold Fielding's long *Gone With the Wind* occupied Drury Lane for a twelvemonth; *I and Albert* (Lewis M. Albert and others) had pretty sets; *Jesus Christ Superstar* (Robert Stigwood) flaunted a razzle-dazzle direction that was vulgar, idiotic and giggly by turns.

Thankfully the year ended with the witty lyrics and zestful music of *Joseph and the Amazing Technicolor Dreamcoat.* In this bright, perfect gem of a show, narrative and action were integrated in a swift-flowing stream of song and dance. A distended version, burdened with an inferior prologue later came in to the Albery Theatre (the old New renamed) but Frank Dunlop's staging was better suited to the arenas of the Young Vic and the Roundhouse. A happier solution to the problem of making a fifty-minute pop musical commercially viable in the West End might have been to perform it twice, once before the interval and again afterwards. I could have watched *Joseph* a second time quite happily.

I had hoped that by naming the producers responsible for presenting the past year's shows some pattern and perhaps even an argument might emerge. But I am defeated by the cluster of people and companies that brought *Joseph* into the West End:

By arrangement with Donald Albery
ROBERT STIGWOOD
in association with
QWERTYUIOP PRODUCTIONS
MICHAEL WHITE and GRANADA
By arrangement with DAVID LAND
presents
THE YOUNG VIC PRODUCTION

What can one make of all that except to conclude that a lot of people like to dip their hands in a good broth. Even the less complex associations will often be found to interconnect, manager with manager behind the anonymity of company names.

Some managements limit themselves to serving up titty tat. Others mix poor fare with marginally more substantial stuff. (Even Delfont, one should remember, brought *Kean* in to the West End a couple of years back.) Codron's productions are better than most more often than not. Eddie Kulukundis gets some good things going. The tastes of Michael White (*Arturo Ui, Oh! Calcutta!, Sleuth, Dirtiest Show*) are incalculably catholic. A pattern begins to emerge only when one contrasts the commercial theatre with what has been presented at the National, the Royal Shakespeare, the Royal Court and the Mermaid. Set against these the determined frivolity of the commercial plays makes a disheartening picture.

If there were no division between subsidised and unsubsidised it is possible that one or two of the plays put on at, say, the Court might have been seen at the Criterion or the Duchess instead. One or two. For commercial managements the costs, taxation and risks are high. Nonetheless, it would have been possible this past year to ignore the commercial theatre entirely, restrict one's visits to the four major subsidised theatres, to Hampstead Theatre Club and the Fringe (chiefly Open Space and Theatre Upstairs), yet to have missed no play of consequence, only some accomplished performances, some pretty sets and jokes.

Notes from the Underground

The arts reporter of the Guardian *looks back at the past twelve months on the 'fringe'.*

The patient is sick. He lies with his recent defeats ranged depressingly about him, while a chorus of critics hover about the place preparing their memorial phrases and funeral tears: the underground theatre in its metropolitan manifestation is grievously sick and a remission is not yet expected. That is the chief and unreassuring message from the fringe this year gone; but because we are careless with titles and definitions we need to distinguish. For if the 'underground' theatre is sick, the 'fringe' theatre is still alive and well. For the 'fringe' describes those cellars and pubs, the casual resting places of all manner of conventional and one-act lunchtime plays. The term 'underground' suggests the small troupes of performers who wish to revive the forces of questing experimentalism, the spirit of Artaud, the living example of the Living Theatre and La Mama: for them death arrives with the linear play, though their commitment to this form of theatre has never necessarily connected with any general alternative counter-culture. If 'underground' in theatrical terms refers to a specific world it has not fully become the dramatic bearer of truths for any alternative society.

This, though, is the area where the deaths have occurred. The Pip Simmons' Theatre Company, The Traverse Theatre workshop have perished this year, the Freehold have declined and the People Show alone has remained true to its original self. In saying a regretful goodnight to these companies we need to stress the economic facts which have made their lives difficult: none achieved financial stability until the beginning of touring abroad and, to a lesser extent, in this country. Such travel imposes a strain which few are able and willing to endure for long: the companies are dying partly because they have completed the contributions they can make, but also because they need relief from the pressures of being an 'underground' troupe.

If there has been any pattern this year it has been discovered in the resurgence of music-theatre. Pip Simmons' Theatre Company in *George Jackson and the Black and White Minstrel Show,* The Red Buddha Theatre and the Tokyo Kid brothers and even Jerome Savary's *Grand Magic Circus* belong loosely in this genre. Music-theatre hardly means Wagner or some such but an action in words or ballet which enjoys a symbiotic relationship with music. Where would Red Buddha have been without that crescendo of music which ushered in its days in the life of Hiroshima, or the entry of the coffin carrying a resurgent George Jackson? In each the emotional impetus and development depends partly on the accompanying music. The potency of the word may be disparaged in the process and the whole provides little in the way of experiment, but it is indicative of the underground situation.

George Jackson and the Black and White Minstrel Show, seen at the Oval and the Theatre Upstairs was a satirical recreation of those original nineteenth century black and white minstrel shows of which we know little. With white American southerners dressed and blacked up as negroes they provided evenings of vicious mimicry and abuse for the pleasure of their own kith and kin. Here were bland Southerners, calmly despising all things black and living black. In a crude, jumbled fashion this aspect of the evening had certain success, but the inventive and sustained metaphors of the second stage were on a different plane. The idea, with metaphor within metaphor, was to show the fashion in which all chance was set against Jackson: for his last amazing trick, handcuffed and foot-tied, he was thrust in a great sack, and hauled to the rafters while we were urged to watch his struggle for freedom. As if to indicate the scale and character of white indifference to this a white girl, fire-eating efficiently, rushes on stage. In the course of her dancing, a wooden cross is set on fire and there are thus three parallel actions. The movements inside the sack, the girl's dance and the burning of the cross. Each comments on the other. It is the sack and its body which is finally left alone on stage, with all the shackles amazingly flung down and out; and Jackson is poised for freedom when two shots ring out. All movement and all life ends suddenly. The sense of this is strong: to have set the play in the context of the minstrel show shows the extent to which human dignity and aspiration can be ridiculed and tormented by a depraving entertainment.

The Red Buddha Theatre company had greater affinities with ballet than drama. In eight balletic evocations of Japanese myth and history Stomu Yamash'ta, responsible for both the conception and music composition, gave a strong idea of a people: their savagery, sentimentality and grace. The music may sometimes have seemed to have impulses and concerns which did not match or connect with the moods on the main stage, but the quasi-rock sound was appealing on its own account. Lighting and design were unusually sharp: dreading faces of the slaves under pressure of death seen only in shadow, against the glaring white centre-stage backcloth. But everything shrivelled in comparison with the scene's description of the day atomic war came to Hiroshima. On to the stage, accompanied by a serene gentle music came the average Japanese on some apparently average day: schoolboys fighting, young lovers on the verge of loving, a young woman caught in her first pregnancy pains. But each action was suddenly frozen in mid-course until the stage was crammed with these statuesque people. Both light and music began to grow enormous about them until they broke from their stillness, sinking gradually to the ground. It was in its severe stylisation remarkable: for it suggested enormities without the need to describe them realistically.

The Grand Magic Circus seen at the Roundhouse scorned such representational methods: theirs was an exuberant elision of anything to hand and mind: a multitude of stage areas placed about the circular Roundhouse, music and spoken French, songs, pantomime, animals, tricks, magicians, a narrative in which anachronism flourished. The whole was intended to pay some form of homage to Robinson Crusoe as an enduring example of our loneliness and isolation. But the memory is of chaos, a narrative line lost again and again as if it was some theatre-of-the-absurd action without the character or intention to support it. Jerome Savary, the theatre's group founder, may have blown his trumpet literally and superbly but the evening's hybrid nature and intentions meant that all expectation was defied. That, a form of negative anarchy, may have been a reason for its popularity.

Actual experiment, new forms for old themes, was strictly confined during the year. On the verge of theatre here was found underneath the arches of Charing Cross station a thing called Global Village, a series of rooms and cellars. In this was Liquid Theatre whose unusualness for Britain lay in the nature of the relationship between actor and individual member of the audience. With debts to contemporary American methods of therapy we were involved in group game-playing and exercises which demanded much mutual touching of flesh. Such pleasing idiocies as admiration of the shape and taste of an orange suggested the aim and pursuit of the whole was a simple affirmation: for everything that lives is Holy. Beyond that there was a concern to relax our urban and repressing bodies, thereby allowing us to leave with some illusion of personal liberation from restraints by being touched and felt but it was no more than a minor flesh party, incomparably purer than an orgy I suppose.

In the experimental dispensation it was the year of Charles Marowitz, the Open Space's artistic director. His productions are experimental in that they begin as experimental writing. Marowitz produces his textual reworkings of Shakespeare and Buchner in a form which reduces, reorders, transposes and alters. The narrative line disappears, displaced by something expressionistic: a line of action which has an emotional rather than linear sense to it. Thus his Hamlet depends upon the Marowitz view of the Prince as an impotent wordmaker, whose emotions are consumed while worshipping at the altar of his own incapacity to action. The play is a mockery of the Prince for this. But *An Othello* which followed later in the year was radically different. He invested the play with contemporary overtones by making Othello the house negro who has more hope or expectation than to integrate at the humblest level, and Iago the field negro conspiring to destroy and disrupt the white scheme of things. Although this does not altogether bear justification in terms of Shakespeare it does provide a series of fascinating parallels with the original, and these were sparsely and clearly brought out by the company.

The third in the series of transpositions, Buchner's *Woyzeck* was a variation on these methods but, a week's gastric virus kept me away and unable to comment. The trio of plays does however suggest Marowitz's successive attempts to take us away from the strait-jacket of realistic and linear theatre. In comparison James Roose-Evans's reworking of Oedipus Rex, under the title of *Oedipus Now*, was disappointing. There were remarkable images which were genuine creations of theatre in the sense that they suggested and shaped original Sophoclean insights in fresh terms: at the outset the oracle gradually emerged from the swirling mist as from a tunnel or womb. It was a response to the theme of the play – the secret reaching the light of day. So too the idea of Oedipus being blinded by the mirror of enlightenment suggested that the secret the king was trying to discover was in himself alone. But these images were not sustained. There was too much mere recitation of an inadequate Sophoclean translation, debts to old and modern ballet decoratively rather than dramatically exploited: obvious power yet to be completely fulfilled.

The People Show depends upon Surrealism and a spontaneous reaction to the company's stage surroundings. It suggests a stage experiment which does not know its end or means. Yet out of this, after our suffering of stretches of private dementia, much may come. The year has yielded no more powerful image of farewell than theirs: the music of an unaccompanied Bach cello suite, the sound of waves ebbing and flowing, children's voices faintly and incessantly calling good-bye, a girl lapsing into silence. It suggested both peace and resignation in farewell, allusive and surely to be exploited or explored by other people.

Political theatre continues to be cherished by some of my colleagues who would not normally be described as tea room revolutionaries or cocktail Maoists, but the underground's direct contribution to the awakening or striving of political consciousnesses is not high. *England's Ireland* written jointly by such as Snoo Wilson, Howard Brenton and David Hare, was allowed one night at the newly unadventurous Royal Court which now rests on its large laurels. It manifested, in its terse chronology of English immersion in Ireland, a catholic-provisional bias and a hostility to the English soldier serving and torturing abroad. The purpose was to affirm our island history of both imposing upon and ignoring Ulster. But only with its scene of undivine hysteria, with an analogy between a crucified Jesus and a tortured Catholic innocent, did the play tend towards politically motivated bathos. The Ardens, who wrote *The Ballygombeen Bequest* at the Bush, used the case of an absentee landlord trying to evict an impoverished Irish family as a microcosm of all Irish suffering. The aspiration was excellent but the rendering diffused and melodramatised hostility to the ruling class which suggested a narrow political view.

In preference to this was a form of grotesque farce employed to mock socio-political mores. Colin Spencer's *St George and the Dragon* at the Soho Poly owed everything to the *Oz* trial: the bizarre functioning of the judiciary in that case was ridiculed in the course of a trial where a man was tried for having a penis which had been transformed into a dragon. This had caused scandal and concern to neighbour and family alike. In the best absurd tradition Mr Spencer treated his farcical theme with a strict legal logic, which made both judge and judicial process as absurd as you would wish, and it deserved. David Edgar's *Tederella* at the Bush was also in this vein. The attempt to take Britain into Europe was transposed into the Cinderella legend with Cinderella masquerading as Edward Heath, a girl finding true love in the hands of an uncharming Prince Pompidou, and Wilson and Jenkins as as two most ugly sisters also longing for European bliss.

By making these two Labour politicians absolute drag queens, weighed down by a host of envies and longings, Tederella managed to see political aspirations as no more than a self-seeking urge for success, loosely equating sexual and political desires, though a writer of Mr Edgar's socialist commitment surprisingly provided a sympathetic study of Edward Heath.

Another socialist writer, John McGrath, provided ammunition for liberals of all parties – pleas for resources to be shared, cottage industries to be spared from destruction. But *Plugged In* at the Bush succeeded best with its middle-aged, middle-class woman on a park bench, in an encounter with a young man. She can do no more than repeat newspaper headlines of suffering and horror, and cannot escape the way the outside world has utterly become hers, any more than he can coax her into a world of private failure. It made a stronger point than McGrath's *Out of Sight* at the King's Head which was an elementary attack on crooked and vulnerable hippies.

Otherwise social concerns loomed small: John Grillo's *Mr Bickerstaff's Establishment* pleaded for sexual emancipation. But his proponent Mr Bickerstaff, a murderous fantasist who wished to set up a network of brothels, was immersed in a melodramatic farce which did not repay much scrutiny. Howard Barker's Open Space play *Alpha Alpha* was less an exposé of murderous East End twins than a witty comment on mammas who make their offspring devious and deviant. Sam Shepherd's *The Tooth of the Crime* had some form of social concern beneath its modish surface – a concern for the way one generation's style of things is ruthlessly challenged by the next, neither able to accommodate the other. The method of suggesting this, with two pop singers of two generations and another boxing ring to achieve it, was striking though perhaps slightly frivolous: pathos not withstanding. Two Howard Brenton plays *How Beautiful with Badges* at the Open Space and *Hitler Dances* at the Young Vic marked firstly a concern with the potency and danger of uniforms and secondly the danger and durability of wartime myths.

For Sylvia at the Lamb and Flag took a far slighter and gentler view of those same wartime myths. Its range was limited to a duo of English officers and their ladies (all played by two men). With the Sportsfield as a microcosm of wartime England there was yet something more than a parody of those men's brief and finest hours. The old clichés were spoken with solemnity and sincerity and therefore suggested a time when we unquestioningly accepted that personal demands must be surrendered to those of war. Emotion was as strongly defined in the Soho Poly's rediscovery of Chekov's *On the road* and David Warner provided a portrait of a drunken failed aristocrat an indictment of a society where only castle and money mattered. Matching and surpassing this was Doreen Mantle in William Trevor's *Going Home* with her stupendous portrayal of a life of the emotions when all restraints and inhibitions are struck down.

It is not an imposing catalogue. Expectations were not fulfilled and expectations were never great during this year of little grace. The intimacy of fringe theatres should allow more than a naturalistic presentation of life. The time should have passed when time, space and place are regarded with the sober reverence of an estate agent. The dominance of the performer rather than the writer or director has not yielded rewards. We have hardly touched realism in the theatre when compared with the examples of painting, sculpture and film. The theatre remains much in the last century and the first decades of this. Its complex of resources, this year suggests, are neither fused nor greatly explored except on the level of display and exhibitions. We need new exposures to and of life.

Writing on Sand

The Artistic Director of the Royal Shakespeare Company and the company director of its London home survey the 72–73 Seasons at Stratford and the Aldwych.

TREVOR NUNN: I am probably the last person who should write about the RSC's 1972 season at Stratford-on-Avon. My memory of it is a blurred triple montage: three separate visions superimposed on each other, like the painted gelatine layers which build up a film cartoon. First, there's the background: a calm, carefully composed landscape brushed in by a senior studio artist. That's my bird's eye view from the chair of artistic director of the RSC. Then, framing the scene, comes the foreground, drawn by the film's designer. That's my view from under the hat of director-for-the-season of our Stratford theatre and company. Finally, there are the moving figures, drawn by the animator – me in my capacity as director of four of the season's five plays. In fact, most of the time I felt like a cartoon figure myself: frantically running on the spot while a diorama of nightmare artifice swam past me.

It was the Olympian view as the RSC's artistic director which first yielded the plan to mount Shakespeare's Roman plays in a single season. Or rather, it yielded to the logic of a decision which largely took itself. At Stratford, the RSC works within two defining parameters: its duty to Shakespeare, and the size of the canon. Within them, I have to programme seasons which offer lines of parts to specific actors, and mix surefire money-makers like *Hamlet* and *As You Like It* with what can be less popular works like *Timon* and *Cymbeline*. Most of the thirty-seven plays turn themselves over once every five years rejoining the queue for revival the moment they drop out of repertory. In 1972, the queue was headed by *Antony and Cleopatra*, not seen in Stratford since the Ashcroft-Redgrave partnership of 1953, and *Titus Andronicus*, neglected since Peter Brook's production in 1955. Both required enormous casts which, in a normally varied season, would mean many of the actors suffering from boredom and frustration for much of the year. It made economic and psychological sense to surround them with plays their own size: two of the most obvious were *Julius Caesar* and *Coriolanus*. By doing all four Roman plays together, one could make maximum use of the mammoth company needed to stage any one of them, and help pay for it with savings on costumes and set changes.

Thus the cold administrative logic of the idea. But, more important, there was also the fascination of examining the four together, with one director and the same group of actors. Obviously they would not form a cycle like the history plays – they were too disparate and self-contained for that. Not only did they belong to different phases of Shakespeare's development – *Andronicus* to his apprenticeship, *Julius Caesar* to his mid-maturity, *Antony* and *Cleopatra* and *Coriolanus* to the last years before his final romances – but they dealt, if you except the semi-continuity of *Caesar* and *Antony*, with quite separate periods of Roman history. Still, it seemed remarkable that four times in his life Shakespeare should have returned to the subject of Rome and, at least for the three last plays, created an identifiable Roman style – spare and bleak in *Julius Caesar*, rich and blown in *Antony and Cleopatra*, taut and dialectic in *Coriolanus*. Exploring the plays as a group might turn up other connections, shed cross-lights between them and over an oddly neglected area of Shakespeare's work and imagination.

Even before work started, one other connection was obvious. The Roman tragedies are Shakespeare's most political plays. The matter of Rome, mirror for empires, lawgivers and civilisations, gave him a freedom lacking from his English chronicles. In them, Tudor power dictated a religious argument. The primal sin of Richard II's regicide wastes England's other Eden, and is purged only when another Richard's death on Bosworth field ushers in a new golden age of Tudor legitimacy. Rome could be discussed without religious preconceptions, in terms of pure political theory. How should states be governed? What is the individual's relation to society? What power should rest with the people? What are the dangers of dictatorship and world domination? What gulf can we tolerate between private truth and public artifice in pursuit of power? Behind all these questions lay an all-embracing one: how can subsequent civilisations avoid a fall such as plunged Rome and mankind into darkness? What the Roman plays lacked in continuity compared with the histories, they might make up in contemporary relevance.

So much for the bird's eye view of artistic director. From the point of view of the Stratford company director, such a season provided a splendid opportunity to buy *out of running costs* (this wasn't generally grasped) a new, marvellously flexible stage whose machinery would not only create an infinitely fluid series of settings for the far-striding Roman tragedies but be permanently available to the company thereafter. With it, the problem of directing four productions in one season would be enormously simplified. Each play could evolve a natural, organic shape in rehearsal. When the production was ready to move into the Stratford auditorium, the stage would simply shape itself into appropriate settings. At a stroke, the company director could halve the work of the man under my third hat – the one who would actually have to set the figures moving within that frame.

That was the theory. Buoyed up by it, I started rehearsals of *Coriolanus* and *Julius Caesar* at our London rehearsal rooms in Floral Street, behind the Royal Opera House, in January 1972. Those early weeks were golden. Free to let the plays find their own shapes, we improvised all round them: sensitivity exercises, physical exercises in release and coordination, exercises based on parallel modern instances of political violence and on Goya's war etchings. With the help – no, the inspiration – of Kristen Linklater of New York City College, we explored the language of the plays. Slowly, painfully, lying on the floor or slumped in corners, actors would let the words resonate inside them, gathering associations and force, then ooze or spill out of them with a life of their own. 'Drop the word in and let it bang around inside,' Kristen would say. 'Let it use you.' Her technique, totally individual and brilliantly original, brought a special excitement to those first weeks, and with her

1 *Laurence Olivier, Ralph Richardson in* Q Planes (1939)

2A–F WORLD THEATRE SEASONS AT THE ALDWYCH

2a (*above*) *Peppino de Filippo Company* (*1964*)

2b (*left*) Hedda Gabler (*1964*) *Gertrud Fridh*

2c Der Hauptmann von Köpenick (*1970*)

2d *Noh Theatre of Japan* (*1967*)

2e Un Fil à la Patte (*1964*) *Jacques Charon, Bois d'Enghien*

2f Yerma (*1973*) *Nuria Espert*

3a (*left*) *John Clements, Artistic Director, Chichester, 1966–73*
3b (*right*) *Keith Michell, Artistic Director, Chichester, 1974–*

3C–K PRODUCTIONS AT CHICHESTER

3c An Italian Straw Hat (*1967*)

3d Vivat! Vivat Regina! (*1970*)
Sarah Miles

3e Vivat! Vivat Regina! (*1970*)
Eileen Atkins

3f The Taming of the Shrew (*1972*) *Anthony Hopkins, Joan Plowright*
3g The Cocktail Party (*1968*) *Alec Guinness, Eileen Atkins*

3h Caesar & Cleopatra (*1971*) *John Gielgud, Anna Calder-Marshall*
3i The Unknown Soldier and His Wife (*1968*) *Peter Ustinov*

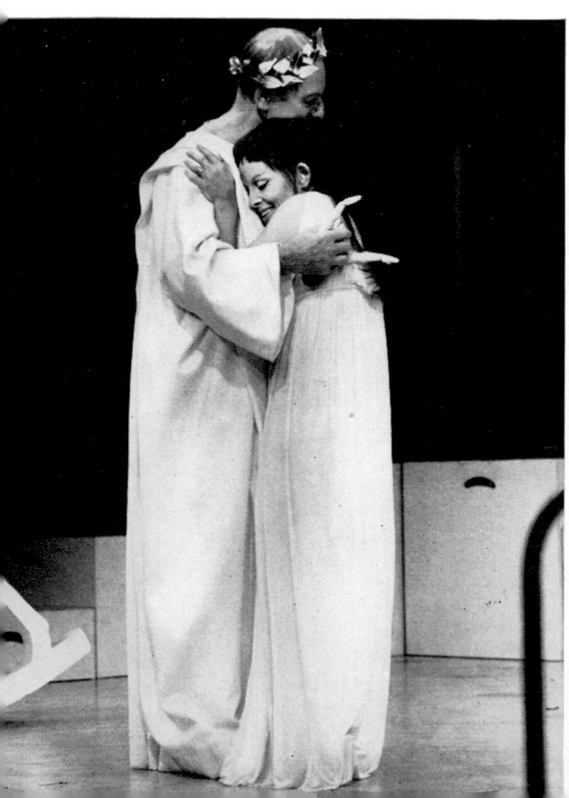

3j The Clandestine Marriage (*1966*) *Margaret Rutherford, Alastair Sim*

3k The Caucasian Chalk Circle (*1969*) *Topol*

return to New York at the beginning of February some of the brightness dimmed.

Still, there was a run-through of *Coriolanus* after four weeks which ranged unpremeditated all over the rehearsal rooms, upstairs and downstairs, and even out among the lorries and squashed vegetables of Floral Street. It was a kind of climax to this period, and wonderfully inspiriting. *Coriolanus*, rehearsed through the days from eleven till five without a lunch-break, took shape as the more strenuous of the two productions, physical, energetic and anarchic. *Julius Caesar*, rehearsed in the evenings after a break for supper, emerged cooler, more reflective and deliberate, gaining a stillness and economy from our tiredness after the day's exertions. One night we rehearsed the conspiracy scene in total darkness. The sense of danger, furtiveness and fright was extraordinary. On another, there was a long, disturbingly messy improvisation of Caesar's murder, Mark Dignam taking what seemed hours to die, after which everyone had to describe their reactions. The senate guards, who had stood rooted to their posts throughout, had an odd but convincing explanation of their inertia – none of them dared interrupt such famous, excited statesmen arguing over the dictator's body with waving, bloody arms.

All this was still without organised staging of any kind. Relying on the new Stratford stage to accommodate whatever groupings we arrived at, everyone moved as the necessities of each scene drew him. The exodus to Stratford came early in March, just as the miners' strike was causing the first major power cuts. It was not until we got there that its full relevance dawned on us. The machines for the new stage had been held up by the strike. Until they were successfully installed, there was no stage at all – no floor to support either actors or the necessary pre-opening work of rewiring our new lighting system. *Coriolanus* and *Julius Caesar* moved into the rehearsal hall, trying to force themselves into shapes arbitrarily dictated by unsatisfactory experiments with a toy model of the new stage. I moved into a state of trauma, in which I seemed to spend twenty-four hours a day wearing all my three hats at once.

Our opening dates had been long announced, and tickets sold for the first six weeks. No postponements were possible. As artistic director of the RSC, I authorised myself as Stratford company director to spend whatever was necessary to keep two teams of workmen hammering around the clock so that the stage should be ready by the date of the first public preview of *Coriolanus*. As director of the plays, I struggled to keep my focus on them unblurred by days which began with urgent technical conferences at eight a.m. and ended with design-production meetings over supper at ten or eleven to plan the next day's crisis strategy.

In the end, the technical rehearsal period was insanely short, especially as it covered the first use of the new computerised lighting system, but *Coriolanus* opened on the announced day. To me, its mangled rehearsal history was all too obvious – the new stage seemed to be giving a performance of its own, only at points dovetailing with that of the company upon it. Technical, stylised or naturalistic solutions had been imposed on problems rather than organic acting ones – apart from costuming, I realised, I had done too little to distinguish patricians from plebeians in terms of behaviour, a fairly serious fault in a play which hinges on their difference. Still, in spite of indifferent reviews, it was a production which, right up to the end of the season, always got very enthusiastic final applause from audiences. I set this down to its own astonishing richness – certainly, of the four Roman tragedies, it was the one I most itched to return to and explore more deeply.

With *Coriolanus* established, we returned to *Julius Caesar*. John Wood as Brutus and Patrick Stewart as Cassius rehearsed marvellously, exploding like rockets in the tent scene where, for the first time, Brutus loses control and shows himself angrier than the myopic, irascible, dangerous Cassius. Richard Johnson as Antony found a fine, brooding disquiet for his speech over Brutus' body. As he said 'This was the noblest Roman of them all', he managed to convey Antony's troubled sense that the Rome he belonged to had died with his adversaries: a first glimpse of the Antony of *Antony and Cleopatra*.

Then, on the day before the first preview, I was struck down by the accumulated tensions of the previous weeks in the form of a blinding migraine. A doctor ordered me to bed, and John Barton took over chairmanship of our production committee in my place. Through meetings at my bedside, I tried to keep tabs on the production's last stages. At the opening, John Wood and Patrick Stewart fulfilled all the promises of their rehearsals, and I felt we had succeeded in showing that the play doesn't effectively end with

Caesar's murder. I was pleased with the response of audience and press alike to the insight, superbly realised by Wood, that Brutus is a figure close to Hamlet in his attempts to resolve an impossible moral dilemma. But although we had got the structure right in our heads, I did not feel we had managed to execute it entirely. Something in the ending – the contrast between Brutus' and Cassius' deaths, still believing in heroism, the classical virtue of personal combat, and the warfare of great, armed automatons which replaces them – eluded us.

Our third production, placed to give me a break before *Antony and Cleopatra* and *Titus Andronicus*, was *The Comedy of Errors*. Its director had dropped out, and for a few mad days it, too, threatened to become my responsibility. Then Clifford Williams nobly stepped in to recreate his brilliant 1962 production, and the doctors sent me away for three weeks with dire warnings. Translated into terms of the possible, they meant I would have to take it easy with *Antony and Cleopatra*: avoid stresses and enjoy it. I had been frightened. The season was less than half over, with two major productions still before me. I took their warnings to heart, and came back to work in June determined to enjoy myself.

It would have been difficult not to, in any case. After the strains of our opening productions, the great play took off with the ease of a huge, perfect sailing ship. Its structure unfurled itself smoothly, and the company expanded within it in an atmosphere of lightness and gaiety. Stratford was bathed in summer, and it was no hardship for our Egyptians to rehearse, as they were to play, in bare feet. Relaxed and happy to be working with a company that I knew well, which had been joined by Janet Suzman (whom I also knew), I did not press the actors into the nervous crises which push performances beyond themselves, and for once no accidental crises pushed them for me. On opening night, one could feel the audience sharing the pleasure of our rehearsals. The play rose luscious and shimmering as the canopies which Christopher Morley floated over the Egyptian scenes. Richard Johnson was excellent as the declining, bibulous ruffian Antony, Janet Suzman totally pulled off Cleopatra the politician, and Cleopatra the vixen. Their passion for each other was physical and rough, a kind of battle. What we missed between the three of us was Antony the Emperor, Cleopatra the Queen, and the liquid moments of gentleness that they share.

As for the production, I realised as I watched the first night performance that the tone of the rehearsals had coloured the performance. It was bland.

And so to *Titus Andronicus.* From the beginning, we had known that it would be the odd play out, a kind of coda to the three mature tragedies. Its whole idiom was different, cruder and wilder, like popular sensation-journalism after their achieved poetry. They were epic. It had to be nightmare – 'When will this fearful slumber have an end', cries Andronicus. So we improvised dreams. Dreams of violence. Dreams of orgy. Dreams of rape, torture and wish-fulfilment. Dreams of dreams. More than any of the preceding productions, it detached itself from the stage and became a series of pure, acted sequences. Possibly a firmer historical approach would have fitted it more neatly into the season, enhancing the sense of a 'cycle'. But from the first we had promised ourselves that each play would take its own shape; that the season was to be a voyage of discovery, an inquiry rather than a report of findings. In that sense, *Titus Andronicus* was a satisfactory end to it, taking us further from shore than any of the other plays.

Satisfactory to us, that is. In my view, Colin Blakeley had given one of the finest performances ever seen at Stratford, but to be perfectly satisfying, the season would have had to take audiences and critics with it too. After a shaky start, it seemed to take many of its audiences, but its major disappointment to me was the number of critics who lacked the space or the inclination to see the season as a whole and discuss it as a project. (The most personally irritating, I suppose, was Robert Brustein who, having deliberately satirised baroque excesses in *Titus Andronicus,* proceeded to generalise about RSC extravagance and a changed house style.)

Contrary to popular myth, we think critics necessary, and desirable. The theatre is a collaborative art. The final judgment on anything it does must be, like my memory of Stratford 1972, a triple montage – a collaboration between the critics' verdict, the public's verdict and our verdict on ourselves. I can't help feeling that the final judgement has a layer missing.

DAVID JONES: The work of the theatre is written on sand. You may regard that as a matter for regret or celebration; but if the theatre is where you work, you learn to accept that what you do is transitory. The movement must always be forward, echoing the Baron in *The Lower Depths* – 'Very well then, Further!'. The best of drama critics manage to catch a few moments of performance in aspic, and, hopefully, the really good productions go on reverberating in the memories of those who have seen them. There's a vast and salutary gap, though, between the fading yellow press cuttings, and the impact and now-ness of the original event that passed between actors and audience. The most important show must always be the next one, and you don't start glancing over your shoulder if you want to bring Eurydice back out of the final darkness.

You'll have gathered I'm allergic to retrospective surveys. Written by outsiders, you give them swift marks for perception or pig-headedness, and move on. To attempt to survey your own work, and the work of close colleagues, with a proper detachment and the right balance of hard salesmanship and touching diffidence . . . well, I suspect it's impossible, but we can but try. And perhaps it's worth saying that one of the best things about working for the RSC is the continual and tough interchange of opinion between directors, between actors, between directors and actors, about the quality of what you're engaged in. The best way of recording a year of work might be a collage transcript of all the discussions that took place in pubs, in dusty rehearsal rooms, under the glare of stage lights, in small offices. It might be libellous, but it would be a dialogue and alive, not a Papal pronouncement, or a chiselled epitaph for the dead shows of one more season.

The value of the 1972–3 season at the Aldwych may turn out to lie as much in what we didn't do, as in what we did. The season continued our regular London policy of playing Shakespeare (*Othello* and *The Merchant of Venice*) alongside neglected or undiscovered classics, foreign or home-grown (*The Lower Depths* and *Murder in the Cathedral*), with the vital injection of new writing of stature (*The Island of the Mighty*). It's an ideal that stems back to Peter Hall's first season at the Aldwych. Before that, it was formulated by that neglected prophet of nearly every principle that informs the work of the RSC and, indeed the National, Harley Granville-Barker.

Trevor Nunn and I, over the past four years, played certain variations on that theme. We felt that Shakespeare must be permanently available throughout the London season, not crammed into the intensive cultural ghetto of a three-month run. We asked that successful Shakespeare productions transferring from Stratford to London should undergo intensive rethinking and re-rehearsal designed to narrow the gap between intention and achievement. Our criterion for selecting other classics became even more stringently geared to whether they had something to say at this particular moment in time, particularly in their social and political implications. As to new writing, we felt that the most dynamic and exploratory work available was often ill-served if we planned to produce it in the traditional proscenium setting of the Aldwych theatre: it's become increasingly crucial to have access to a second auditorium in London which would allow us greater freedom of presentation and the chance of contacting new audiences. Finally, we believed that a healthy theatre should be a full theatre: to play to critical acclaim and half-full houses may flatter the artistic ego, but it wasn't a country in which we wished to pitch our tents.

For three seasons, from 1969 to 1971, the Aldwych grew and prospered on these ideals. Box Office and attendance figures mounted steadily, as did the appreciation of the company's work from critics and audiences, both for its aesthetic and for the discoveries and content of the plays we presented. Our first season outside the Aldwych, at the Roundhouse in 1970, was traditional in its repertory, but established contact with new young audiences, and began to experiment with a freer use of dramatic space. In 1971, at the Place, we got nearer to what we wanted with a raked arena auditorium of our own design, and the production of Trevor Griffiths' remarkable political study of Gramsci in Italy in the early 20s – *Occupations*; Robert Montgomery's free-wheeling musical adaptation of Dostoievsky in *Subject to Fits*; and a hypnotically naturalistic production of *Miss Julie* by Robin Phillips. Everything looked set for an even more adventurous season in 1972–3.

In the event, it proved to be the season in which ideals hardened into formula; and where the difficult logistics of staffing two auditoria from a single company of actors finally defeated us. Maybe that's a harsh judgment, but as Company Director I can't evade the gap between what we hoped to achieve at the start of the year, and the much smaller body of work that finally surfaced.

Both Shakespeare productions were immensely creditable, and on the whole, well received. Neither, however, quite underwent that creative rebirth between Stratford and London which in the past had turned, for instance, John Barton's *Troilus and Cressida* or Trevor Nunn's *Revenger's Tragedy* into new and definitive experiences. *The Merchant of Venice* started with the commendable intention of pruning away some of the more picturesque and romantic elements that had blurred its impact in Stratford. It ended with an excessive simplicity and bareness that never really allowed the story to catch fire. Emrys James' Shylock remained a remarkable and daring attempt to embrace the clown, the villain, and the human being that exist in the part within a single performance. Susan Fleetwood managed to succeed Judi Dench as Portia with distinction – a lonely heiress, who could never quite trust the protestations of those who said they loved her. Bernard Lloyd was dashing and eloquent in the difficult part of Bassanio, and Tony Church was rightly commended for the depth and humanity of his presentation of Antonio. The production had many insights: it did not shirk the anti-Semitic streak in Shakespeare's writing; it convinced you that the carving of the pound of flesh was about to become a physical fact before your eyes; in its treatment of the Gobbos it tapped a vein of cruel almost tragic humour that started echoes of Samuel Beckett (Peter Geddes' performance as Lancelot was little understood and less appreciated for the really original interpretation it was); and above all, it was full of reminders that in a world where money is king, emotional happiness is the most fragile and dispensable of commodities. A pity that all these points remained rather abstract and above the eyebrows; the conventional fairy-story approach was thrown out, but the materialistic world of Venice was too sketched-in to give the action a new foundation in reality.

If *The Merchant of Venice* became too schematic on the road South, the danger with *Othello* was that it became too cluttered with detail. John Barton is certainly the most erudite, probably the most purist of Shakespeare directors in England today. His decision to set the play in the costume and ambience of a Crimean War outpost was a startling and new approach for him, abundantly justified by the way in which the tensions and gossip of a military frontier community suddenly rationalised all that seems ridiculous or melodramatic in the plot. The reality of that world was totally achieved in Stratford; all that was missing was a final tragic resonance in the central performances. Both Brewster Mason (Othello) and Lisa Harrow (Desdemona) developed their interpretations considerably for London. Mason was infinitely more vulnerable and dangerous in his capitulation to jealousy, and the Desdemona was now able to break out of the decorum of Victorian bustles and corsets much more passionately. Emrys James, presenting Iago as the life and soul of Sergeants' Mess Night, continued to give the production a spine of steel; and Roger Rees' fragilely aggressive Roderigo, Heather Canning's cynically experienced Emilia, and David Calder's Sandhurst Cassio, succumbing to alcohol and the brothels, were further fine performances. But the 'verismo' aspect of the production, which should have transferred marvellously to the more intimate setting of the Aldwych, was no longer so persuasive; and the addition of a wealth of new detail – cafe scenes in Cyprus, Arab street life, additional arms drill for the garrison – simply accentuated the drift towards the operatic rather than the believable, and obscured the main emotional drives of the play. It remains a remarkably achieved and original production of perhaps the most difficult of Shakespeare's tragedies, but somewhere along the line, it lost the ring of total truthfulness.

It didn't altogether surprise me that *Murder in the Cathedral* was the runaway success of the season, playing to packed houses throughout its run. Whether that proves there are more Christians in London than we realise, or more advocates of the poetic drama, I'm not sure. It was given an immensely assured production by Terry Hands, which interwove music and speech to great effect, had a marvellous sense of Eliot's language, and made the most of the comic possibilities of the T.V. Jury Panel of Knights in the second half. I never saw Donat's performance as Beckett. Richard Pasco, for me, gave one of the finest performances of a distinguished career, and those who saw both interpretations seem to feel that Pasco's may have the edge because he managed to express far more tension and uncertainty before choosing the road to martyrdom. Eliot's message is a thorny and unfashionable one today, and some people found our choice of the play reactionary and irrelevant. In reply I can only point to the vast number of people who found the play worth their attention and were deeply moved by it. Spiritual experience cannot be denied out of hand, even if it may not be your particular road to salvation.

What can I say of my own productions of Gorky and Arden? Gorky I consider as one of the great neglected dramatists of our time, and I would be happy to direct a play a year by him for the next five years until he begins to achieve equal status with Tchekhov. He deserves it! *The Lower Depths* is one of the most difficult projects I've tackled. To really penetrate that world of poverty and deprivation needs a major act of the imagination on the part of a basically middle-class, protected group of actors. And if you make the discovery, you still have to persuade an equally middle-class and protected audience that what you have found is worth their attention. The play is deceptively simplistic; like the *Book of Proverbs* or the *Thoughts of Chairman Mao* it reveals nothing to the man who refuses to be impressed. It appears photographically realistic, but is, in fact, a highly orchestrated psalm to man's ability to survive the most degrading circumstances. I think it's been wrongly enshrined as Gorky's major work – I believe he wrote at least three better organised, more comprehensive studies of the human condition – but it was good to return to it after the totally fresh discovery of *Enemies*, and the ensemble playing of the Company in this production gave me, and its audiences, great pleasure. To select arbitrarily from an interlocked set of performances, the bleak honesty of Morgan Sheppard as Klesch; Peter Woodthorpe's pathetically comic fragmentation as the Actor; Alison Fiske, inarticulately assertive as Nastya; and Bernard Lloyd, sinking himself into an enigmatic character role as Satin, were particularly fine. Gordon Gostelow's Luka was every bit as individual as Wilfred Lawson's famous performance in the role, but much truer to Gorky's intention, I feel, as he managed to present both the consoler and the cunning peasant, the bringer-of-hope and the evader of reality. Gorky always complained that Luka was sanctified in Russian performances, and this danger Gostelow triumphantly avoided. I must record that the critics found much of the performance coarse and over-raucous. Barrack-rooms and doss-houses have a funny trick of being that way. Life we know is not art; but I'd like to feel that Gorky would have backed us on this. He strongly criticised the original Moscow Art production because it was tactfully begging for sympathy from the audience instead of making it uneasy with the vulgarity and danger which he felt should be in the play.

Finally, the Arden saga. It's been sufficiently pursued in many other journals not to need re-embalming here. I would simply say that I don't believe it provides any kind of test case for the conflict between director and author, or for that between author and monolithic subsidised company (whether its source of money be red or blue). To me, the argument simply underlines the perils of co-authorship, both for the production team, and the co-authors themselves. I am very proud to have directed a play of outstanding originality and comprehensiveness by someone I consider one of our greatest living dramatists. I am very sorry that he should have felt compelled to disown the production after helping radically to shape it during six weeks of rehearsal, and before seeing what the final fortnight of work might make of it. That the critics, after two years of complaint about the safe, minor, small-scale ambitions of new works, were unable to embrace the sprawling, eccentric daring of the piece, seems to me ironic. And that, as a result, so few people had a unique and unlikely-to-be-repeated theatrical experience, fills me with considerable sadness. Patrick Allen and Estelle Kohler returned to the company to give outstanding performances as Arthur and Gwenhwyvar. Emrys James' Merlin combined bardic fervour with a gift for real-politick that might even have survived Stalin; Bernard Lloyd sang the final Lazarus Song with a haunting vehemence; and the whole company responded remarkably to what was often difficult and alien material. Arden has enough of Yorkshire in his veins to survive the vicissitudes of this particular production, and continue to write some of the most profoundly poetic plays of our time. It's interesting that the speech that Harold Hobson chose to quote as proof of the author's verbosity is, in fact, a direct and familiar quotation from *The Mabinogian*, a classic of Welsh literature.

I started this piece despondent, but have been slightly cheered by going through the roll-call of the productions. Yes, a lot was achieved. But there should have been a second auditorium season. There should have been many more new plays. The irony was that the plays existed, but not the facilities. Not enough money to cover production costs, not enough actors to cast the plays – in the end what scuppered us was that all the new work we had encouraged, or found, or commissioned demanded large casts; and to run the

Aldwych and a further auditorium out of a single company demands quite a few small-cast plays along the way. So work like David Rudkin's *Cries from Casement*; a new American farce by Philip Magdalany, *Section Nine*; Melvyn Bragg's musical version of *Animal Farm* – all these, and others, have had to be put aside for the moment.

The tide is well in now over that particular patch of sand. What you remember is what you didn't do, what you didn't achieve. That's what's valuable for the RSC as it looks to next year. Theatre companies, like football teams, can have their muddy seasons. To know that 1972–3 may not have been a vintage year is the best incentive I can think of for making sure that next year *is*.

Top Banana?

The two great successes of Laurence Olivier's penultimate season as director of the National Theatre (Long Day's Journey Into Night *and* The Front Page) *both stemmed from the United States and it is an American, the ex-editor of* Plays and Players, *who here looks back on a year in the life of the Old Vic.*

It was the year the National could do no wrong, even when it did wrong. And it did. Success piled on top of success, award upon award, records were broken, deficits eliminated, and doubting questioners hushed as everybody stood around congratulating themselves on being supermen.

It was also tenth anniversary time, ten years riding the treacherously fickle theatrical waters, more often through than over, getting washed overboard a lot, but never drowning, and shivering in the wet most of the time, but never catching the deadly pneumonia. But anniversary surveys are a bore. What makes ten years different from four years or four months, or six performances, other than the time span?

Still, a marker of sorts, one supposes, and time for a change. Not that the National hasn't been changing all along, but this time it was one of significance and a new direction was in store. Where or why is beside the point; growth and evolution are all important in anything ponderously labelled 'national'.

But is it a 'national theatre'? A 'theatre' yes, and of that there can be little argument for it is, and rightly so, a *traditional* theatre, conventional without being stagnant, responsible without playing it safe, and certainly not afraid of getting its experimental fingers scorched, but as a daring 'avant garde' (shudder) card-carrying leader of the community – no, it isn't and probably never could be.

Theatre in itself is a traditional and dated form of communication. Its validity, excitement, entertainment value and obvious attractions remain – perhaps ever more so in the present papland of intellectual starvation, but as a viable organ of the community, it serves an extremely minor function.

How then can it be truly national when by its very nature it remains elitist? Thank God it has never become a propaganda arm of our so-called dream society (and contrary to the hysterical cries of a few, neither the National nor the RSC, nor for that matter any of the subsidised provincial theatres, are temples of bourgeois culture, whatever *that* means) but equally, unfortunately, neither is it an accurate reflection of our contemporary society. It exists, primarily and simply, to serve a relatively small public, and that service is essentially one of high-level entertainment. It is a museum, or better still a gallery, that displays works both old and new, both worthwhile and not so, in the best possible light. Its works are theatrical and so are its workers, but national, is there such a thing? Certainly it provides a better service to the community than any other nationalised industry one can think of, and as a crowd-puller it ranks up there with such other nationalised prestige institutions as the Royal Family and the Houses of Parliament. The variety of accents audible in any National audience suggests that it might be better under the auspices of the British Travel Association; then perhaps we could more fully appreciate its titled status.

The question of National, to be or not, is merely one of either chauvinism or semantics, both great time-wasters. Enough to say that it represents the nation to the world at large, even if not a great part of that world is British.

And this it did better over the last year than it has in a long time, mainly because it had more critical and popular successes and thus was seen and appreciated by more people. It didn't give a particularly strong showing of English works (although more than half of the repertoire was British born, the three major triumphs started life in America and France) or of new and experimental plays. One new play and one new adaptation out of seven productions is, to say the least, a fairly conservative average. But this was the year to pull in the horns, to play it on the safe side, and to consolidate strength with internal development. The previous year was one of over-expansion and extension which led to disaster, and the years to follow are destined to be even more expansionistic and experimental by necessity. This was the time to work from the inside out, and this was exactly the way the game was played.

A lot of the deadwood was trimmed away – although some remains – and a few of the lightweights who had been thrown in out of their depth were allowed to scramble onto safer grounds. Again the emphasis was put on ensemble playing – once the National's hallmark, but lately bypassed for star turns – and there was a greater concern for total cohesion between direction, design, and acting. Style returned to the Old Vic and again, the company was a Company.

This upswing and reversal of attitudes was clearly and curiously announced by Michael Blakemore's production of *Long Day's Journey Into Night.* An almost flawless production of a very flawed play, it was initially greeted as a tour de force for Laurence Olivier who nobly stepped into the breach to save his theatre from going under. That may have seemed the case during the ill-fated season at the New, but with its transfer to Waterloo Road, it became apparent to the hasty judgers that this was ensemble work at its finest. Blakemore's direction was supreme. He charted the extremely long, difficult play with the confidence of an explorer who knows what's waiting at the end of a long voyage; sure-handed and confident, he never allowed a star-filled event to degenerate into a star vehicle.

In his designer, Michael Annals, he found the ideal partner, and their work in two subsequent productions confirmed that this was not to be a lucky strike, but two men working and thinking as one within the company structure. Where they succeeded, they and the National did so together; where they failed, everybody went down with the ship.

And to those who insisted on referring to *Long Day's Journey* as 'Olivier's personal magic show', what then of Constance Cummings and Denis Quilley? Any production that can boast three such performances out of a total cast of five is far from being a one-man band. No, this was the product of a strong company that knew where it was going.

But exactly where that was took a little longer to figure out, especially after the next production, *Jumpers*, the surprise controversy of the year. A surprise because no one, least of all those at the National, expected it to be the hit it became, and controversial because even after it received enough praise and plaudits to raise it to the status of an instant classic, most astute observers refused to acknowledge that it was all *that* worthy. Yet there it stands, hailed, by default, as the cleverest, wisest, wittiest, most original play of the year – to name but a few of the quotable quotes. It was of course none of these things, except perhaps clever, and that too much by half.

After a brilliant, surrealist opening scene that promised great things to come, it quickly spiralled downhill into an undergraduate panto/word game that belaboured every point and ran out of fresh ideas before we were half way through the first (very long) act. Tom Stoppard has a way with words along with a knack of dreaming up some very lovable losers and placing them in ridiculous situations, but he is too easily overextended. *Jumpers* would be overextended as a BBC Play of the Week; on the stage of the Old Vic it was one long, juvenile exercise in rib-jabbing asides.

Yet it could not – or would not – fit anywhere else but here, and its great success I credit almost entirely to the splendid production mounted in its favour. Peter Wood, back with the National after far too long an absence, pulled every trick in the book to make *Jumpers* move, and by parrying Stoppard's weight of palm with his own sleight of hand, it *almost* did; yet because of the play's pretentiousness, it may look like it's running and jumping, but it's always going around in circles.

The central core of the play's structure – and I use the term loosely – is Michael Hordern's bemuddled philosopher known simply as George (now What could he have meant by That?) who spends most of his time, and ours, preparing, and in the process delivering, a ridiculously irrelevant sermon questioning the existence of God, or Nature, or Man, or the World, or Whatever. It's the kind of psuedo-intellectual maze that dragged me out of bed at 8:30 in the morning when I was a 19-year old student waiting to be delighted and stimulated by that crazy old Professor of Philosophy who stood on top of the desk, stamped his foot, shoved his hands deep into his pockets, and wheezed at us through pinched eyes with questions – and pauses, and raised hands, and every other cheap trick he could think of at 8:30 in the morning – all about the existence of God, or Nature, or Man, or the World, or Whatever. My that was good stuff back then; but then that was a long time ago.

Perversely, *Jumpers* became a snob hit. Most newspaper critics were tricked into assuming there was more to it than met the eye – when in fact there was a great deal less – and being on the defensive about not getting the full impact, rushed to judgement pronouncing it an intellectual triumph. (Or as one put it quietly, 'It's the kind of play they wished they'd written or could write – if they could write.') As a result, audiences were tricked into thinking they were getting something special, whether they liked it or not, and the only one in on the joke from the beginning was the chief trickster himself. With *Jumpers* Stoppard may indeed have proved himself 'one of the most dazzling wits and surprising minds ever to turn up in the history of British theatre' (as the *New York Times* so modestly put it), but it had little to do with the quality of his play.

A definite Plus in the production's favour was Michael Hordern: it was a performance and a character we have seen before, most recently in David Mercer's *Flint* and in Stoppard's *Enter A Free Man*, but over the years Hordern has polished his convoluted metaphysician to a high point of perfection. In this case familiarity breeds enjoyment, but please, let's not confuse *that* with originality.

The remainder of the cast did their duty with a kind of brave hysteria, and Diana Rigg took off most of her clothes which was a very nice gesture, but no matter what the programme stated, I kept thinking I was watching rejected bits of Joe Orton, Peter Nichols, or Monty Python – as well as the first draft of a Tom Stoppard sketch. Nevertheless *Jumpers* was unique in that it not only took everybody's award for the year's best new play, it was the *only* new (as opposed to original) play produced during the year at the National, and that *is* some form of uniqueness.

Shakespeare was next, and although the National as a national must have some Shakespeare in their repertoire, they've never had much luck with him. Over the years, yes, there have been a few, but they depended on either big star performances or a special director's touch (both of which may be valid and even preferred, but neither of which seem to fit into the current policy), so this year they tried it straight; and it didn't work.

Richard II arrived first, at the end of March, in an honest, clear-cut interpretation that few could actually fault, but fewer still could enthuse over. *Macbeth* came some seven months later – again fairly straight – but by then one didn't feel obligated to be nice to the National and faults aplenty were found. Both productions seemed best suited for a school's outing or a beginner's primer to 'Shakespeare the Dramatist'; neither were up to the National's standard.

Of the two, I preferred 'Richard' simply because it's a much better play, but David William's unimaginative production bordered on the pedantic. Respectful Shakespeare is a non-event, and Richard particularly requires a sweeping central performance. Without it, the characters, the conflicts, and the plausibilities are swamped in a confused, jingoistic, and rather inaccurate history lesson. Ronald Pickup's Richard was reasonable to the point of being moderate, but devoid of any powerful magnetism. Perhaps one can't ask for these elusive qualities all the time, but then a company shouldn't attempt a play of Kings with a cast of Senators.

Richard is obviously a charmer from the word go and very used to getting his own way – only a spoiled and successful child could become so unreasonable when his toys are taken away – but he is capable of rising above himself and his enemies with great, tragic dignity when faced with unthinkable defeat. Effeminate surely, effete never, yet in William's production and in Pickup's playing, the two became confused.

Quite the strongest performance in the production was Denis Quilley's Bolingbroke, whose natural strength and open manner overbalanced the title role. How appropriate that Quilley should start his Shakespearean year playing the lesser parts of the winner so that he could graduate into the bigger ones of the loser, as he did when he took over from Anthony Hopkins in *Macbeth*.

I missed this production when it initially opened in November, but caught up with it after the first of the year. By then there had been a few cast changes beyond Quilley, but one had the impression that it was a 'second company'. And it was a poor impression. In our most famous national company – even one whittled down to the bone – there shouldn't be anything resembling a second string, yet the group I witnessed was clearly not up to the demands of Shakespeare. Far too many couldn't even speak the lines as they were written, let alone understand what they were all about. It's more than an embarrassment when we can't even do as well by our own plays as we do by foreign works – it's almost an emergency.

But is it entirely the fault of the company, or is it something more? *Macbeth* is not only a bad play, it's unplayable. A silly, obvious, creaky pot-boiler with nothing much to say and no new ways to say it, though God knows they do keep on trying. Maybe because it's never been done well everybody feels they've got to have a crack at it; a bit like Everest, and strictly for the climbers.

Michael Blakemore's production was not so much ill-conceived as unconceived and if it had a point of view, it escaped me completely. At times there was a smattering of the pageant – with marching boots and waving flags – then it turned into a touch of the Grand Guignol before settling down to straight melodrama (and not forgetting the Black Magic bit). None of it worked, from the cackling hags who uttered their non-harmonious curses in a variety of unutterable accents, to the slow-motion death scenes that looked astoundingly like a television commercial. I was waiting for the strobe lights to switch on.

Much of it was all simply laughable – the villains were of very curly lip, the disappearing acts would have been hooted out of a road-show pantomime, and all of that flowing blood was of the bright red, high gloss variety – but alas, not enough. Michael Annals crowded the scene with massive grey battlements which were hardly ever used – and then they were hopelessly ineffectual – and their most positive feature was to make the Old Vic's forestage look pitifully small.

Of the company I saw, Quilley made a likeable if somewhat confused Macbeth, but Jeremy Clyde's interpretation of Malcolm appeared to be inspired by one of the Rover Boys setting off on a jolly-super New Adventure. Alan MacNaughtan's Duncan was grand and wise, but he was swift dispatched leaving only Diana Rigg unscathed by the curse of this doom-laden featurette. Her tight lipped, bossy social climber made sense of the only interesting character, and of her transformation into the lost and wretched creature of the sleep-walking scene. A formidable performance in a non-formidable production.

But while *Richard* came early in the season and *Macbeth* late, Shakespeare was the year's odd man out. Neither was a total washout (and in fact *Macbeth* did well at the box office, a primary consideration in any theatre, national or not), but neither did they enhance the company's reputation or further its ensemble spirit.

Jonathan Miller's production of *School For Scandal* however did both. It showed yet again what this ever strengthening company could do if given the guidance. Playing Sheridan grotesque – almost to the point of caricature – and agressively eschewing the pretty, pretty look that has been standard *Scandal*, Miller and designer Patrick Robertson created a vulgar, bawdy Hogarthian world where rampant seediness never did much to cover up the dirt. Gossip, weary intrigue, and wasteful minor treachery were right at home here. Certainly a deadly attack on the petite bourgeoisie masquerading as the aristocracy, but done with broad good humour and a delicious sense of style that never collapsed into easy camp.

And again it was ensemble at its purest, most integrated, yet again it was Denis Quilley who gave the greatest individual pleasure. There was a freshness, even boldness that he brought to all of his roles at the National during the year, along with a strong scent of vaudeville, and it was never put to better purpose than in *Scandal*. There's a hunger within Quilley's charismatic throwaway, and we're going to hear a great deal more of him in the years to come.

Not that we hadn't seen much of it already, and especially in *The Front Page*, in which Michael Blakemore supplied the year's true joy. Exactly what prompted the National to come up with this play at this time is anybody's (and everybody's) guess, but it couldn't have been timed better. Perhaps it was the Broadway revival of a few years back that won over the doubters (but by all accounts that was a pretty heavy-handed affair), or maybe just an itch to cash in on the nostalgia; either way it was a perfect example of the right play at the right time.

Certainly the Ben Hecht/Charles MacArthur tough-as-nails comedy has been a known commodity for a long, long time. It made household names out of its original leads, somebody is always making some kind of movie out of it, and it's tops of the required pops in any course in the American Theatre – not only for reading, but for playing (and I can say with all modesty that my undergraduate Hildy Johnson was one of the highlights of an unmemorable year). Be that as it may, or was, the National's production was its first in Britain. Amazing.

What took them so long? The size of the undertaking is mammoth, as is the cast, and the possibility of doing *any* American comedy has always been doubtful – there couldn't be a more American play than this – but encouraged by the success of O'Neill's *Journey*, the team of Blakemore and Annals (the resident American specialists) got hold of *The Front Page* and exploded with London's best production of the year.

Slow to start – but not as slow as some have claimed – the press room of the Chicago Court came alive with restless energy until it burst with the kind of frenzy that comes from mixing your bourbon with bennies. Fast talking, fast cracking, heartless and sentimental at the same time, too true to life yet romanticised out of all comparison, it has theatrical fireworks all the way.

What *The Front Page* demands, and what it got for the most part, is a totally integrated company playing with jet fuelled intensity. There are two superstar parts – complete with mouth-watering entrances and exits – and a number of meaty bijous, but they all have to fit into an intricate puzzle, and the production is the puzzle. Break-neck speed is the rule of the day, hard-punched laughs and shock tactics. It's a cruel play, jaundiced really, corrupt and corrosive, which makes it just about perfect for our time.

Quilley, by now the National's most valuable asset since – well, since Maggie Smith – made a meal out of Hildy. Brash, bull-headed, quick and conniving, he was all toothy grins and sharp-eyed glares, the perfect student of (and foil to) Alan MacNaughtan's growling Walter Burns. Between the two of them they barked and bit, chewed and spat, lied and cheated, and created enough electricity to supercharge the play on their own.

But they weren't alone; far from it, and in the entire cast hardly a false note sounded. No easy trick that.

All of Hecht and MacArthur's ghouls are really caricatures and the only way to play them and make the play work is to do it all out. It's all a farce, a broad charade, performed directly to the audience who are in on the joke but who must be continually surprised. Without a sense of wonderment and innocence, *The Front Page* falls flat. Blakemore recreated the period atmosphere and the unwholesome setting with infinite detail and kept this feeling of naive innocence going right up to the never-to-be-bettered final curtain joke.

The production was strongly cast right down the line – a necessity since there's not a weak part in the writing – and the accents, a fundamental stumbling block, were, contrary to some critical carping, dead-on throughout. Except for a general lack of sparkle among the ladies, the rewards were rich indeed, worthy of any national company regardless of the nationality.

The exception on the female side was an amazing performance by Maureen Lipman who gave Molly Malloy a hooker's desperation and pathos that went far beyond the character's original conception. Shaking and straining with every drugged nerve on the needle's edge, her final plunge through the shattered window became the natural impulse of a half-crazed fluttering failure whose birdlike existence never seemed capable of confining itself to the floor of the stage. I doubt if any Hecht/MacArthur character has ever been performed so well.

The Front Page was a solid success, both critically and publically, and it highlighted the National's weakness as well as its strength. The harder the job, the better the results; the more familiar, the more simply adequate. With that in mind, one approached their final production of the period, *The Misanthrope*, with caution. Possibly the most difficult to pull off and certainly the most problematic Molière just doesn't work in English, and *The Misanthrope* least of all. Wordy, formal, actionless, a critique of a society far removed, its universal relevance – and appeal – is subtle to the point of obtuseness. Yet it has had its champions and not all of them have been academics or Francophile theatre critics. After the National's triumphant production, their meagre ranks have swollen.

But was this Molière's *Misanthrope* or Tony Harrison's? I've read the former more than once (in translation) and seen the play performed innumerable times (in both original and translation), but I've never been able to get through it – literally. 'Oh God' one moans, 'Yes, of course it *is* important and all that, but it *is* deadly dull.'

Harrison's version, however, is something else altogether. It remains long, subtle, and of course actionless (I say of course because I'm sure it *is* the same play and yet . . .) but now there doesn't seem to be a word, a phrase, a rhyme, a scene out of place. Witty, wise, and suddenly relevant, it becomes more than an adaptation or updating of a 17th Century court piece; with all due reverence to Molière, I'd say that Harrison's *Misanthrope* is the best *new* play of the 70s.

It was a stroke of genius to remove the setting to Paris in the late 60s, thus retaining a period flavour while giving a whole new dimension to the meaning of Period. It works there and then, where it couldn't here today. And while great pains were taken to draw exterior equations between De Gaulle and Louis XIV, they were totally unnecessary. Harrison's work stands on its own in this snobbish, intellectually void, beautifully and carefully cluttered world where chic is the only fine art worth pursuing. This *was* the Paris of less than a decade ago (perhaps it still is, as well as it could be New York or Rome of today, or London of tomorrow) but whether it was a product of him or visa-versa is immaterial, for only in such a world of glamorous vapidity could Alceste exist and persist, and that world is only to be found in certain places at certain times.

In the National's production, the period reconstruction takes on almost as much importance as the literal. The set, a vast, sumptuous adult playroom, had obviously been planned by the most fashionable decorator in Paris to incorporate the vogue befitting the personality of its tenant. Rich and comfortable, but cool and unattainable, full of gadgetry and the latest toys, thick plastic furniture, books by the metre, and all encompassed in luxuriant drapes to link up with the past; this is Rheostat Land where anything or anybody can be turned on or off at the touch of a switch. Celimene is Queen here.

Director John Dexter and designer Tanya Moiseiwitsch built an existing dreamworld with the kind of detail and perfection that only the National seems to know how to do anymore. This was the 60s to be sure, from the flamboyant clothes – Nehru collars and all – to the furtive giggling and dope-smoking among the intelligentsia. They even remembered the *round* Crickets in the fancy, phoney Cartier cases.

But it was not just a beautifully dressed paradeground for Harrison's beautifully dressed words. The company matched the physical glitter with style, grace, and above all, intelligence – particularly Diana Rigg as the svelte, consciously empty, and finally pitiful Celimene – and not a false or confused word or action was to be seen.

Funny how the English can make sense out of Harrison's Molière, but don't seem to have the slightest idea what Shakespeare's Shakespeare is about. And if any overall weakness is apparent in the present company, that is it; they're on far firmer footing in strange or new territory than they seem to be going over their own familiar ground.

What this signifies – if anything – and where it will lead over the next few years will become apparent as changes and personalities overtake events. The decade has passed, successfully certainly, but with rather less fanfare than one might have thought. Olivier has stepped aside – not down – and will remain very much in the picture, but sadly Kenneth Tynan has left, and I feel he will be sorely missed. Obviously with the new complex on the South Bank nearing completion, a vast and careful expansion programme is a necessity, and the new Director, Peter Hall, is one of the best expansionists and administrators in the business. Whether or not the 'Merger' talks prove conclusive, Hall brings with him to the National a whole crew previously associated with the RSC, including Harold Pinter, John Schlesinger, and John Bury; but if interplay between the two big companies is a natural and desireable thing, let's hope it doesn't destroy the National's sense of unity, nor the unique style that has re-emerged over the past year.

If these go we may end up with a lot of overcrowded stages facing a lot of empty seats, and it wouldn't be the first time a powerful national company found itself completely isolated from the community it was pledged to serve. Just a little something to think about while we're all patting ourselves on the back.

Love-Song for the Young Vic

Composed by the drama critic and arts editor of the Financial Times.

You'd have to go a long way to find a more uncomfortable theatre than the Young Vic. Its seats are plain wooden benches, painted pillar-box red. The floor is plain concrete. The square shell housing the auditorium, which flatters itself it's an octagon because the corners have been blunted, is plain breeze-blocks. If you want a drink in the interval and are not one of the privileged classes who are slipped a glass of wine in the studio or one of the upstairs rooms, you may have to stand for a long time among a crowd of young people who tend to be ordering coffee or milk or toasted sandwiches. I think it is the nicest theatre I know.

I knew it was going to be the nicest theatre on the night it opened, September 11, 1970. A pop group was playing in the foyer. (I hate pop music.) The House Manager was letting off fireworks from the roof. Inside was *Scapino*, with Jim Dale climbing all over the furniture. Outside a little bunch of local kids were still asking to come into the foyer at the interval, though it was probably the music rather than the Molière that attracted them.

And there was *Scapino* again on January 1st of this year, celebrating our entry into the European Common Market with an English version of a French play about Italians. There was Jim Dale again, still climbing the furniture, though without quite the agility he displayed in 1970. The house was packed. The Young Vic had staked its claim to a permanent place on our theatrical scene.

The Young Vic has developed so far precisely on the lines laid down when its existence was first announced. 'Here,' Laurence Olivier said, 'we think to develop plays for young audiences, an experimental workshop for authors, actors and producers; a kind of Young Vic like that in which I and all my generation were able to cut our teeth on the big classic roles without being too harshly judged for it.'

It certainly started with big classic roles. Jim Dale's *Scapino* gave way to Ronald Pickup and Annabel Leventon as Oedipus and Jocasta in Yeats's version of Sophocles; and after Sophocles, Shakespeare, Jim Dale again as Petruchio, with Jane Lapotaire as Katharine. 'Developed for young audiences', too; already the Frank Dunlop touch was showing. In *The Shrew*, Christopher Sly was replaced by an apparently tiddly visitor in the front row of the audience, and only after a bit of Cockney backchat did we slide into Act One, Scene One.

Oedipus, however, was played absolutely straight. One wouldn't want tragic plays given that special treatment, and the Young Vic has always been scrupulous about it, to its own gain. When they played *Romeo and Juliet* in 1971 (Richard Kay and Louise Purnell) Peter James's production was wholly serious, with perhaps a little more movement than usual to keep the young people's attention firmly anchored. On the night I went, a girl opposite me wept helplessly and noisily through the last 20 minutes: laughter is not the only reaction the Young Vic can extract from its patrons. At their *Measure for Measure* I saw people sitting on the edge of the benches in their excitement, wondering how on earth all that cliff-hanging complication could be resolved. This pristine impact is one of the Young Vic's most valuable assets.

Experimental work has been generously offered, with Ionesco, Beckett, Genet and other contemporaries imaginatively presented. The small studio theatre alongside the main auditorium seems to suffer from too many claims; it stores scenery, it accommodates rehearsals, it serves coffee and ices, and only too seldom houses a play. In the past year, most of the experimental work has been done in the main room. One recalls Ionesco's *The Chairs* with Denise Coffey and Gavin Reed; the Genet double-bill, *Deathwatch* and *The Maids*; a thoroughly Dunlopised version of *The Alchemist* set in modern Chelsea. And, for the Edinburgh Festival, the hilarious *Comedy of Errors* and the enchanting *Joseph and the Amazing Technicolor Dreamcoat,* developed from its status as a popular cantata for schools into a superb half-hour opera. Too good to discard when Edinburgh was over, it moved, with its preliminary Mystery Play, to the Roundhouse; and from there to the Albery Theatre (formerly the New), where public indifference to the Mystery Play had to be conceded and a new first half was substituted, a preface to *Joseph,* though with spoken dialogue that to my mind marred it. It was, and at the time of writing still is, a great success.

I give it what may seem disproportionate attention because it exemplifies what seems to me the foundation of the Frank Dunlop production. Dunlop's mission is to get people into the theatre who don't normally think of it as their cup of tea. Before the Young Vic, he ran a company called the Pop Theatre. The Pop Theatre, also at the Edinburgh Festival, produced among other things a version of *A Midsummer Night's Dream* with a wonderfully comic Puck by Hywel Bennett, a score by John Dankworth to be sung by Cleo Laine as both Hippolyta and Titania, and a pack of hounds that was brought each night to the Assembly Hall in a van. (Robin Bailey's apologetic delivery of the line 'My hounds are bred out of the Spartan kind' was a masterly example of how to get a new sound from a familiar text.)

Absolutely no wrong was done to the play; but the comedy was played whole-heartedly for comedy, the romance for romance, and encrusted tradition was thrown to the winds. This is the principle on which, it seems to me, the Young Vic's style is based; and its success is clear from the packed houses there night after night, both for familiar plays and others less familiar.

And, as Olivier said in that introductory speech, fine chances are given to young players that they might not otherwise find. The established theatre is excessively cautious, and is slower to take a new artist to its bosom than it ever has been. The Young Vic therefore casts its star parts from actors of proved popularity in other media who have not yet been recognised as potential star material by the sluggish commercial managements. Where else, as at the Young Vic in 1972–3, could Hywel Bennett have played Julius Caesar? or Peter McEnery have been enabled to present his own adaptation of a long narrative poem, Ted Hughes's *The Wound*? or Richard Warwick have been cast as Len in Pinter's *The Dwarfs*?

What other company would give Denise Coffey such free rein for her abounding sense of comedy, or provide Nicky Henson with roles extending from Goldsmith to Tom Stoppard?

Not, as it happens, that the Young Vic audiences appear to worry much about who is playing for them. They are as omnivorous a bunch as you could ask for, crowding the house as enthusiastically for what seemed to me an indifferent production of *Look Back in Anger* as for the brilliant productions of *The Alchemist* and *Scapino*.

They are in fact the kind of audience such a house needs. Most of them are quite young, and a high proportion comes from the slice of society where the theatre is not taken for granted. Moreover they are not by any means uncritically appreciative; being free of preconceived ideas about the stage they are curious to explore what is going on, and accept or reject without reference to accepted notions. The fact that Vanessa Redgrave was a person of repute both on the stage and in the newspapers did nothing to help *Cato Street*, which had to stand or fall on its own merits as a night out. This general unfamiliarity with received theatrical standards is a marked advantage, for even quite unorthodox procedures, like the playing of the two girls in Genet's *The Maids* not by girls, or even by boys (as Sartre claims Genet wanted), but by adult men, Nicky Henson and Andrew Robertson, are coolly weighed up on the merits alone of their dramatic effect.

The fact is that the young generation today are extremely confident and critical, and to play down to them is disastrous. See them, not only at the Young Vic but at the Proms, another great democratic arts manifestation in our midst: they are not reacting on any traditional lines, or in accordance with instructions from tutors and school-masters. They are very firmly making up their own minds.

This is one reason why I believe that a theatre of the Young Vic pattern is the proper model for theatres in the regions rather than the conventional, or fashionably unconventional, million-pound monsters being built all over the country. The Young Vic cost £60,000. Today I suppose it would cost £120,000. Its interesting design, with an apron stage in front of a wide platform stage, allows for all kinds of varied productions, even accommodating visiting theatre-in-the-round productions without trouble. Communication between actors and audience is ideally intimate; there is virtually no barrier between stage and audience, and it is interesting to watch people walk across the set during the intervals on their way in and out without any kind of self-consciousness. The sight-lines are perfect from any part of the house.

Of course if one were going to start again from scratch detail changes would no doubt be made. The Young Vic was thought of in terms of young audiences who would not mind much about the hardness of their seats, which are, after all, more comfortable than the seats at football grounds. Still, a little padding would do no harm. Building from scratch (the Young Vic incorporates the shell of a standing building) one might make room for easier access to the refreshment counter. And when I win the Pools I am going to buy them an improved sound system. In Peter James's generally imaginative production of *Julius Caesar* the crowd had to be conjured up by way of relayed rhubarb, and the crowds I conjured up myself were pretty sparse.

The future of the Young Vic, as I write, is uncertain. It began as an offshoot of the National, and its Arts Council subsidy was a part of the National's cheque. But there are changes afoot in the National Theatre; they are headed for their great new house, which has no accommodation in it for any Young Vic, and they are under new artistic direction. As Lord Olivier told the Press at the meeting where he announced his reversion to co-director with Peter Hall, 'We gave birth to the Young Vic, but now under Frank Dunlop's care they have grown up.'

There is all the same some doubt about whether they should go out into the world on their own. This is a matter still under discussion. What is more worrying is the distant loom of the end of their lease in the Cut. The building was never intended to be more than temporary; but if they should lose it, where would they go? The West End would clearly be a wrong site; a lively, democratic theatre like the Young Vic needs lively, democratic surroundings. Yet it must be reasonably accessible from all parts of London.

Well, that bridge can be crossed when it is reached. Meanwhile we have this likeable little house by Waterloo Station, where I have spent some of my happiest evenings in the theatre. It hardly seems possible that it should only have been going for three years. To me at any rate it is already indispensable.

The World Coarse Acting Championships

The acknowledged leading authority on Coarse Acting, author of the definitive text-book on the subject, here reports on a recent contest at the Questors Theatre in Ealing.

Ever since *The Art of Coarse Acting* was published some ten years ago, people have been writing to tell me about splendid examples of that black art that they have seen or been involved with on their local stages. Which only confirms what I have felt for a long time, namely that the coarse version of the craft is often more interesting than the genuine thing. And why not? It's so much more spectacular when an actor tugs at a vase glued to a shelf and brings down the entire set, than if everything goes smoothly.

The idea gradually came to me that it would be fun to have a whole evening devoted to Coarse Acting. And thc vaguc idea crystallised when the Questors Theatre, Ealing (who, as usual, were trying to raise an impossible sum of money for a further extension) asked if I would do something to raise funds, and actually suggested a Coarse Acting Competition. So thus, last year saw the Questors as host to the first (but not, I hope, the last) World Coarse Acting Championships.

Actually the use of the word 'world' was a slight exaggeration. Four out of the six teams entered came from Ealing. but the other two were important exceptions. One was from students of the famous Rose Bruford College and the other from the Royal Shakespeare Company. I decided against individual turns as I thought team-work would be more interesting and give an opportunity for that ensemble disaster that is the hallmark of the true Coarse actor.

Each team appeared twice. In the first half they had a free choice to perform, maximum length 10 minutes and in the second half they were given impromptu tasks. Rules were drawn up, while the adjudication was given and the winners selected by Richard Gordon, author of the Doctor books.

The first-half choices ranged far and wide. The Royal Shakespeare Company for instance, found themselves in a genuine Coarse Acting situation. Two of their team of four couldn't turn out through illness and they had to work out something at short notice. So the two survivors – Anthony Pedley and Roger Rees – contrived a new act consisting of the box-tree scene from *Twelfth Night* with Anthony Pedley as Malvolio while Roger Rees played all three characters behind the box-tree. A team calling themselves The Hammersmith Hams performed an excerpt from a genuine opera, only they said the words instead of singing them. They brought the house down when the heroine found her lover dead amid bloodstained bedclothes and cried: 'Oh Sheet! He is dead!'

The palm, however, went to the Mike Langridge Anti-Theatre with an original murder mystery with the somewhat ambiguous title of *The Butler Did It And Judging By The Smile On His Face He's Been Doing It For Years*. This opened with a body on stage transfixed by a poker through the chest. But it took the detective ten minutes before he triumphantly announced, 'I believe I've discovered the murder weapon!'

The second half was slightly more informal, with the impromptu tasks. These were not entirely unrehearsed – to ask for genuine impromptu acts would have been risking disaster – but teams were only given their assignment at short notice. The tasks were suitably outrageous and consisted of such demands as 'Perform *Macbeth* in three minutes omitting no part of the plot.' Incidentally, the company which received that did it to music in brilliant style and had actually got as far as Birnam Wood before the hooter went to signify their time was up. Another company, who had over-run their time badly in the first half received a special punishment – *War and Peace* in three minutes. I don't think it bore much relation to Tolstoy but it was so funny when they came to the Battle of Borodino that we let them over-run again.

The Royal Shakespeare were asked to perform a death scene 'in the manner of the Hanwell Amateur Dramatic Society'. They chose *Julius Caesar*. Never has Caesar died so dramatically. To start with Anthony Pedley had hidden several quarts of blood under his toga which he released in little squirts. His death agonies lasted five minutes and involved being pursued right round the auditorium by Roger Rees as Brutus. The audience was as exhausted as the actors by the time Caesar had received his *coup de grâce* while trying to escape out of the emergency exit.

The surprise of the second half was a brilliant piece of dance-mime from the Rose Bruford students, who had been asked to perform *The Merchant of Venice* in the inevitable three minutes. Although largely improvised, it was so polished and ingenious that it won the loudest applause of the event and the audience rose to them.

Richard Gordon, in his adjudication, awarded the World Trophy (which looked suspiciously like a decorated chamber-pot) to the Mike Langridge Anti-Theatre, who promptly started singing 'Who Beat the Aldwych?' to the tune of Sospan Fach. Mr Gordon said that they had come nearest to the spirit of Coarse Acting with their first-half murder mystery. His judgement was generally agreed with. The M. L. Anti-Theatre had given a very good impersonation of a play in which everything was not quite right. Lines were not so much forgotten as obviously half-invented, and delivered with that split-second wrongness of timing that is the hallmark of the Coarse Actor. In addition the characters were all so obviously themselves. The charwoman was plainly being played by the vicar's wife whose idea of working-class characterisation was to spit every ten seconds. The assistant detective was goggle-eyed and moved as if he had stilts in his trousers. The detective was clearly someone pretty important in village life, judging by the way he strode round the stage masking everyone, prompting them when they forgot their lines and even rebuking the prompter when she wasn't loud enough.

Although a great evening, but if any theatre should think of doing something similar, a word of advice: in a Coarse Acting competition it is not enough just to come on and act badly. It has to be bad acting with a purpose. And it also has to be funny, or the evening will be positively painful. A lot of rehearsal may be required. The M. L. Anti-Theatre rehearsed their tiny scene for three weeks. A chairman to compère the evening is essential and so is an adjudicator. And finally a delicate hint: the title Coarse Acting *is* copyright but permission to use it, along with the rules of a Coarse Acting competition, can be obtained from me through the publishers of this book.

4a *Her Majesty's:* Applause (*Lauren Bacall*)

4b *Mermaid* and *Cambridge:* Journey's End

4c *Palace:* Jesus Christ, Superstar

4d *Royal Court:* Not I (*Billie Whitelaw*)

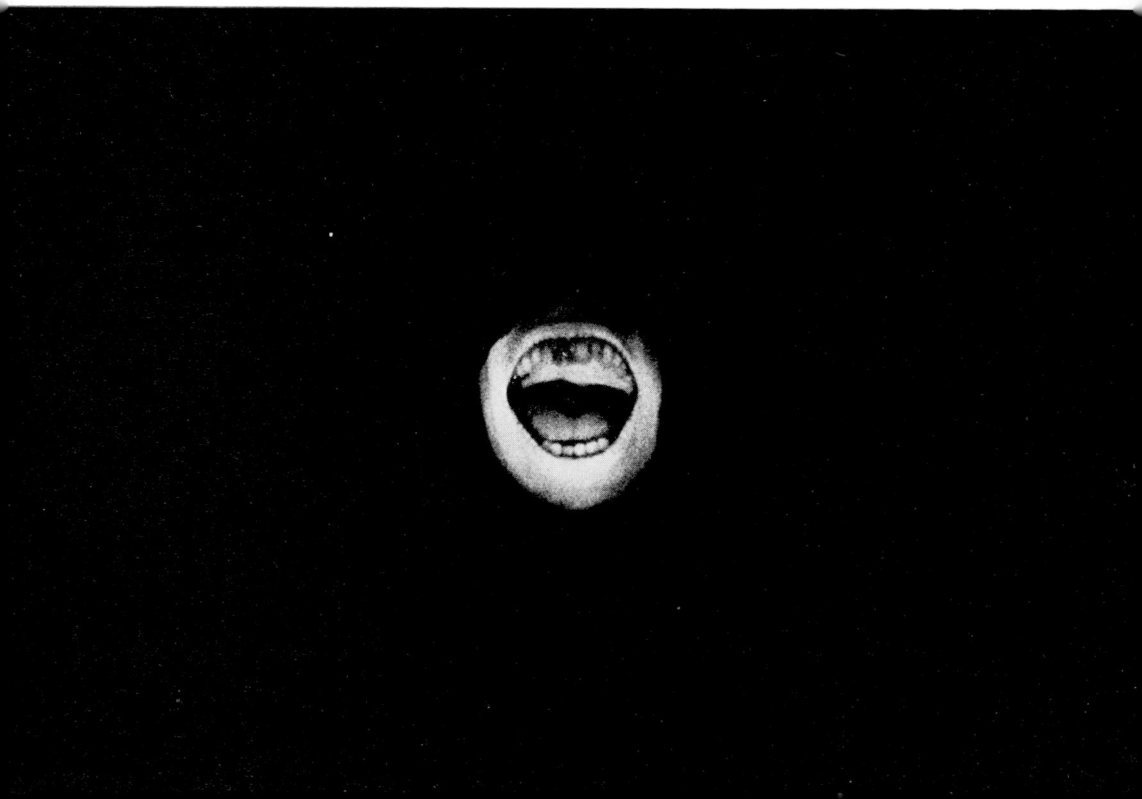

4e *Hampstead:* Po' Miss Julie (*Gabrielle Drake, Lon Satton*)
4f *Savoy:* Lloyd George Knew My Father (*James Grout, Ralph Richardson, Peggy Ashcroft*)

4g *Queen's:* Private Lives (*Robert Stephens, Maggie Smith*)

5a *Roundhouse: Stomu Yamash'Ta's Red Buddha Theatre*

5b *Open Space: Charles Marowitz's* An Othello

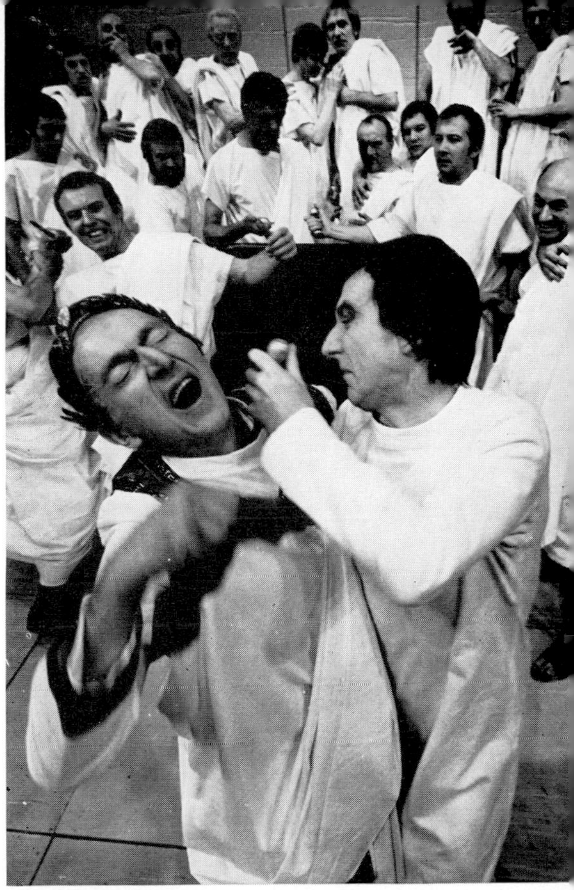

6A–C RSC STRATFORD

6a Julius Caesar (*Mark Dignam, John Wood*)

6b (below) Antony & Cleopatra (*Janet Suzman, Richard Johnson*)

6c Titus Andronicus (*Colin Blakely*)

6D–F RSC ALDWYCH

6d The Island of the Mighty (*Patrick Allen, Estelle Kohler*)

6e The Lower Depths (*Bernard Lloyd, Gordon Gostelow*)

6f Murder in the Cathedral (*2nd from Rt: Richard Pasco*)

Opera: Perilous Freight in International Waters

Feeling that a detailed survey of a crowded and diffuse year in Opera would require a book rather than a chapter, the Guardian *critic has here chosen to defend his beloved medium from increasingly vehement enemy attack.*

Why does opera make so many people angry? So asks an operatically hostile friend of mine. Oh yes, I do have some such, and pity them, which makes the relationship worse. One such I persuaded as a favour to sit and watch with me a television performance of Verdi's Macbeth. He stuck it out nobly: sleep walking scene, Birnam Wood to Dunsinane, even the last battle. But when baritone Macbeth was finally toppled to his knees, this robust John Bull exclaimed, 'If he starts to *sing* again I shall bloody well shoot him'. Good practical criticism of the genre, I would not deny. Another case is even more striking: a Wagnerian girl of my acquaintance got engaged to a non-operatic fiancé. I thought that under the influence of that *possente dio amor*, the madness of first love, this fellow might be converted, in both their interests, to a love of *Tristan and Isolde*. I bought them tickets. Did you like it? I asked later. The man's face puckered with rage. 'Frightful, appalling, worse than all my years in the RAF'.

And what about all this booing we read of: poor Miss Shuard in Naples, poor Miss Jones in Vienna? True, one seldom reads about ecstatic applause but then that is in the nature of news coverage. We read about derailments but news editors are chary of stories about trains which actually do arrive on time. Evidently opera makes enemies as well as friends, though one should note that booing is often a kind of idealised applause, saying, 'Not good enough in the thing we love most'. But I mean here is Monsieur Pierre Boulez who is rightly revered, a conductor of *Pelléas et Mélisande* out of which he has no doubt made a tidy little sum of money, saying that all opera houses should be burned down *because they are no more than museums*! (My italics.) As if that were not a very good reason for building more of them. As a conservative, in the arts at least, I find such a view wholly preposterous. Not to digress too much I think that what Boulez probably meant was not so much museums as mausoleums and there his view begins to corner into that of Benjamin Britten who has some very sensible notion about not limiting opera to our idea of an opera house but getting it (the thing, opera) out into the classroom, the village hall, the church (where in a sense it may be said to have begun life). It was in Orford parish church, I remember that, at the first performance of *Noye's Fludde* with the use—surely it would have been approved by Meyerbeer—which Britten suddenly made of Dyke's hymn, 'For those in peril on the sea', that I found myself crying real operatically engendered tears. Not in amphitheatres only . . . then.

Well, in a sense the liberation is made already: opera comes to us at home, by television screen (as I reminded you at the start), by radio (why bother to sit in the dark at Bayreuth?) and above all by gramophone which except in the case of some comic operas by Rossini or Mozart is almost as good as the real thing if you can visualise the action to some extent in your mind's eye. Furthermore you can follow with a score or a libretto in your hand just as our great-grandparents did in the opera house in the days when the chandelier remained ablaze throughout the performance. (It was Wagner who had it dimmed, then extinguished.) Undoubtedly, we could almost get on with opera even if M. Boulez had his way. But to revert to the matter of hostility to the genre as such. Could it be that we ought to measure the intensity of the hatred – opera as a dirty word – by the intensity of the love also aroused by this, to some of us, the most powerful and rich of all forms of poetic and dramatic communication? If it affects people so strongly *against*, may it not simply be that it also affects people *for*. One seems to hear in that question a vague reflection of the endless to-ing and fro-ing of the pro and anti censors: if no one is ever made the worse by pornography, why is it deemed so dangerous, unless damaging? And so on.

Your true believer in opera probably finds this case self-evident to a point where he never even stops to examine it. If oponents cannot see that the second act of Mozart's *Marriage of Figaro* is not only ten times more pungent than the comedy of Beaumarchais played as a straight play then the opponent must be wilfully blind – or deaf (because one must concede that to the tone deaf, to those to whom music is a language without meaning, opera must forever be a closed book). I would of course go as far as to say that the second act in question of Mozart's opera is the finest flower of comedy in *all* drama: a pretty hefty claim. Try it out. It might sort out for good and all your real opera-addicts from the goats. Let me make a further claim: I would say that the only drama which can measure up to the stupendous stature of Wagner's *The Ring of the Nibelung* is the *Oresteia* of the ancient Greek theatre and that Wagner's opus is the greatest artistic creation of the nineteenth century.

How dare I advance such extravagant claims? Because after sixty years of addiction I am more than ever sure that opera as an art form has the edge on every other medium. I am convinced that opera alone can bring to bear the greatest eloquence, the greatest pungency of allusion to a dramatic situation that is needed for full expression. It lies in the nature of music-plus-speech, in the form of song, that this should be so. Hamlet's death is noble, poignant, eloquent. But consider what Wagner is able to 'bring to bear' at the moment of the death of Siegfried: allusion and reminiscence of a whole life-time, from three previous operas, three previous evenings in the theatre. What would not a Henry James have given in the climactic scenes of a novel to be able to condense, in musical comment, every allusion simultaneously? It is music's power of simultaneous commentary which gives it this unique dramatic power. Ernest Newman pointed out, unerringly, that the orchestra (specifically Wagner's in the case he was quoting) was able to do what the ancient Greek dramatist expected from the Chorus in tragedy (who probably chanted, anyway). In what other dramatic form (or what poetry or prose either) can the creator (composer) enlist as many as six or seven separate voices to express contrasting opinions simultaneously? Think of *Cosi fan Tutte*, *Fidelio*, or more down to earth, the sextet in Donizetti's *Lucia di Lammermoor*. The ensemble of disparate emotions: there's a prize unique to the opera.

The idea widely held by opera's enemies was once epitomised as 'les choses trop bête à dire, on les chante' simply does not hold water. Why do we sing the National Anthem, not merely speak it? (I once heard a poetry recital which began with Lewis Casson saying 'Now, if you will all stand up, Sybil will *speak* the National Anthem'. And we did. And she did.)

Of course to people to whom song is not a language at all, who would never in a thousand years find drama in *Malbrook s'en va-t-en guerre* – Yvette Guilbert used to make us cry with it – the whole notion of opera must be a mystery: Johnson's 'exotic and irrational entertainment'. Well, against stupidity, as Schiller said, the gods themselves strive in vain. Voltaire thought Shakespeare a barbarian.

Is not Heine plus Schumann twice as strong as Heine on his own? Is not Mörike, through Hugo Wolf, ten times stronger than Mörike off the printed page? Who dares refute the fact that opera is ideally the dramatic art at its richest?

Now for the economics of the thing: the proof of the pudding, so to speak. Does it 'pay'? Of course not. Is not this damnation enough? Some would like to think so.

Opera in its very nature is spendthrift of talent and when talent has to be paid for – the unions see to that – the consumption of money is always bound to be relatively greater than for simple drama or even ballet on its own, where sometimes, for example in the highly succesful Chopin ballet by Jerome Robbins *Dances at a Gathering*, a solo pianist provides the accompanying music. But a symphony orchestra in charge of a virtuoso conductor, a large chorus, exorbitant singing stars and acres of elaborate scenery cost a lot of money. Whether they always need cost so much is a later consideration but opera is hardly likely to run at much of a profit, more likely at a heavy loss. Where patronage is no longer forthcoming – even in America it is practically dry – the state or the municipality takes on the burden out of a sense of civic if not artistic pride. The amount provided by different countries for the upkeep of opera differs widely. Huge subsidies in the USSR and Germany seem hardly to be questioned. Huge, that is, by our standards; some of these subsidies, for example in France, prove inadequate and 'there is trouble up at t'mill' for week after week in Paris. In Germany one feels that something like prestige comes into the reckoning a bit too clearly. The demand for opera in Germany is obviously too great for them to reduce the number of opera houses (some sixty or seventy in West Germany alone), though it is difficult to find the singers to people the stages (a great chance for our unemployed and vociferous Welsh for example, Joneses abounding up and down the Rhine and hardly to be kept up with). Demand has probably contracted in Italy on the other hand; where once opera had the immense popular appeal of football in this country, you will now find the famous opera houses more often 'dark' than full of shouting claques and fans. In other countries, England or even Japan, strange though that may seem, the demand is increasing. It is also resisted as money down the drain, and one can hardly fail to see why. Germans accept the abonnement system, but Britons who tire not of singing that 'they never shall be slaves' will not be co-erced into accepting what they do not want. Even at Covent Garden where the demand for the plum performances, the Callas nights, the Birgit Nilsson nights, would sell the house ten times over, the accepted German trick of forcing opera patrons to take the rough with the smooth – 'either you take a pair of stalls for the whole series of productions in the season or stay away even from the great evenings' – is not even envisaged. Rightly perhaps? Certainly it can make for dreadfully bored audiences. I have known German and Swiss performances where one guessed that fifty per cent of the audience has been induced to use their seats only because they had had to pay for them in advance.

Yet the demand for the best opera remains very strong. What one wonders is why in this day of technological and logistic miracles the best opera is not more readily distributed. This might not benefit tourism: in the sense that if you know you are to get Bayreuth or La Scala performances of opera in your home town you are that much less anxious to scramble onto a plane for the Festival at Salzburg or Spoleto. But the trouble is that no two opera houses are alike; occasionally Covent Garden and Dallas or some such far-apart houses will find that they can borrow each others' clothes, but moving whole casts, orchestras and productions about is as awkward as trying to distribute films would be if every projector worked to a different size of reel. Some practical solutions however should be found for reducing production costs and making travelling less cumbersome: notably, I should have thought, the use not of cut out canvas scenery but of light projection. It might be duller but it would be far more practical if all Wagner settings, say, were . . . what is the word? *gleichgeschaltet*: treated on equal terms as the Nazis used to say about Austria, before they grabbed it by force.

Again with good forethought and planning there are an enormous number of repertory works which could be done in more or less neutral settings. I have never been able to understand why for example Covent Garden finds it necessary to re-do *The Magic Flute* every five years or so, why the sets for *Die schweigsame Frau* could not have served for the revival of *Don Pasquale* (perhaps they have all been cannibalised already). My suggestions that too much is spent on production do not of course meet with smiles from people who make livings out of producing (as opposed to singing or playing in) opera. Is it possible that opera suffers more than it gains from the tyrant producer? It is surely in that department and not among the singing talent that economies could best be made.

But now I can no longer refrain from touching on the great stumbling block in the matter of getting opera around and about more freely. It is in a phrase the Curse of Babel. If some of the biggest and best opera houses of the world (even Paris where the vernacular so long obtained even with Wagner) are showing a tendency to play all operas in the language in which they were originally set to music, there remains a stubborn hard core of audiences who very naturally and quite rightly want to know *what* is being sung. Ideally opera patrons should be exceptional linguists, with a ready understanding of four or five languages. The facts are otherwise. In comic opera especially it is particularly unfortunate when the majority of an audience does not follow the gist of what is being sung on the stage. To revert to that second act of *The Marriage of Figaro*, the difference between audience participation when the piece is played in the audience's own language and the comparative lack of response when it being performed in the no doubt more elegant sounding Italian is strongly to be noted. Even in opera which is not comic – and not even its worst enemies would say that of *The Ring* – recent experiments with *The Ring* in English at the Coliseum suggest a far fuller audience appreciation. English Wagner by the way is not new at all, as early as 1908 Hans Richter conducted *The Ring* in English. And yet and yet. . . . Figaro's *Brollop* (as it becomes in Stockholm), *Carmen* in Dutch,

Lakmé in Russian – I testify that these and other such have struck me as barbarous and isn't that just what I strive to avoid and make others avoid feeling? But I fear of all opera's problems the language barrier is going to be the hardest to cross.

Ballet: Moving From Centre

The Editor of Dance and Dancers *finds dance theatre spreading to new areas in Britain.*

If anyone, even as recently as thirty years ago, had publically declared that Britain would soon become one of the world's major ballet powers then that person while not burned at the stake might well have been considered as mildly moonstruck. Probably not even Ninette de Valois could have foreseen that the major company she founded would inspire at least two other companies of international reputation, and lead to the formation of several distinguished contemporary dance companies, regional companies for Glasgow and Manchester as well as smaller units working with education authorities and touring schools, colleges, small towns and villages.

It became obvious, early in the post-war years, that ballet and dance theatre couldn't hope to survive without a form of subsidy and it was at this time that the Arts Council (formerly CEMA) started to replace those vanished pre-war patrons of the arts and benign commercial managements who had been responsible for ballet's precarious existence. Unfortunately the Arts Council's concern for ballet was pretty meagre, extending to little more than one company, until Lord Goodman instigated an enquiry into the state of opera and ballet existing in Britain. As a result of the recommendations from the Report which eventually followed, there has been a tremendous widening of the whole range of dance theatre activity throughout the country. Not only has dance moved out geographically with the establishment of two regionally based companies – Scottish Theatre Ballet in Glasgow, Northern Dance Theatre in Manchester – and with the constant touring of smaller groups through the remoter areas, but the whole attitude to contemporary forms has strengthened with the changed policy of Ballet Rambert and the establishment of London Contemporary Dance Theatre. In fact the plan for today, first envisaged in the Report, has become a reality, automatically forming a clear vision for a future in which dance theatre will play as important a part in the life of the country as opera, straight theatre, orchestras and art galleries.

Possibly the most encouraging aspect of dance theatre in Britain in '72, has been that both regional companies became more established in their respective areas. Although ballet companies have flourished in Europe's opera houses for a great number of years, the very idea of a dance company in one of Britain's principal regional cities was considered as an extravagant frivolity by most local authorities who have been slow in realising that a company based in their region could be beneficial to the area. With a great deal of prodding from the Arts Council there has now been quite a break-through.

When a company starts up in a region it is obvious that the only way to succeed is to form a policy and then stick to it, although there should be enough leeway for it to bend a bit according to how the situation develops. The first thing to do is to catch your audience and Peter Darrell, Scottish Theatre Ballet's artistic director, soon realised that the quickest way to the Scottish heart was through a well-known classic and his production of *Giselle* in '71 did the trick. With his eye still on the box office he repeated this success in the following year with a three-act ballet based on Offenbach's *Tales of Hoffmann.* Closely following the opera story, each act was concerned with one of Hoffmann's three abortive love affairs – with the doll Olympia (Hilary Debden); with the dying Antonia (Marian St. Claire), with the treacherous courtesan Giulietta (Elaine McDonald). The whole idea adapted itself admirably to choreographic treatment and Darrell ingeniously fashioned the production to the nature of the Offenbach music and to the different qualities of his dancers.

In a further move to build up a repertory of classics suitable to a company of such modest size, only 26 dancers, Darrell also put on the second act of Tchaikovsky's *The Nutcracker* as a first step to mounting the complete work in '73. With a basic repertory of popular classics it is then possible to introduce more experimental works into triple bills. It was perhaps a diplomatic move on the part of Stuart Hopps to create a work based on Scottish folklore. His *An Clò Mor* to traditional Gaelic music reflected the life, marriage ceremonies and fears for the safety of fisher folk in the Western Isles. The work was the first to reflect the rich folklore of Scotland, a good way for getting ballet over to the Scottish people, also excellent for the programmes of the splinter group, Ballet for Scotland, which tours through the smaller towns. The varied repertory, suitable for these small theatres, was enlarged with Cranko's *Beauty and the Beast*, Gore's *Peepshow* and Tudor's *Soirée Musicale*. In addition to this group Stuart Hopps, SDT's associate director, has built up links with the Scottish education authorities not only with classes and lecture demonstrations but with 'Moveable Workshop', devised by Remy Charlip, which as well as getting professional dancers and students together in a workshop situation, stimulating for both parties, also helps to build up audiences for the future.

It is remarkable what Scottish Theatre Ballet has achieved in less than three years but at least Darrell was able to build up on the established foundation of his former Western Theatre Ballet although the structure and nature has changed considerably since the transformation. Laverne Meyer started with no such advantages in Manchester although he was given time by the Arts Council to explore the possibilities of dance theatre in the North West Region. As a result of his feasibility study, Meyer started Northern Dance Theatre with little more to build upon than enthusiasm and a small collection of experienced dancers. In a few years, he has developed a repertory interesting by international standards as well as to the local audiences. By '72 the company really started to find its own identity and a distinct personality.

One of the advantages of starting from scratch has been that NDT had to develop choreographers from within its own ranks. Jonathan Thorpe, whose second creation *Quartet* was justly praised when first given in '71, has shown with his third work – *The Wanderer and his Shadow* (to Brahms' Four Serious Songs), a male duet meditating on life and death – that he possesses a rare sensitivity towards the music and movement relationship as well as an unusual choreographic ingenuity remarkably similar to the best years of Antony Tudor, whose work Thorpe has never seen. As well as the works created by Meyer himself – a pas de deux to Sibelius's *Valse Triste* and a company work, *Schubert Variations* – other dancers in the company who added to the repertory were Suzanne Hywell with *Threequarter Profile*, Simon Mottram with *Tchaikovsky Suite* and John Haynes's *Within Walls*.

What is heartening about Britain's first two regional companies is that each has something entirely different to offer without in any way playing down to the kind of thing that so many people imagine to be the staple diet of provincial audiences. Both Scottish Theatre Ballet and Northern Dance Theatre appear to have taken their rightful place in the life of their respective areas so that when, in the problematical future, Edinburgh and Manchester have opera houses of their own it is to be hoped that both companies will become as much a part of these theatres as the Royal Ballet has at Covent Garden.

The unfortunate aspect of any company being permanently attached to an opera house is that everything tends to take on the refrigeration of a museum run on civil service lines. The Royal Ballet broke through the restrictive barriers of established classicism when in '70 Glen Tetley, foremost contemporary choreographer working outside America, was invited to create a work. The performance that his *Field Figures* (to a Stockhausen score) got from both sections of the Royal Ballet proved that those who have sound academic training can, provided they are guided by someone like Tetley, move naturally into more contemporary forms. This was later emphasised by the performances of Nureyev, Seymour and six other dancers in Tetley's second creation for the Royal Ballet – *Laborintus* (to Berio's 'Laborintus 11'). Here Tetley takes his dancers down to an underworld in which Berio and his collaborator, Edoardo Sanguinetti, 'tried to relate (Dante's) Inferno and *The Divine Comedy* to the chaos of present day capitalism'. Although the disturbingly beautiful choreographic images which Tetley created appeared to pay little attention to capitalistic chaos (referred to in the text sung by Cathy Berberian) there was a restlessness and disquiet in everything the dancers did in the labyrinthine inferno of Rouben Ter-Arutunian's impressive settings.

It is encouraging that organisations established as the Royal Ballet recognise the need to move on from the traditions of the past without in any way destroying their essential classical structure. That the company's classicism, far from being impaired, seemed revitalised with a revival of *Swan Lake* in the autumn of '72. This was in no way a new production but a sorting and sifting out of the best from several rather unfortunate revivals and integrating it into a proper choreographic reconstruction of the Petipa/Ivanov masterpiece as it had originally been given to the Sadler's Wells Ballet by Nicolai Serguéef from what he remembered of the original Maryinsky production in St. Petersburg. Now the ballet has been restored to its former eminence it is to be hoped that in future the pitifully few classics of ballet will be preserved for what they are rather than tampered with by those who foolishly think they can do better.

Apart from the Tetley there was little other outward movement from the Royal Ballet at Covent Garden although '72 had started with a new work, *Triad*, from MacMillan which looked as though he was shaking off a creative run of bad luck during which he had been roughly handled by some critics. To Prokofiev's D major Violin Concerto, MacMillan evolved a choreographic triangle with two brothers (Anthony Dowell and Wayne Eagling) wanting the same girl (Sibley); finally Dowell gets Sibley, leaving Eagling, the eternal outsider, alone. The choreography expressively worked on the changing emotions of the three protagonists and was as inventive as anything MacMillan created in his early years when new ways of moving appeared to flow from him unceasingly.

As a vehicle for Fonteyn during the Royal Ballet's New York season, Cranko's *Poème de l'Extase*, originally created for her in Stuttgart, was revived. In spite of Fonteyn's touching performance as a 'fin de siècle' Diva, lifted around by a series of lovers and an infatuated boy, the main impact came from Jurgen Rose's art nouveau sets and dresses.

For the Royal Ballet's other company, now called the 'new group', there was much more creative activity. Joe Layton, whose *Grand Tour* had successfully married Coward music to 'twenties personalities, moved back in time to the Yellow Book world with

O.W. (to Walton music). It emphasised the high camp of Wilde's life and resulting confrontation with Bosie's father, Lord Queensberry, without implying anywhere that Wilde (magnificently played by Michael Somes) made any contribution to the greater glory of English wit and literature. It was also disappointing that the promise of *Triad* at Covent Garden was not followed up in MacMillan's two works for the new group. *Ballade,* a game for three men and a girl to Fauré music, was an unresolved piece which didn't get anybody anywhere except the girl got the man she wanted and he didn't seem very happy about it. MacMillan's other piece, *The Poltroon,* took stock Italian Comedy figures and attempted to show that their on-stage behaviour, Pantaloon and his nasty household beating down the hapless Pierrot, reflected their real life characters off-stage when Pierrot, the worm finally turning, slaughters the lot. An ugly black comedy, not redeemed by any striking choreography, saved by the performances of the dancers.

Far more successful and still in the traditional sense was Ronald Hynd's *In a Summer Garden* where a lady with a past (Vyvyan Lorrayne), chaperoning four children on a river outing, has a brief encounter with a rakish gentleman (Barry McGrath) who espied her from a passing boat. To two Delius tone poems, Hynd managed to evoke the sensuality of Edwardian afternoon seen through the almost French impressionist haze of Peter Docherty's designs. It was one of those rare pieces in which the relationship between music and design worked in complete harmony with choreography creating a mood and emotional tensions.

With Hans van Manen's *Grosse Fuge,* originally created for Netherlands Dance Theatre, the new group moved out into the classic/contemporary amalgam. This erotic battle of the sexes, to Beethoven music, became a stark ritual for eight dancers. Seemingly naked, apart from the black Dervish skirts later removed from the four males, the dancers responded with the same enthusiasm and dedication that they had shown in the previous year when Glen Tetley mounted *Field Figures* on them. This work was the only one to underline the 'new' in the group's title since the remainder of the repertory consisted principally of revivals from the days of the old Sadler's Wells Theatre Ballet of twenty years ago.

Britain's other major classical company, Festival Ballet, has made little attempt to move into new fields except that it is physically on the move all the time and that it plays to enormous audiences everywhere. Since the main Royal Ballet refuses to tour the provinces, Festival is the only company to take large scale productions of the classics outside London and in this way is doing great service to ballet as a whole. Beryl Grey refurbished *Swan Lake* on traditional lines and an attempt was made to strengthen the triple bills although out of a programme of three new works only Denis Nahat's *Mendelssohn Symphony*, a rather sub-Balanchine abstract piece, had any lasting value.

Any move towards new areas by any of the companies already mentioned must inevitably be tentative but of all British companies the one that has strode out with no backward glances has been Ballet Rambert which, as well as taking in contemporary forms of movement and music, has now taken dance out of the proscenium arch and into the arena. In a programme 'Dance for New Dimensions', devised for the many thrust stages increasing throughout Britain, nine members of Ballet Rambert each created a work for a season at the Young Vic. Not all the nine completely understood how to cope with the wider dimension but at least four emerged as first rate works – Joseph Scoglio's *Stop-Over* about a man's desire for solitude in spite of his temporary involvement with a friendly couple; Norman Morrice's *Ladies Ladies!*, another variation on the Women's Lib theme; Christopher Bruce's *For these who die as cattle*, a deeply penetrating work about the fears and loneliness of war. John Chesworth's *Ad Hoc* was virtually a game for dancers improvising to a given situation which changed at every performance which was as good for extending the dancers as it was entertaining for the audience. Chesworth later added to the thrust repertory with *Pattern for an Escalator*, about the effect of technology on the human being, at the Crucible Theatre in Sheffield. The success of these first thrust programmes means that they will become another regular part of Ballet Rambert's work and by the beginning of 73 there was an impressive hour-long piece by Christopher Bruce. In *There was a Time* he enlarged upon the war theme he began in *For these who die as cattle*. The new work, which at first seemed abstract since nobody was named, gradually revealed itself as a study in the relationship of gods and men resulting in the cause and effect of the Trojan war.

With these thrust programmes, the continuation of the Bertram Batell children's programmes and with the formation of the Rambert Dance Unit, a highly successful demonstration group for instruction in schools, there has been no let-up in developing the regular proscenium arch repertory. Another American choreographer, Lar Lubovitch, created *Considering the Lilies* (to Bach) which got the dancers moving in a variety of moods between jazzy swinging and lyrical solemnity. Jonathan Taylor with *Listen to the Music* went all-out for belly-laughs in a slightly bawdy send-up of those radio programmes in which bright unctuous voices tell children how to find themselves in movement. Both works, in their respective ways, were valuable for programme building.

Britain's youngest company, London Contemporary Dance Theatre, is in constant state of creative activity with workshop programmes for the students in the School, workshops for members of the company and with many of the works developed from these going into the LCDT repertory or into its smaller off-shoot, the X-Group. In a season at The Place in the beginning of the year five works were added to the main company's repertory, of these the most elaborate was Barry Moreland's *Kontakion* which told the Jesus story, from birth to resurrection in 12 scenes, in the form of a mystery play. The most original was Richard Alston's *Cold*, the second act of *Giselle* seen in contemporary dance terms though using the original Adam music. It was witty and showed a very original mind at work. Alston is certainly one of the most interesting young creators to emerge from the workshops at The Place; later he went on to form his Strider group which has done a number of highly original things in a number of places, including Edinburgh and Oslo, and should become an experimental group of great value.

The visiting creators for LCDT were mainly American and while Anna Sokolow's *Scenes from the Music of Charles Ives* and May O'Donnell's *Dance Energies* involved the company in some lively dancing, Remy Charlip's *Dance* was a different kind of exercise since they had to talk about their earliest memories, express in movement the way they fly in dreams, their favourite or unfavourite things and other varied experiences. All this expanded the dancers into other means of expression which could be related to movement. London Contemporary Dance Theatre made more sorties out into the provinces and Robert Cohan's full-length *Stages* was a sell-out in large provincial theatres and was particularly appreciated by the young audiences.

What is now happening to dance theatre in Britain would never have happened were London audiences not so receptive to all forms of dance from visiting companies. Few years pass without a constant stream of distinguished visitors and '72 was no exception. Three from the Commonwealth – Canadian National Ballet, with a varied repertory of classics and more modern works; the National Dance Theatre of Jamaica, mixing its own Caribbean folklore with contemporary themes; Toronto Dance Theatre, a modern dance group decidedly influenced by Matha Graham. American modern dance visitors were the companies of Merce Cunningham, Murray Louis and Dan Wagoner. The Ballet of the Twentieth Century from Brussels returned to the London Coliseum with Béjart's *Nijinsky, Clown of God*, a phantasmagoria based on Nijinsky's diaries, which was spectacular and occasionally vulgar though Jorge Donn's portrayal of Nijinsky/Clown was one of the most moving individ ual performances of the year.

Repertory Round up

The Daily Telegraph's *deputy drama critic, still the best travelled professional theatregoer in the land, looks back over a year of regional production.*

Just as Joxer Daly wondered 'What is the stars?' so the itinerant playgoer who finds himself at, say, Leatherhead one night and Liverpool the next is bound to wonder 'What is the reps?' It isn't just the bars and lavatories and bookstalls and box office manners (beautiful after London's) which differ markedly one from another. It is the policy, the atmosphere, the sense of local ownership; and they all depend on the shape of the place.

If our repertory system has one glaring quality it is this range of character and enterprise. Each theatre is itself, a part of a community; and no community is quite like any other. That is why, although directors are vital to the health of theatres outside London, they are not everything. They cannot change the regional taste. They can only steer it.

Would Val May thrive, say, at Stoke-on-Trent after his years of prosperity at Bristol? Would Peter Cheeseman thrive at Bristol after his years of struggle in the Potteries? Imagine Ewan Cooper of the Greenwich Theatre managing the Octagon at Bolton, or Laurier Lister of the Yvonne Arnaud, Guildford, taking over the Everyman at Liverpool. They are all men of wide experience. They could cope, if required. But their jobs would change overnight.

For if the repertory theatres have one thing in common it is their different ways of life. Unlike the impersonal West End way of treating every play as a separate product to be sold to as many customers as quickly as possible, the repertory theatres can build up a programme of plays from season to season. No need then to fret about hits and misses. No need to fear the butchers of Shaftesbury Avenue; and the audience, knowing the company and perhaps the manager (hands up those playgoers who know a West End manager) will be more sympathetically disposed and less self-conscious than London first-nighters.

There is however a price to pay for the relative relaxation and independence of these provincial theatres. The price is obscurity. Obscurity, that is, for the players, directors, authors, designers; for unless the right people from London have turned up (and with the reps producing roughly 800 shows a year there aren't usually enough talent scouts to go round) the majority of productions which might give wider pleasure are doomed to stew in their own juice. True, there are occasional transfers to the West End. Bristol has always been rather good at that. Its musical version of Pinero's *Trelawny* had a spell at the Prince of Wales during the year under review, and the Cambridge Theatre Company set to music another nice old English farceur, Ben Travers, in *Popkiss* which went to the Globe. Ronald Mavor's *A Life of the General*, after a try-out at Nottingham Playhouse, turned up at the Vaudeville re-cast and re-titled as *A Private Matter*; and Bill Bryden's *Willie Rough*, which set the Clyde on fire with its detailed recreation of shipyard suffering during the first world war, visited briefly the Shaw.

The problem, though, is that the repertory theatres are too distinctive to be of use to one another. Were they all built in the same style as the No 1 touring 'dates' had been built in an age which was so much surer what it wanted (drop-curtains, good sight-lines and class distinctions) they might more often consider exchanging productions or setting up a grid along the lines first mooted in the 1950s. More people might then have been able to enjoy Susan Hampshire in *A Doll's House* after its Greenwich run, or Henry Arthur Jones's *The Liars* which the newly opened Mercury at Colchester (semi-open stage in the Greenwich tradition) dug up after fifty-six years of neglect with surprising success. In a year of conspicuously rare revivals such as Claudel's *Break at Noon* (*Partage de Midi*) at Ipswich, *The Persians* of Aeschylus at Sheffield Crucible, O'Neill's *Ah, Wilderness* and Euripides' *Medea* at Guildford, Etherege's *She Would If She Could* at Bury St Edmunds,

Vanbrugh's *The Provoked Wife* at Watford, Anouilh's *Traveller Without Luggage* at Leatherhead and Ibsen's *Brand* at Nottingham Playhouse it seemed a pity that the curiosity value of such plays could not be exploited. On the other hand anyone who saw a touring revival of Emlyn Williams's *The Late Christopher Bean* at the Sheffield Crucible with its promontory stage and a thin audience sitting round it will confirm that old plays are not suited to new stages.

Anything written for a proscenium arch, drop-curtain or what have you looks awkward in the open. Even a director as experienced as Robin Phillips, who has worked after all at Chichester, seemed embarrassed by the shape of stage and auditorium at Greenwich where his revival of Chekhov's *Three Sisters* in a black and white decor signalled a new era in that new theatre's lively history. This was more exciting in prospect than performance, but popular because a film star Mia Farrow had joined the regular company which Mr Phillips had assembled; and admirable since apart from staging a new play by James Saunders, *Kohlhaas*, a rather monotonous chronicle of a stubborn horse-dealer's search for justice within the Holy Roman Empire, the season offered Miss Farrow again in Lorca's *The House of Bernarda Alba,* a rarity indeed. As Leeds Playhouse was offering at about the same time Lorca's *Blood Wedding* it looked as if Kent and Yorkshire should do a deal.

In fact, people do not know or greatly care what is happening elsewhere. They just take, or neglect, what is in reach; and if they happen to live in Ashby-de-la-Zouch they have the greatest chance of any rep playgoers in Britain of tasting the best shows available, since Ashby is within an hour's drive of five or six reps, thus giving a choice of two new productions a week throughout each season. That is as much as anyone can hope to find in London, and more if you consider that the reps are less exclusively devoted to light comedies and thrillers.

They have them, of course. *There's A Girl In My Soup* has done as well in the sticks as in Shaftesbury Avenue. Feydeau is also well thought of in places far from the Old Vic's area of influence. The Welsh Theatre Company gave Britons a first taste of *Chat en Poche* under the title of *Pig in a Poke* which I saw at Nottingham; and the Pitlochry Festival Theatre included in its repertoire of six plays a week Feydeau's *Tailleur pour Dames* as *A Tailor for Ladies*.

Thrillers occur more often in the South, at places like Farnham, Guildford, Leatherhead and East Grinstead which presumably supply so many Aunt Edna-type playgoers.

The more important repertory theatres have a mind above that sort of trivial thing. Nottingham has, anyhow. When Stuart Burge, for example, returned after a six-month break (during which he directed the successful Paris version of *The Ruling Class*) he dreamed up a season for 1973 which would have looked bold for the Royal Shakespeare Company but which for Nottingham seemed giddily ambitious – O'Casey's *The Plough and the Stars*, Gorki's last play *The White Raven* (*Yegor Bulichov*), John Marston's *The Malcontent* and Ben Jonson's *The Devil Is An Ass*. Is there any other theatre in Europe which could offer such a serious-minded repertoire? There was only one weakness. It had nothing actually new to give us, though apart from the O'Casey everything was novel enough.

Can the reps be expected to find new authors of quality when the West End managers and the chief subsidised theatres naturally have first pickings? Not many budding authors can reject the chance of a London presentation and the attention it draws, compared to, say, a première at Liverpool or Harrogate, Ipswich, Billingham or Swindon. The Leicester Phoenix however has built itself a reputation for trying out very light comedies, some of which are heard of again. Watching them there you might not think they had careers ahead of them, but Robin Midgley, the director, knows how to work up the effects of such plays as *Bodywork* by Jennifer Phillips which placed Jennifer Hilary on a seaside holiday in Spain with a girl friend and boys in pursuit, or Terence Edmond's *Don't Pinch the Teaspoons*, an even slighter bed-sitter comedy of extra-marital Kensington manners. I can imagine either piece turning up again somewhere, just as *The Banana Box* by Eric Chappell, already seen at Leicester two years before, turned up with Leonard Rossiter in the spring of 1973 at East Grinstead and later in the West End.

It would not do, however, for the reps to suppose that new drama was no longer their affair. Pressures and costs are so much lower outside London that a commencing author stands a far greater chance of learning from his mistakes than he might in Shaftesbury Avenue; and if his play seems neither very popular in theme nor skilled enough in treatment to be a highbrow success it may still be worth staging if a company can be found to do it. Iris Murdoch's *The Three Arrows* is a good example of this kind of compromise at which the reps are good. The novelist was perhaps exceptionally lucky to find the Actors' Company, formed for the Edinburgh Festival as an independent group of players intent on reforming the conditions of their work and avowedly democratic in its aims. Thus, stars and lesser lights would shine with equal brightness and all would have the same wages as well as the same say in what plays should be acted. Ian McKellen seemed to head the company which moved on with a repertoire to the Arts Theatre, Cambridge and was generally highly thought of. But did everyone in it feel as keen about *The Three Arrows* as, say, Feydeau's *Ruling the Roost* or Ford's *'Tis Pity She's A Whore*?

It has, as one would expect from a novelist, many literary qualities, and its concern with Japanese medieval mythology worked well on the spectator's imagination. The setting and the acting, both very Oriental, also cast a slight spell, with so much squatting on haunches and the fun of recognising favourite actors despite their make-up; but so little happened in terms of story or characterisation for the first two hours that all the Japanese fringe benefits began to seem nothing more than decorous affectation, and the dry, sardonic dialogue from a donnish English drawing room remained the only steady source of tension, coming from the queerness of its setting. It was hard to see what made Miss Murdoch write it.

Harder still to see the point of John Spurling's *Peace In Our Time* (not to be confused with Coward's post-war melodrama of the same name) at Sheffield Crucible. This was a commissioned skimming of events in Europe leading up to the second world war. It filled the big stage and was presumably meant as a companion piece to *The Persian Wars* which Colin George presented in full regalia with masks, high shoes, outsize costumes (Tanya Moiseiwitsch) and a new translation by the American John Lewin which renewed my faith in the power of Greek tragedy to grip a modern audience. But, of course, Aeschylus knew exactly what he was about; whereas Mr Spurling, for all the jaunty, episodic, cartoon, lampoon style of semi-documented history, seemed uncertain what to say, what to put in, what to leave out.

We met all the top politicians of the time and the temptation to mock them was sometimes resisted, and as schools' history the show might have passed muster. But it remained a wretchedly overcrowded chronicle, uncertain of its tone (if so jolly, why no songs?) and curiously uncritical in its development as study of the anxious 1930s. A sequel was promised on the 1940s but at the time of writing it had not reached the posters. And yet it was surely worth staging, just as Miss Murdoch's Japanese piece had been worth staging because it is important that such writers should remain attracted to the stage, if only in the hope of their improvement.

John McGrath seems already committed enough in both senses. His loyalty to the theatre, especially the Everyman, Liverpool, appears unquestioned; and likewise his loyalty to a leftish not to say Marxist view of how things ought to be. I find his politics monotonous but his insight into how the lower middle class live fascinating; and he seems always anxious to take theatrical risks. In *Fish in the Sea* at the Everyman, for example, a local pop group, the Petticoat and Vine, blurted out deafening comments on the rambling tale of young people growing up in and around Merseyside today; and although I can't be sure what the music was saying since I had to put my finger in my eardrums at the time there is no doubt that as an additive to a domestic comedy it helps to give a sense of pace to episodic writing as well as filling gaps while scenes are changed.

Whether a management always ready to put on your plays is the best kind of management for the health of your art is a point that might be raised in relation to Mr McGrath and the Liverpool Everyman where he seems to have also a ready audience. We must be glad he has a theatre willing to put on his plays since other managements might consider them too untidy or similar to one another, and they always prove very actable and diverting. It is just that the eye of a less sympathetic director than Alan Dossor might be more ruthlessly artistic in its search for the best things in Mr McGrath's writing. (Might not the same point be made about John Osborne, for example, and the Royal Court Theatre? Playwrights in residence can sometimes be too comfortable for the good of their art.)

Peter Cheeseman's theatre-in-the-round at Stoke-on-Trent has its own playwrights too; and the latest in my experience is C. G. Bond (Peter Terson still being the best known). Mr Bond's *Downright Hooligan* took a rather conventional look at back-street life in the East End. It was set in a betting shop; and it told in a series of flash-backs how a lout came to be murderer – how it was hardly his fault when you considered his upbringing and the hostile or indifferent people in his life. He had no Dad. His Mum was flighty, and the only relative who showed him any love died while he was still a small boy. This was less sentimental than it sounds because it was so tautly acted and directed, and its time sequence was handled with skill; but it couldn't help looking dated, like re-vamping a Ted Willis social drama with Freudian overtones. And the London setting sounded odd at a theatre which dedicates so much of its new work to the Potteries.

No odder, though, than J. B. Priestley's *Open House* sounded at the Phoenix, Leicester, where Leslie Sands, that much admired Yorkshire actor, had extracted from the fellow-Yorkshireman's writings a delightful anthology for four actors to pay tribute to his art. Luckily Mr Sands was one of the actors, and Priestley himself had turned up to cast an eye over the staging of these bits from his plays, books and essays. But why wasn't it being done at one of Yorkshire's theatres – especially one of the new ones at Leeds or Sheffield where presumably the art of this neglected dramatist is unknown to their young audiences? Could it be the discouraging open-ness of their stages, or that Priestley is now reckoned old hat, like so many pre-1956 writers?

Jean Anouilh, for example, still so strong in Paris, is lucky if he can get beyond the provinces in Britain, which is of course pleasant for the provincial playgoer but it does mean that he does not always get the best possible performance; and thus his reputation fades further.

But Chichester appears to have some faith in him still. So did the University Theatre at Newcastle-upon-Tyne, where Gareth Morgan directed on a too-spacious open stage *The Baker, the Baker's Wife and the Baker's Boy* with some very odd casting – Freddie Jones as the frenzied, wayward husband and Yvonne Mitchell as his frivolous wife. The joke against middle-class wedlock and the exigencies of family life came across amusingly but the dream sequences and many of the emotional points were blurred by the author's usual technical demands, unmeant for this kind of theatre. The Thorndike, Leatherhead, reminded us more memorably of Anouilh's early days in a revival of *Traveller Without Luggage* with Jeremy Brett playing the man in search of his identity, literally, after a spell in hospital: a superbly sensitive performance which received less assistance from the rest of the production than it deserved.

To what extent are the provinces prone to spoil the future chances of a play's revival by themselves reviving it limply? It is a risk, of course, which has to be taken; and more often than not a rep revival can be revelation. But sometimes you are left feeling that a play has been done for and that another decade must pass before anyone will try it again. I felt like that after both of those Anouilhs, and feared the same thing would happen over Rattigan's *The Deep Blue Sea* which Eric Thompson directed for Nottingham Playhouse – the men seemed so wrong and the first-act craftmanship so creaky.

Then gradually it all came to life in the acting of Isabel Dean as Hester Collyer, a performance to set beside Peggy Ashcroft's at the Duchess twenty years ago; and one realised again how it is possible in the theatre to see the wheels of a play going round and be moved emotionally at the same time. Or if not moved extremely pleased, as I found myself at that rare revival of Henry Arthur Jones's *The Liars* at Colchester, a well-made comedy if ever there was one with a now impossibly Victorian last act of general self-renunciation and submission to the best public school values. Played without the least sign of the tongue-in-cheek temptation to which old plays are often exposed, this social satire had more than a touch of Wilde, and I am not surprised to hear that when it first came out there were rumours that it was Wilde's own work (written at Reading).

Revivals, in fact, are the staple of the reps, as Birmingham roundly and sensibly decided with its *Macbeth* played more or less in whispers in a huge sort of saucer by Keith Baxter and Sara Kestelman but marred by the director Derek Goldby's use of exit doors and aisles within the auditorium for spooky effects and withcraft. *Man and Superman* with Jennifer Hilary and Patrick Mower was better than any version I can recall since John Clements and Kay Hammond did it; and for those playgoers who must have script-less experiments the Studio Theatre went to work on Aristophanes' *Plutus*, re-titled *Grab* (disastrously I thought) and David Edgar gave them a violently sexed-up version of *Romeo and Juliet*, all orgasms and fascist oppression.

For sheer experiment however it would be hard to beat *The Real McCoy* at Worcester where *Macbeth* had been turned at the cosy Swan Theatre into a London suburban ballad opera, all the characters being seedy crooks. No names, no pack drill. But you have to admire the nerve of such failures; just as you have to admire the nerve of an actor like Derek Jacobi who took on the old Olivier roles in a double bill at Birmingham of Sophocles' *Oedipus* and Sheridan's *The Critic* – a nerve which this time proved justified since Mr Jacobi is much more of a powerful actor than his popular reputation for camp-like comedy might suggest.

But perhaps the most courageous performance of the year outside London was Richard Briers as Richard III which Prospect Productions sent on tour with Chekhov's *Ivanov* re-titled for no good reason *Crisis of Conscience*. Did Mr Briers explore the gruesome-comical side of the king as might seem obvious for such a skilful farce actor? He did not. You could see him trying not to. The result was a somewhat negative interpretation – an actor suppressing years of stage instinct and finding nothing very thrilling to replace it, except integrity. A pity, in a way, he could not have come on in the Chekhov where his talents might have found a more natural outlet as the agonised egotist Ivanov.

As it was Derek Jacobi caught a good deal of the irony in the man's melancholia. Hugh Griffith's Prospero in *The Tempest* for Nottingham Playhouse seemed to be all irony, an example of that fine actor's penetrating gaze and evocations of Welsh wizardry overcoming any awkwardness with Shakespeare's verse, much of which appeared to have been cast away with a sort of depleted passion and weary resignation. Yet he was plainly a man with magical powers even if he couldn't take them seriously, and that is what counted for so much in the end.

In the rescuing of old plays which would need stars for anyone to present them in London, and in the rescuing of old or would be stars otherwise doomed to television acting, the repertory theatres have a valuable function; and they can also make an outlet for authors whose art is not automatically up to National Theatre standards (such as David Turner's *The Prodigal Daughter*, a jovial picture of a Roman Catholic household of priests with a pretty Protestant spinster for housekeeper – sex, religion, and theological issues having combined at Colchester to suggest that Mr Turner had another play in him apart from *Semi-Detached*). But stars in need of vehicles and authors in need of stages and directors in need of jobs may be all very well. It isn't the work which it provides for the theatrical profession that renders the regions important. It is the audiences, the playgoers; and they are proving every year that they are ready to turn out to support their local reps in greater numbers than ever before. They like a name, they like a star, they like 'something to go on', as with playgoers everywhere; and it is obvious from the programmes of the better reps that not many names or stars in the West End sense can do the work of, say, a name like Mia Farrow at Greenwich. The theatre itself however often 'stands in' nicely. Its traditions, prestige, management, and mood – so evident as soon as you step in the door at, say, Pitlochry, Exeter, Ipswich or Watford – are often enough to the discerning playgoer to know if he'll be suited or not. And more often than not (apparently) he is.

On and Off Broadway

The drama critic of the New York Times *surveys a 'so-so' season*

The important thing about the New York theatre is, oddly enough, its quantity. It would be impossible for any man to see everything that is staged in the New York theatre – which is probably one of God's kinder dispensations. In the 1971/72 season there were fifty-three productions on Broadway (compared with forty-five the season before and sixty-six ten years ago) and ninety-four Off-Broadway (compared with ninety-eight the season before and seventy ten years ago) but this is nothing like the half of it.

Apart from Broadway and Off-Broadway there is the spreading morass of Off-Off-Broadway. These references are not incidentally geographical – as a matter of statistical fact there are more Off-Broadway and Off-Off-Broadway theatres *on* Broadway than there are Broadway theatres on Broadway (if you see what I mean) but in fact refers to the union contracts the producer undertakes in each particular show. Financial considerations are different for each type of theatre, and indeed in the Off-Off-Broadway theatre the actors quite probably will not be paid at all, and the unions will regard it as a 'showcase' production.

Off-Off-Broadway productions normally run from either Thursday or, less usually, Friday, until Sunday each weekend. They take place in attics and cellars, in converted garages and transformed movie houses. There are about fifty productions any given weekend and they vary from the world-famous presentations of La Mama (which is the queen of Off-Off-Broadway), to the somewhat square Equity Library showcase revivals, to shows that cater for the very specialised sexually orientated public. It is all the great wide world of show business – and there is more of all of it in New York than anywhere else.

I make this point most forcibly because it is so obviously unrealistic to talk about the New York theatre without stressing our *avant garde*. After all in Europe the Off-Off-Broadway troupes of, say, Robert Wilson or André Gregory are probably better known than the activities of David Merrick or Joseph Papp. However, to be honest I find myself getting to Off-Off-Broadway comparatively little. Yes, to be sure, I do see things such as Wilson and Gregory, and Ellen Stewart of La Mama has a hot line to my heart, so I do go to see anything at her place she tells me I should go and see. (In every producer there is a grain of a critic – and, I suspect, vice, for what it is worth, versa.) Yet my regular theatrical beat – apart from my official dance and clandestine opera attachments – is pretty much establishment. And the New York theatrical establishment rather tediously emulates Caesar's Gaul in being divided in three. (And history informs us that this is almost always a mistake.)

The largely unrespectable respectable theatre in New York consists of Broadway theatre, Off-Broadway theatre and institutional theatre. No species of theatre on Broadway genuinely makes a profit. Often, admittedly producers do make shabbily small profits from the follies of backers, but most plays lose money. The now common expectation of this fact has led to the rise of the institutional theatre – sometimes called the resident theatre – which is to be found all over America, including New York. Its premise is simple. It does not want to make a profit. It wants to exist, with the help of some kind of subsidy, and it wants simply to be responsive to the needs of its audience. It wants to make a convert rather than a buck.

In many respects it seems to me that London copies the worst of New York at a ten to fifteen year time lag. But in theatre New York is most beneficially following the pattern of London. We are learning about subsidy. And we are learning that it does not have to be politically controlled or even governmentally influenced.

There was a time when America looked at government subsidy

as an instrument of the devil destroying the artist's precious freedom. The country looked, as an instinctive example, toward Soviet Russia rather than the United Kingdom. This was a grievous mistake, for the example of Britain's subsidy to the arts (which after all only started in World War Two) is much more relevant to the United States than any other form of arts subsidy. The enormous success of the Arts Council, despite its continuing poverty – and this success is possibly more easily assessed from New York than London – is the real message to America about the arts.

By and large the arts do not have to be political. Now and again, even in the best regulated systems you will run into misunderstandings about, say, a Hochhuth play describing Churchill with perhaps more truth than tact, and a few things will run awkward. But normally the Arts Council system, beautifully bureaucratic and prejudiced, with a defiant bias towards the best, works very well indeed. It is a system which we in America need to take to our hearts or die. We will take it to our hearts. To die is the most unfashionable thing you can do in America. It is the one social act regarded in bad taste.

This present season was not particularly better nor particularly worse than its predecessors. But it did show a certain realisation of changing times and the need for a theatre rather larger than can be easily envisaged by an entrepreneur cheerfully out for a quick buck. It was in the late forties, early fifties, that the London theatre inexorably moved towards the public and institutional style of theatre. It is precisely at that point, here and now, that the New York theatre is tremulously finding itself. It is a very exciting moment in New York theatre history. Once we can get our financing right, we are about to achieve miracles. But the financing is still not easy.

In the theatre – British, American or Serbo-Croat – we always talk of seasons in a totally unrealist fashion, which personally worries me. Theatre critics solemnly look back on a year and assess the new works. This was not as good as Molière – Jesus! that wasn't even as good as Pinero. In no art other than the movies (whose critics have taken on our worst habits and wear them with a shameful pride) is the immediate given such stupid currency.

How good is the theatre? How good was last night's play? We judge the health of the theatre – fundamentally, and admittedly more fundamentally in New York than in London – on the acceptably commercial new works of the last three or four years. Imagine a concert programme based on such a premise. Or an opera company. Or, even, an art gallery. 'What have you done for me lately?' is a question that in the arts applies particularly to the theatre, and particularly it applies in New York City. New York wants something new. With horror I am occasionally forced to recognise that my adopted home-town would prefer a bad new play to a good old play. This would not be so dangerous to the theatre were it not for the town's practically notorious propensity for closing the bad new play in one night. Consider this for a moment.

The record of the year was moderate but decent enough. It did not come up with the premières of four Shakespeares, three Molières, one Vondel and two Schilling. It wasn't that kind of season. Yet we survived. On Broadway we had Harold Pinter's *Old Times*, with Rosemary Harris, Mary Ure and Robert Shaw. I personally happened to prefer them to the original London cast, but that is totally unimportant. We also had the world première (taken from our institutionalised New York Shakespeare Festival) of David Rabe's fascinating excursion into American family life and its Vietnam picnic, *Sticks and Bones*.

Neil Simon, who remains America's most under-estimated playwright – Americans generally and the Revenue Department specifically find it hard to accept that a simple hayseed city boy like Doc Simon is making as much money as he is making – gave us *The Prisoner of Second Avenue*. New Yorkers laugh at it with tears on their rear retina. Mr Simon is enormously funny to everyone in New York except the insecure. New Yorkers are not too secure about whether they are insecure. Often they go to a Neil Simon play in order to find out. This has made Mr Simon very rich. But I suspect that Mr Simon does not want to be rich, he wants to write good comedies responsive to the temper of his times.

What has been particularly disappointing about Broadway for this season in review was the failure not just of Michael Weller's excellent *Moonchildren* to find an audience despite four different rave reviews from the supposedly omnipotent *New York Times*, for Mr Weller's play with its background of student unrest could never be common or garden Broadway fare, but the comparative failure of more conservative plays one would have expected to have succeeded. I am thinking of plays such as the thriller *Night Watch*, George Furse's *Twigs*, even Robert Bolt's *Vivat! Vivat Regina!* which only mustered a relatively disappointing 117 performances. It also became very evident that fine, even virtuoso performances in flawed plays could not help very much, as they can occasionally do in London. A perfect example could be seen in the fate of Simon Grey's *Wise Child.* In London it received rather carping notices, and yet the virtuoso performance by Alec Guinness in the lead secured it a respectable run. On Broadway it received much the same kind of notices, most of them cold for the play, but lavish in their praise for Donald Pleasence who was playing the Guinness role. The result was a mere four performances and a certain amount of ill-feeling on the part of the understandably disgruntled actor.

Although Off-Broadway plays did not have a good 1971/72 season there were three fairly solid successes – Tennessee Williams's *Small Craft Warnings* (in which towards the end of the run Mr Williams, armed with a brand new Equity card, appeared himself), Arrabal's *They Put Handcuffs on the Flowers*, and Tom Stoppard's *The Real Inspector Hound* and *After Magritte.* Incidentally Stoppard does seem, if anything, to be more popular in New York than in London.

In musicals the story was as murky and as patternless as in recent other seasons. Although *Jesus Christ Superstar* did moderately well with the public (but rather badly with the critics) it was not the smash-hit expected. Indeed the surprise of the season – in Broadway argot it would be termed 'the sleeper', was a revival of *No, No, Nanette* with Ruby Keeler tap-dancing.

Two more conventionals came with *Sugar*, a musicalisation of the Billy Wilder movie *Some Like it Hot*, with Bobby Morse hilarious in the old Jack Lemmon role, and another nostalgia trip, this time only into the early Presley age, *Grease*, which after a slow start has done very well.

Probably the big musical money-maker, oddly enough, was Off-Broadway rather than on. This was *Godspell* and it has made a fortune, by mingling Jesus Christ with Commedia dell'Arte and praying for the best. I found it self-consciously cute but this was clearly a minority view. Where *Godspell* cleaned up was its marketing, for although it could not make much money in its tiny New York home, companies formed for international consumption, and soon the royalties were rolling in.

Anyone looking at the Broadway area today is bound to notice that it is largely a black district. As you might expect most of the movie houses have what are known as 'black-exploitation' movies, such as *Shaft* or *Superfly*. And yet the theatres were predominantly white. There were hardly any shows on Broadway catering to the black audience, even though elsewhere the black theatre has shown a remarkable health and vigour.

This season the film-maker Melvin van Peebles decided to do something about it, and presented two black musicals, the bitter and corrosive *Ain't Supposed to Die a Natural Death*, and the lighter and amusing, *Don't Play Us Cheap*. Another black musical – full of blues and gospel – was Micki Grant's *Don't Bother Me I Can't Cope*.

Another Broadway development is the coming together of Broadway and the institutional theatre. The previous summer Joseph Papp's New York Shakespeare Festival had a highly successful musical version of *Two Gentleman of Verona* in Central Park. It had music by Galt MacDermot (who composed *Hair*) and new lyrics by one of America's most promising playwrights, John Guare. It was decided to take the production and put it on Broadway, and it proved a substantial success. As I mentioned earlier another Papp production, David Rabe's *Sticks and Bones*, was also transferred from its down-town home to Broadway, where it won many plaudits, including a Pulitzer Prize.

Which brings me to the institutional theatre. This is really the equivalent of the London nationalised theatre, the National, the Royal Shakespeare, the Royal Court, the Mermaid, and the rest. Everything that is outside the West End gambit, but could not be considered fringe.

Of course the most important of these theatres in New York is the Lincoln Center repertory company, which operates two theatres in the vast Lincoln Center complex – the Vivian Beaumont and the Forum. The Vivian Beaumont is the larger, but both theatres use the same company and have the same director, Jules Irving. Perhaps the best major production here was a stylish revival of

7a (*left*) *Laurence Olivier, Director, National Theatre 1963–1973*
7b (*right*) *Peter Hall, Director, National Theatre 1973–*

7C–E PRODUCTIONS AT THE NATIONAL

7c The Front Page (*3rd from Left: Denis Quilley*)

7d Macbeth (*Gawn Grainger, Anthony Hopkins*)

7e Jumpers (*Diana Rigg, Michael Hordern*)

8A–C THE YOUNG VIC
8a Look Back in Anger (*Nicky Henson, Mel Martin*)

8b (*left*) Oedipus (*Ronald Pickup, Desmond MacNamara*)
8c (*right*) Scapino (*Jim Dale*)

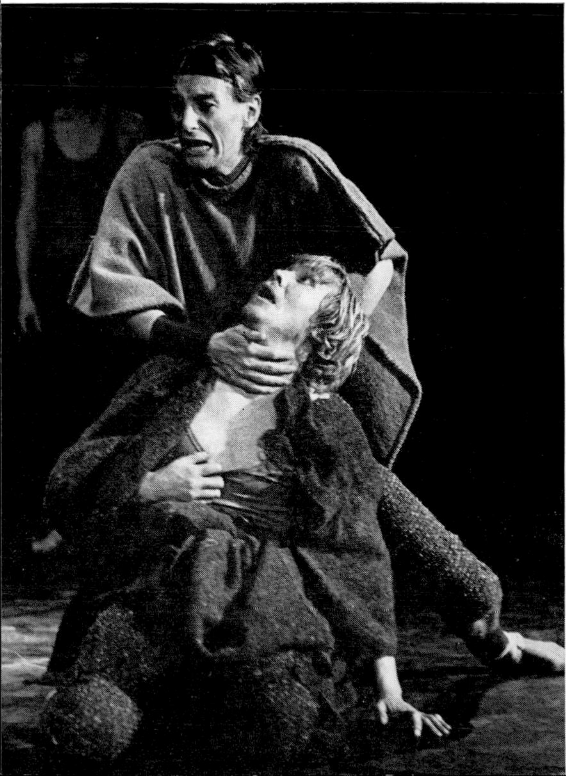

9A–D SOME EXAMPLES OF THE ART OF COARSE ACTING

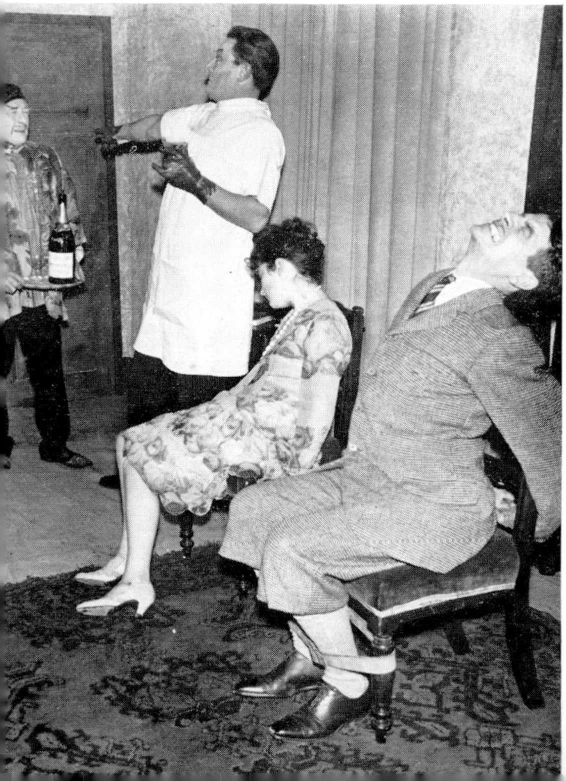

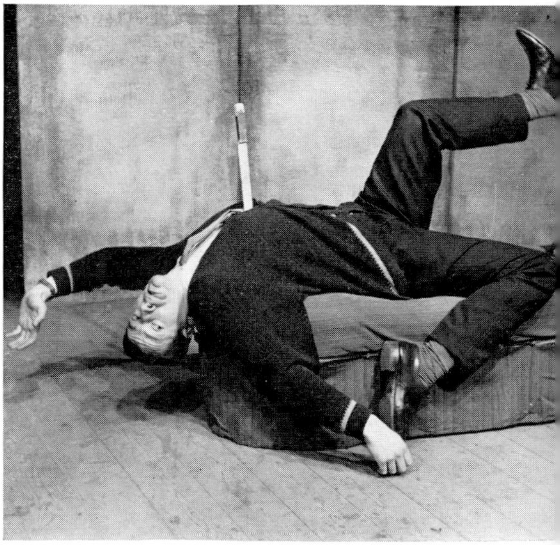

11a (*left*) *Northern Dance Theatre:* Cinderella (*John Fletcher*)
11b (*right*) *Ballet Rambert:* There Was A Time (*Julia Blaikie, Leigh Warren*)

11c *Royal Ballet:* Poême de L'Extase (*centre: Margot Fonteyn*)

12a *Prospect:* Richard III (*Richard Briers, Derek Jacobi*)

12b *Birmingham:* Macbeth (*Keith Baxter*)

12c *Nottingham:* The Tempest (*Hugh Griffith, Angela Scoular*)

12d *Actors' Company:* The Three Arrows (*Ian McKellen, Juan Moreno, Jack Shepherd*)

13A–C BROADWAY 1972–1973

13a (*left*) The Prisoner of Second Avenue: *Art Camen, Barbara Barrie*

13b (*right*) That Championship Season: *Richard A. Dusart, Walter McGinn*

13c Old Times: *Robert Shaw, Mary Ure, Rosemary Harris*

Arthur Miller's *The Crucible.* Although I was personally disappointed by the New York première of Edward Bond's *Narrow Road to the Deep North,* Schiller's *Mary Stuart* emerged fairly well, and a rather glossy staging of *Twelfth Night* by Ellis Rabb rounded out the main season. Downstairs in the Forum, I enjoyed a controversial black play by Ed Bullins, *The Duplex,* and also Peter Handke's strangely haunting if ineluctable, *The Ride Across Lake Constance.*

Mr Papp and his Shakespeare Festival had a good year. In the Park it gave a very interesting *Hamlet,* with Stacy Keach in the title-role, and in its down-town home – an elegant rabbit-warren of about six theatres – it had some notable productions. The best, apart from *Sticks and Bones,* was Jason Miller's *That Championship Season,* a realistic and strong work, that later also transferred to Broadway.

The American Place Theatre is a club. It is run by Wyn Handman and offers nothing but new plays by American authors. This season it moved into a new and handsome theatre, and its inaugural season was as successful as any season of experimental plays by young authors has a right to expect. The Negro Ensemble Company scored with Philip Friend's *The Sty of the Blind Pig,* the Circle in the Square succeeded with a new production of Saul Bellow's *The Last Analysis,* and the Chelsea Theatre, directed by Michael David, and based in the Brooklyn Academy of Music had a most successful season producing a very lively new production of *The Beggar's Opera,* the American première of Jean Genet's *The Screens,* and an unusual autobiographical piece by Allen Ginsberg, called *Kaddish,* which used both film and television very imaginatively. In most ways this Chelsea Theatre is the best of the truly adventurous companies in the country.

There are however the genuine *avant garde,* such as André Gregory's Manhattan Project. Mr Gregory is a disciple of Grotowski and an admirer of Brook, and his production of *Alice in Wonderland,* which subsequently went on a European tour, is inventive and important. Robert Wilson, with his extenuating of dramatic time, and productions that last six or more hours, is another of New York's theatrical experimentalists. Then, of course, there is La Mama, and the entire Off-Off-Broadway scene, sometimes brilliant, sometimes dingy, always energetic.

A final word for a couple of little classic theatres, operating on a shoestring, the Roundabout Theatre – which this season gave, among other things, a respectable *Master Builder* – and the CSC (Classic Stage Company) which will do anything from Pinter to Shakespeare with unusual zest.

In many ways it is in such grassroots of the New York theatre that I perceive the most energy and in which I take the most hope. The theatre is still very much alive in New York City, and best of all it is plentiful.

Edinburgh's Traverse Now and Then

As he leaves the theatre he has directed for four years to take charge of the Hampstead Theatre Club, Michael Rudman looks back over the past and present history of Scotland's foremost experimental playhouse.

Ten years ago in a small room in the English colony of Edinburgh one or two gathered together to watch two foreign plays in what used to be a brothel not far from a well known castle. This was the official opening of Britain's most unofficial theatre. The Traverse was never born; a botanical image is more precise. Seeds were scattered on the granite ground of Scotland. Manure was spread and still is. (Don't look a gift horse in the arse is our official attitude towards the Scottish Arts Council.) Playing the leading role of Johnny Appleseed was one, or possibly ten, called Jim Haynes, recently released from the American Air Force where his main activity was reading *Das Kapital* while his official duties were to screen and censor all telegrams sent from Europe to America. Jim Haynes started a paperback bookshop where plays were sometimes produced and this bookshop is considered to be the beginnings of the Traverse. Ronald Mavor gives this account:

'(Jim) started a paperback bookshop where you got a cup of coffee and someone was always tuning his guitar in the back shop – a situation now commonplace but then unique. At successive Edinburgh Festivals Jim and some friends from Edinburgh University Dramatic Society put on readings at about midnight, somewhat dramatised, in costume, with claret included in the seat price, of the works of David Hume and others. These entertainments ended with violent public debate and the then still extant walls of George Square echoed with perfervid Scots debating their ways home in the early hours.'

In our nows we see our beginnings. Now at the Traverse debates are held, often involving city councillors, M.P.s and long haired radicals (the latter sometimes including the former). These are called Traverse Trials and cannot be bested as documentary theatre, involving as they do men and women speaking extemporaneously on subjects close to their hearts and minds before an audience, often perfervid, ready to jump on every remark. If these gatherings were to become the Scottish Assembly (and in all modesty we can claim that the constituency of that projected body will not be so different), the following would have been instituted:

(1) Comprehensive education for Edinburgh
(2) Gay Liberation
(3) The centre of Edinburgh limited to public transportation
(4) A Scottish Government controlling Scotland's oil
(5) An Edinburgh Festival with some official relevance to Edinburgh.

It will become increasingly clear that the thesis of this article is that the Traverse now is very like the Traverse then and that Harold Hobson, when he wrote about the National Theatre, was right in saying that men do make theatrical history. Men like Jim Haynes for example:

> A great feature of those days was Jim. Everybody's easy friend and always on the verge of getting Orson Welles to play King Lear with music by either Lionel Bart or Stravinsky on a cart in James's Court. Jim's greatest gift was to believe anything possible and, by gentle enthusiasm, to keep everybody's daft notations alive until, almost as often as not, they began to take shape. Everybody went to the Traverse and Jim would introduce you to Timothy Leary, the Lord Provost and a man who was growing blue carrots in the interval between acts. (*Ronald Mavor*)

These days the bar of the Traverse is decorated with posters, some of them designed by the daughter of Jack Kane, the present Lord Provost, and Jack Kane will go on television and say that the Traverse is good, and he will help the Traverse to a grant from the Corporation of £2,000 a year, and he will bring his wife to a show where the word 'fuck' is used 296 times.

The impetus of the Traverse was to keep the spirit of the Festival going fifty-two weeks of the year. Now the Traverse receives considerable help from the Royal Lyceum Company, Scottish Opera and the Scottish Theatre Ballet. But in those days there was very little. Jim Haynes writes of the beginnings:

It began in Ricky Demarco's flat, in my wee basement in Dunne Terrace, and it was a product of the Edinburgh International Festival. The Festival brought people from all over the world for three short exciting weeks, and some of us wanted to keep that spirit around us all year round. But specifically it was Jane Quigley, Red Williams, Ricky Demarco and Tom Mitchell who one way or the other, inspired me to attempt to do something concrete.... I was in love with Jane. We considered getting married. I wanted her to stay in Edinburgh. In fact, Ricky and I wanted every one we like to stay in Edinburgh. One way to get these people to stay was to make the city exciting. And this is what we attempted to do....

Tom Mitchell, farmer, owner of Workington Rugby League Football Club, world traveller and now President of the Traverse gives a vivid account of how Jim Haynes' dream became fact: 'If we are to be reasonably accurate about the origins of the place perhaps now is the time to place a few credits where hitherto there have been none. It was profusely red-bearded College of Art teacher, soft-spoken gentle Peter McGinn who said to me one day, "I would like to show you something." "Something" turned out to be a cobwebbed dirty, decaying building in James Court that had once been the last model lodging house of Edinburgh. Kelly's Paradise had been one of its many names. Said Peter McGinn going over it with the eye of a romantic, "It's coming down, you know." His momentary cunning challenge did the trick. One year of tracking down absentee owners – one an absconder doing the Corporation more for repairs than the building was worth – proved a frustrating, even painful business. On the day I got the key Pete McGinn and Tamara Alferoff went down into the basement with me. Pete brushed the cobwebs away from the half-open door under the creaking stairway and peered into the gloom. "Poor bugger," he said, I froze – I could see an inquest coming. When I mustered up enough courage to look – the poor old bugger turned out to be a pair of crutches propped up against the wall topped with an old trilby hat. Phew!

'Getting the place approved as a Theatre Club was an unbelievable exercise. Some of the City Fathers assumed it was to be the Edinburgh equivalent of Raymond's Strip Club. And next door to the Royal Castle at that. 'Twould never do. The original idea was to use the building for painters to paint in – painters of Edinburgh and itinerant painters. I was not encouraged by the head of the Art College – "A place for coffee and red wine? That's all that painters are doing these days – drinking red wine and not doing any damned painting." I had met Ricky Demarco two years earlier. An advance party of the Cambridge Footlights led by undergraduate David Missen and their meeting up with Ricky did the trick. We met. The building was named *The Sphinx* and a sign was erected to that effect. Lord Kilbrandon, an ex-Cambridge man himself met the Footlights people and sustained them in one way or another. So *that* was the first use of Kelly's Paradise as a theatre!

'The roof was bad. It came off. The plumbing was rotten – it had to be renewed. About this time I collected typhoid during the Algerian troubles. Enter John Malcolm – professional actor working at the Citizens. Sitting the required six paces from my bed in the City Isolation Hospital he propounded the idea of using the Traverse for professional theatre. By the time I was out of hospital John Malcolm, assisted by Terry Lane, had virtually gutted the old cookhouse and had scrounged theatre seating and a host of other things. They lived in what later became the restaurant. They were incompatible. We were a committee of three. Ricky Demarco was the first addition. Then followed John Martin, Jimmy Walker, Andrew whose second name escapes me and Sheila Colvin, who was our first real secretary. There were storm clouds ahead. What was originally meant was an acting commune where the box office take and coffee sales would be all the financial support required. Equity said bollox to that and there we were in the fertiliser business. As I said, the two heavies were not in accord. They rowed. It was a toss-up but it was John who got the "golden handshake" in the form of lunch at the Wee Windaes, a bottle of wine and a large brandy. He was not pleased and quite disillusioned – after all, it was *his* idea. Terry had gone into hiding in the Dean Village. He was coaxed back. We opened with an unfortunate stage stabbing with Colette O'Neill taken off to hospital. I didn't know until much later that she was almost a goner – news given to me in the middle of the night in hospital by the surgeon who had operated. It could have been the end of the Traverse (the name chosen by John Malcolm and Terry Lane). The adverse publicity was bad enough as it was with one national (you know which) newspaper not at all happy about the Traverse idea.

'Ricky Demarco was a tour de force – very often at seven p.m. there was not a single booking yet by half past he had the place full. The steady hand of John Martin saw us through the ever recurring financial crises. He took over from me as Chairman. Terry Lane was our Artistic Director. Jim Haynes returned from America after a while, replacing John Martin as Chairman. Terry had many outstanding productions to his credit. Jim and he didn't see eye to eye. Terry was the one to go and Jim became in charge of direction with Andrew Elliot as his Chairman.'

Once established in the Lawnmarket the Traverse began with the introduction of European plays to Britain. Ten years on, especially through groups like Freehold and The People Show it still gives Edinburgh audiences their first taste of faraway ideas and new-fangled notions. But the main business of the Traverse, since Jim Haynes introduced the policy, has been to discover and produce British plays that might not otherwise have been performed.

David Story says that had he not received a letter from Gordon McDougall several years ago asking for permission to do *The Restoration of Arnold Middleton* he probably wouldn't be writing plays. Robert Kidd saw the production on its last night at the Traverse and a Royal Court production followed. Cecil Taylor, a fairly undistinguished record salesman, became a playwright through Jim Haynes as did Heathcote Williams (not, strictly speaking, a record salesman) and Stanley Eveling is one of ours. Max Stafford-Clark, both as Artistic Director and later as Director of the Traverse Workshop Company made a significant contribution to the careers of Howard Brenton and Stanley Eveling. The main point, however, is not 'look who we made famous' because these men would probably have emerged as playwrights without the Traverse. The point is that they emerged 'well' and are still writing plays. The reason for this lies not so much in the talents of the men who ran the Traverse as in the ethos of the place and its audience.

In August 1969 the Traverse moved to a former machine shop in the Grassmarket. The auditorium there is a black box, partly filled with cushioned seating units, and on a first night these units are packed tight with people. These people are part of the cast of every play or theatrical invention that opens at the Traverse. Firs would call them a 'job lot'. Some actors, several lawyers, two city councillors (one red, one blue) a man who claims to work on oil rigs, two schoolteachers (one retired) a few stray Americans, a policeman (Hamish McFuzz we call him) some people we've never seen before and, of course, the village critics.

I should say a few words about the Scottish critics. They write so well and with such witty invention that one might well wonder why they have not taken Dr Johnson's famous road to London. The reason is simple. They miss every boat. This is not a mixed metaphor. One of the main reasons they miss boats is because they look for them on roads. There is a positive correlation between their liking for a play and the number of yawns it will raise in our audience. They never pan a play – oh no – the Traverse and the London critics have taught them not to do that. That could be dangerous. But if they like it, really like it, compare it to Oscar Wilde and give it the highest accolade ('literate') then you can be sure that it had better not cross the Pennines.

I hope that I don't sound ungrateful. I do, but I'm not. As journalists the Scottish critics are unsurpassed in their support of local theatre. A great deal of the success of the Traverse can be attributed to the *Scotsman* and its drama critics. They may reserve their accolades for the struggling reputations of Chekhov and Miller but they lash out column inches on even the oddest offering from the Traverse and the dreaded Glasgow duo of Havergal and Prowse. If the Nottingham Playhouse had even half the coverage the Traverse gets in the local press (if indeed there were a notable local press there) it would never have an empty seat.

But I should be talking about the Traverse audience which seems oblivious to what it reads. Often they frighten me with the anticipation they bring at a first night. I find myself wishing that they didn't care so much. Think what they saw before we did. Storey, Abelman, La Mama, Heathcote Williams, Arrabal, Freehold, The People Show, Bellow, Jarry, D. H. Lawrence and on and on. I've seen them carried away with such joy and hilarity that I was certain the actors would lose control. I've heard them silent with thundering dread as they realised that their worst fears were coming true. One of them burned an American Flag because Pip Simmons suggested it. ('I'm sorry Mr Consul, sir. Of course we'll buy you a new one. I had no idea they burn so easily.') And afterwards. What about 'I didn't like the play at all, Michael, but it was so well acted I'm coming again next week.' What about the Bishop who involuntarily lit up a cigarette as seven nude bodies writhed, genitals pressed together, two feet from him in bright light. Afterwards he said that it was 'very enjoyable'. There is a lot of talk in the theatre about 'training audiences'. As a group ours must have a D.Phil. being for the most part professional men and women and therefore practically itinerant workers in Britain today. Most, incidentally, lived in various parts of the world before settling in Edinburgh.

Where our now chiefly differs from our beginning, is in the relationship between the Traverse and the Edinburgh Festival. Whereas Jim Haynes wanted to keep the Festival spirit going all year the Traverse now has quite a job to keep the Festival spirit alive during the Festival. In Drama the Festival has, quite simply, lost its excitement. In the past few years there have been exceptions, like the annual Dunlopmobile, André Gregory's *Alice in Wonderland* and the 7/84 Company but generally it has been a case of playing safe with oldies. The excuses for this are legion but the reasons are seldom stated. To paraphrase Ethredge there is nothing older than an old play. Unless there is a Brook or a Guthrie involved, acting as a kind of co-author, an old play at the Festival perpetuates the myth that old is good and new is dangerous, especially financially. Worthiness has been all and even Ricky Demarco, perfectly cast as Sir Novelty, has failed to generate more than the requisite number of column inches. Like the Presidency of the United States the job of Drama Director of the Edinburgh Festival seems to be too important to give to anyone at all.

During the Festival the Traverse is the unofficial centre of the Fringe. The Traverse Tattoo provides a nightly sample of everything that is going on. It is a free entertainment in the courtyard where many festive things have occurred. Yehudi Menuhin fiddling followed by Lindsay Kemp... Jack Shepherd declaring Armageddon while the Director of Productions of the Royal Lyceum Theatre threw water over 300 people... John Neville throwing and getting custard pies... *The Ken Campbell Road Show*... the emergence of the *Low Moan Spectacular*... Harold Hobson being introduced to *The Great Northern Welly Boot Show* and on and on. Meanwhile, on the inside, the Traverse auditorium, designed by

Nick Groves-Raines, is extraordinarily gifted. I've called it a black box. It has certain advantages over John Bury's grey box. Used properly all attention is focused on the actors and the play. By obviating the phoney magic that comes from flies and wings the audience can relish better the magic that is conjured up before their very eyes. When I hold up these two fingers, spread like a pair of scissors, then that's a hole in a wall, you see. Unfortunately not all productions at the Traverse take advantage of its qualities. But when they do, in *Lay By*, *Curtains*, *In the Heart of the British Museum*, *Carravaggio Buddy*, and *Pantagleize* you have what the Edinburgh Festival should provide: a show for that time and that place, in complete control of the room, brooking (pardon) no criticism from outside and spreading the word that Edinburgh is a place to see good theatre during the Festival. The answer is not, definitely not, to turn the Festival over to the Traverse. The answer is to find the right men and women (Bill Bryden, Frank Dunlop, Nancy Meckler, Mark Long, Terry Hands – there are lots) and put them into the rooms, while providing the audience, as the Traverse does, with food and drink in the same place. The aim of the Edinburgh Festival should be to make the Traverse superfluous.

One feature of the Traverse which might well prevent its becoming superfluous, is the composition of its staff and its management committee. The Traverse Committee of Management should be hailed across the country for the complete freedom it gives to the Artistic Director, and for the degree of financial responsibility individuals take in the form of signing leases, guaranteeing overdrafts and fund raising. Unencumbered by any knowledge of show-business ('Who is Barbara Jefford?' was one of my favourite questions) or how other theatres work they will argue for hours about a five per cent drop in bar takings while the Artistic Director vainly attempts to relate the programme for the past three months. In my three years I never heard any serious criticism of the artistic policy of any of the five Artistic Directors past or present.

Partly because of this attitude the staff of the Traverse has a loyalty which I have never seen matched. Penny Richardson, the General Manager, and Sheila Harborth, the Production Manager, consider the Traverse their own, as indeed it is, partly because everyone is paid the same, partly because most decisions are taken in consultation, but mostly I think because the Traverse is needed in Edinburgh and by writers (and this need communicates itself daily to the staff) the men and women who work there consider themselves permanent. The Traverse is not a stepping-stone or a training ground. It is the only theatre of its kind and to leave it is to leave a world behind at considerable risk.

The Stagestruck Cecil Beaton

A profile by the author of Erté *and* Bakst.

Cecil Beaton's success, in so many fields, has been fed by two basic ingredients – an unshakeable belief that he possessed artistic gifts and a determination to succeed in his own way. His father's efforts to impose sound academic achievements, and when that failed, a career in cement – if you can believe it – were swept aside for what the youthful Cecil knew were better things.

Nothing is more central to Beaton's biography than the image of the ten year old stage-struck boy. That was in 1914. He would gaze wistfully at photographs of Edwardian beauties outside the theatres, and when inside he stored away visual images of splendid spectacle and colour. This love of the theatre made him take up photography, first borrowing his Nanny's Brownie, and then persuading his mother to buy a 3A Folding Pocket Kodak as a birthday present. He began by posing his mother and his sisters in imitation of the theatrical photos of the time, with draperies and flowers.

For a stage career Beaton had almost no professional training; as he himself says – 'My gift is largely an intuitive one, for colour and for supervising the making of costumes – I think I must have been born with it'. Nevertheless he understands the importance of sound technique and has always used first-rate assistants, respecting the professional contributions of costumiers, scene painters, builders, on whom so much depends.

The third important factor is a personal nostalgia for his own childhood, or rather for his own life-span. Beaton is not a scholarly recreator of the past, like the remarkable designers of Russian historical films, a Visconti or a Tosi with a gimlet eye for detail and atmosphere, or a Zeffirelli whose realistic recreations are like academic Victorian painting.

Beaton's preference for Edwardiana represents a perfect understanding – instinctive or calculated, I'm not sure – for his own gifts, and a nostalgic desire to immerse himself in the period when perhaps he felt most secure.

Certainly Beaton's best work has revolved around the turn of the century. Even Sheridan's *School for Scandal*, (designed both for London 1952, and the *Comédie Française*, 1962,) which is, after all, a prototype of Edwardian elegance and wit – beyond the bleak hinterland of Victorian drama – was grist to Beaton's nostalgic mill. *School for Scandal* he considers 'the best thing I have done, particularly the French production'.

Let us, however, retrace his steps. Cecil Walter Hardy Beaton, since made a Commander of the British Empire, and more recently Knighted, was born in London on 14th January 1904. Educated at Harrow he was sent up to Cambridge, to read History and Architecture. He admits to never working, never attending lectures, spending his time – appropriately – designing and acting for the Marlowe Society – among other productions Pirandello's *Henry IV*. London was never too far away, for the joys of the theatre, exhibitions of Lovat Fraser's stage designs at the Leicester Gallery, and then the ravishing spectacle of Leon Bakst's designs for the Ballets Russe, the intoxicating colour and splendour of *The Good-Humoured Ladies*.

Down from Cambridge his father remained obdurate; it was all very well for the boy to want to be an actor, to write plays, to design, but could he, and if he could, where, how? Beaton *père* sent the aspiring artist to work with a friend who sold cement; in his spare time the young Cecil hawked book jackets and illustrations round the publishers.

As we know, photography first won him fame – 'taking pictures of that extraordinary tall and gothic-looking Edith Sitwell lying on a chequered floor like a Renaissance figure on a tomb'.

In his early thirties he got his first chance in the theatre from

C. B. Cochran. Beaton created a tropical island, influenced by the Douanier Rousseau, which proved a disaster. He feared that this first chance might well prove his last. But wily old Cochran must have recognised something and gave him another chance, a ballet called *The First Shoot* by Osbert Sitwell, choreography by Frederick Ashton, music by William Walton. How's that for a bag of future Knights! 'I wouldn't wish to alter any of it to-day' he says. The setting, as one might guess, was an Edwardian photographer's studio. The ballet appeared, with great success, in the 1936 revue *Follow The Sun*, at the newly built Adelphi Theatre.

Young, raw in terms of professional theatrical commitment, Beaton learned some important new lessons.

Firstly that whilst as a photographer and as a writer he is his own boss, satisfying his own taste and standards, in the theatre a designer is part of a group, enormously dependent on the understanding and expertise of others: 'In the early days I would put up a stubborn fight to convince, terribly uncompromising, with nervous storms if I couldn't get my own way'. There is no doubt that since those starry-eyed youthful days his enthusiasm for the theatre has somewhat cooled – 'I'm prepared to work all night, if necessary – painting the scenery, arranging the smallest detail, but what I find irksome is the perpetual banter from everyone involved, big and small'. Later he was to realise that 'the designer must judge at what point to concede something he knows will minimise his effects', and learned that plan as you may 'there is always some chemistry in the theatre which prevents everything being finished before the 13th hour'.

After the 1938 Cochran revue there followed another Ashton ballet, *Apparitions*, to Liszt's music arranged by Constant Lambert, starring Margot Fonteyn, whom he later described as 'of all unselfish dedicated artists, perhaps the most detached and masculine in her approach – she can take any amount of abstract criticism without being touchy or resentful'.

Designing for the ballet presented special problems; 'working within a confined and restricted area, of which the audience has only the slightest semblance of an idea. Unlike opera, ballet relies more on a sense of fantasy – dresses as well as decor, in many cases, must suggest indications rather than realistic outlines'. A later ballet, also with Margot Fonteyn, Ashton's *Marguerite and Armand*,

(1962) was a great challenge. All his serious work is done at his house in Wiltshire, which contains his reference material and working studios. Pondering over this ballet, based on Dumas' famous play, he sought a symbolic theme or emblem; it was winter, a fire flickered in the grate, catching the gilt on a Second Empire screen, the period of Dumas and the story; 'It gave me the clue for my designs – *La Dame aux Camélias* as a bird in a cage – the gilt strips of the firescreen also gave me the theme for the properties, the candelabra and the cornstocks, as well as the applied decorations of the costumes.'

This little story underlines the intensely personal nature of Beaton's approach – the imagery which comes from within himself, his life, his surroundings, his memories and fantasies. His designs are not the result of painstaking research or reconstruction, but a reflection of himself, his life, his instincts and intuition. It is not uncommon. Writing about the Russian-born designer Erté and his work for the French music-hall, I once suggested that one reason for his success was that in some ways he always designed fantastic costumes as though he himself was to walk down the great staircase at the Folies-Bergère.

The only Beaton opera I have seen is Puccini's *Turandot* – designed both for the Metropolitan, New York (1961) and Covent Garden (1963). He found in it,'many conflicting factors – the ancient story of barbaric cruelty is in direct contradiction with the baroque fairy story'. Once again it was a personal possession – some 18th century engravings of Pekin – which suggested the style, quite apart from his own travels in the East. In the New York production he faced the not uncommon problem of other people's views – in this case the conductor Stokowski's insistence on following Puccini's stage directions for a blood-red sunset when the curtain rises. 'I felt that in an opera where there is little dramatic action in the last act, the designer must reserve his best efforts for the later part of the evening'. The production involved him in even more drama! Sitting in the stalls on the opening night, to his horror one of the ladies of the chorus appeared in her own rainbow-coloured costume. 'I could only see a large orange bottom amid an infinite number of subtle blues'. In the interval he rushed backstage and literally ripped the offending skirt from the bodice. The shop-steward of the appropriate Trade

Union demanded an apology, otherwise the chorus would refuse to appear in the second act. Beaton equally adamantly refused an apology and the show went on – as it always does! (His opera designs include *La Traviata* and *Vanessa*, both for the Met. Ballets, *Les Pavillons*, *Les Sirènes* and for New York *Swan Lake* and *Tintagel.*)

As a late-comer to the theatre, conscious of his failings, his lack of training and experience, as well as his gifts and possibilities, Beaton was keenly aware of the status of his two major contemporaries – Oliver Messel and Rex Whistler, the latter killed in the last war. Messel was the master of gay, decorative, rococco, whilst Whistler's sense of period pastiche particularly illuminated the 19th century. Before the war Beaton sought to emulate them; to this day he recalls his sense of inferiority, assuming that his commissions probably resulted from Messel's or Whistler's refusals. By force of circumstances he emerged, after the war, as the most active of the trio, and in a series of stage and screen successes, the only English master of their particular brand of re-creation. 'I never really started in the theatre until after the war', he says. It is not possible to list all his productions, but his comments on some of the outstanding ones are worth noting.

Lady Windermere's Fan was his first important play (1945). It wasn't admired by the great James Agate, because of its Edwardian rather than Victorian setting: 'He was right, but I like the Edwardian period. I am much more disciplined now and in fact when I redesigned the Wilde play I heeded Agate and shifted it back to 1895'. John Gielgud's production of Eric Linklater's *Crisis in Heaven* hardly took off theatrically, but Beaton was greatly stretched to produce ingenious sets, transforming before the audience, with an array of costumes covering a period from Helen of Troy to Florence Nightingale. Other notable productions, in London and New York were *The Second Mrs Tanqueray*, *Charley's Aunt*, *The Chalk Garden*, *Portrait of a Lady*. The period flavour is unmistakable.

In 1953, en route to New York, he received a message to call on Lynn and Alfred Lunt, to hear Noël Coward read his new play *Quadrille*, set in 1866. Beaton enthusiastically tackled the designs. As usual, nothing ran smoothly: 'A certain candy stripe was needed, but it was out of stock. Binkie (Beaumont) would not have it painted; it wouldn't clean. At last some firm was willing to weave the material. Two weeks later the loom broke down, so the dress had to be hand-painted at the eleventh hour. Patterns of fabric, fixed to certain chairs for upholstery, were mixed up and the wrong sofa was covered; pictures were found to be too big for the set'. The designer's role, particularly in the theatre, is as much diplomatic overseer as creator. It is he who must ensure the quality of the scene painting, the making of dresses, wigs, jewellery, props. No wonder that when *Quadrille* arrived in Manchester for a trial run 'the atmosphere was so electric one felt there must be an explosion any minute'.

In the postwar years Beaton occupied an enviable position as almost the only remaining master of a particular kind of period design, and as such began to be in demand for films – *Anna Karenina, The Doctor's Dilemma, Kipps, The Young Mr. Pitt, An Ideal Husband* – mostly for Korda, and *Gigi*. Working in films is quite a different problem; for one thing the standard of technical help is far superior. Period props are expertly recreated, there is excellent professional help immediately at hand, and whilst the designer supervises, he is relieved of responsibility for finish and timing. Large studios maintain detailed archives and documentation, with secretarial as well as manual assistance to facilitate the artist's needs.

My Fair Lady not only represents Beaton's greatest success, it also afforded him the experience of working on one subject in both the theatre and the film studio. The most important single difference is that the original stage production had sets designed by the American artist Oliver Smith. Beaton disliked the arrangement, but in fact the settings were plain and simple, affording a suitable background for his stunning costumes. As the *Sunday Times* later wrote – sentiments echoed throughout the press – 'The costumes he created for it have a luxury, elegance and beauty that have largely contributed to its being the most successful musical play in the century.'

Using a similar idiom in two different media created enormous problems. On the stage a larger degree of formality is possible, and a single frame-work allows different kinds of stylisation. Thus naturalistic costumes might suit the domestic interior scenes, and in no way clash with the famous black and white Ascot scene. 'The gasps of the audience on seeing the motionless frieze of ladies like magpies against a white drop were balm to the designer's ego.'

There had been a battle with the authors and director over the period; Beaton insisted on dressing it in the fashions of the time when *Pygmalion* was first produced. 'Having promised that I could make the ladies of 1913 appear as alluring as those of 1900, my next, overriding, task was to accommodate the pre-World War I styles to the unfolding of the story'.

The film presented other problems. In the first place, whilst in the theatre the designer's total stage picture, his sets and, costumes, are available to the audience for them to see, take in, accept or reject in toto or in detail, in the cinema the audience is presented with a selection-package of details made by the director, cameraman and editor. 'The only solution is to see that there is no bad angle, nothing that must not be shown.' Colours appear different on the stage, and in different lighting, than they do on the screen. Whilst generalisations, even exaggerations, often work best on the stage, on the screen everything must be planned for the scrutiny of close-up.

On the film version of *My Fair Lady* (1964), Beaton faced specific, stylistic difficulties – notably the mixing of realism in the opening Covent Garden sequence, the authenticity of Professor Higgins' study and acoustical machinery, and the heightened stylisation of Ascot. The shock was intentional – 'It is meant to be, for Ascot comes as a shock to Eliza. I knew that the switch in idiom was a risk, that the mixture of painted sets followed by realistic battle scenes had not worked in Olivier's *Henry V*.'

The added responsibility for the total setting in the film gave him much pleasure. 'It is set in my period, the period of my childhood. A lot of the designs are based on actual fashions of the time'. The Art Nouveau rooms and furniture, with strong overtones of Rennie Mackintosh and Voysey, were charmingly conceived and superbly rendered by Hollywood technicians.

Beaton's next musical, for Broadway, proved a great disappointment. '*Coco* was ruined by the fact that the sets were so expensive and heavy they couldn't be taken on a pre-Broadway tour'. The show had six weeks of previews which meant that night after night friends of the director, the authors, the cast, came round with suggestions for the official opening night. 'I then had the tiresome job of having to justify my decisions, or compromising. The show was completely un-Parisian. I'm pleased it didn't come to England, although I loved the *Little Black Dress* number'.

From his now considerable experience we finally discussed general problems. I referred to a growing tendency for designers to be attracted to directing in the theatre. Beaton agreed that the problems of compromise were often disturbing; the lack of rehearsal time, the designer's inability to control the lighting, which could distort, even ruin, the required effect. One understands that his independence as a photographer and writer increases his irritability with the theatre's endless discussions, and often false democracy. As a photographer, he particularly feels a desire to control certain areas of the camera work in films – angles, groupings, the use of colour, all extenuation of design.

The future? For the moment he is immersed in writing, having much to record. If something interesting comes along in theatre or films it will not be difficult to distract him. There are many things he hopes to tackle; *The Tempest* and *Macbeth* – perhaps *A Midsummer Night's Dream*, although his delight with Peter Brook's production has somewhat inhibited this ambition. He deplores the increasing lack of colour on the stage – 'They keep on producing sets in monochromes – yellow, brown, dun colours; Lila di Nobili is a beautiful designer, but her influence has been rather disastrous.' Then there is the classical 19th century repertoire, Chekhov, Ibsen. He still hankers after writing a play successor to his *The Gainsborough Girls*.

Let us leave the final word with Sir Cecil, still as stage-struck at 70 as he was at ten: 'Because it is so satisfying to give to an assembled company a pleasure which has stood the test of time, all the troubles and difficulties that have been faced whilst the play was in production are now forgotten by actor, carpenter, scene-shifter, producer, dressmaker and designer, in the joy of presenting to the world of faces, lit with a reflected glow from the stage, another world – as magical and transitory as a flower.'

Tuning the Instruments

A theatregoer asks: Are drama schools really necessary?

When Robert Morley was a student at the Royal Academy of Dramatic Art more years ago than he cares to remember, he was sent for by the principal, Kenneth Barnes, who informed him that his choice of the stage as a profession was, in his opinion, misguided, and that he'd be well advised to seek employment elsewhere. To the young Mr Morley, who had spent one of the happiest years of his life to date at the Academy, given a 'triumphant Shylock', and been convinced that, had he stayed on a further year, he would have carried off the Kenneth Kent Prize for Attack in Acting, this news came as something of a blow. Lip trembling, he explained to the principal that acting was the only thing he had ever wanted to do. 'In that case,' said Barnes, 'I can only hope you have private means.'

Were he alive today, Sir Kenneth might very well have found himself expressing precisely the same sentiments a good deal more frequently, and not only to those he considered to be without talent. For, as everyone knows, the profession has never been so over-populated and underpaid as it is in 1973. And were some miracle to occur whereby no actor or actress needed ever again to depend on the theatre for his or her living, the only people who'd be likely to find themselves out of work would be Equity. As it is, they thrive on universal uncertainty and end up by being twice as confused as the people whose interests they're supposed to be serving. And if there is one aspect of the profession about which they are particularly equivocal it is drama schools.

'Equity is particularly suspect on this matter,' Peter Plouviez told me, 'simply because we have such a vested interest. Since it is our aim, in the interests of our members, to try and limit the number of new people who can be brought into the theatre, it is assumed that our ideal would be one drama school, run by ourselves, with only five students a year. Far from it. We are the first to criticise the present Government's adverse attitude towards free education. We believe training should become the normal preparation for entry into the theatre; but what we should like to determine first is some kind of standard by which all drama training can be judged. You see it isn't just a question of the 250 or so students who come out of the major drama schools every year; we have people turning up here claiming training at colleges of technology, teacher's training establishments, universities, and sometimes places we've never even heard of. And all the time we have our existing members to worry about. We would welcome a solution from the Government or a private body. At the present time we're very good at asking the questions, but not so good on the answers.'

But is there in fact all that much difference in the aims, methods and standards of the so called major drama schools in this country? I recently visited eight in and around the London area – RADA, Central, Guildhall, LAMDA, Webber-Douglas, Rose Bruford, Drama Centre and E.15. All have been recognised by the Department of Education as being efficient; so at least that's one thing they have in common.

The buildings and their situations tell a tiny tale in themselves. On the one hand you have RADA with its hideously dated but none the less imposing entrance in Gower Street, the entrance hall heavy with busts and portraits of the great, and its uniformed commissionaires, all combining to give the place an air of tradition and authority; and down by the Embankment, the Guildhall School of Music and Drama, like a London teaching hospital with its heavy blackened façade, its motto over the door (*Domine dirige nos*) and inside, in its echoing hall, the large wooden boards indicating which members of the staff are IN and OUT. On the other hand you have the two cosier bedsitter-land schools – LAMDA in the Cromwell Road and the Webber-Douglas in the more rarefied Clareville Street. The Rose Bruford College rambles in and around a large and now slightly seedy country mansion in Sidcup. Central live in a state of some chaos in an overcrowded Victorian house at Swiss Cottage with the old Embassy Theatre as their centrepiece. The Drama Centre lurk behind the forbidding exterior of a converted church at Chalk Farm, while E.15 are to be found eventually, not, as one might have supposed, at Stratford East, but in a lovely Georgian house in the middle of a large housing estate in Loughton.

But wherever they are situated and however good their facilities, they all have their problems. LAMDA has a beautiful little theatre in Logan Place, the perfect setting for a rep. company for third-year students, but is desperately short of funds. They get a lot of work done down at Rose Bruford, being away from the distractions of London, but then they have no London theatre in which to show off the results of their efforts. Central has recently acquired a brand new studio on the other side of the road, but they're still desperately pushed for space. At E.15 they have a choice of outdoor productions in and around the house and nine-acre garden (productions are sometimes done on the trot with the audience in hot pursuit), or indoor shows in the lovely old barn they bought seven years ago for £1,000 and reconstructed themselves in the garden; well, bringing theatre into the midst of the community it may be, but for the students it's still an uncomfortably long way from town.

One thing is perfectly clear: there is, as far as the students are concerned anyway, no question of rivalry between the schools. More would-be students apply to RADA than any of the others but this is probably because it's the best known. Once accepted by a school, however, the question of whether they would have done better to attend one of the others does not exist. This is partly because they have too much work to do to worry about things like that; also because there appears to be very little exchange of information between students at different schools. There are no home and away acting fixtures.

Thus Annabel Leventon is as insistent on the excellence of LAMDA as Penelope Wilton is of the Drama Centre and Christopher Cazenove of the Bristol Old Vic School.

But then how many students do not enjoy their student days, be they at drama school, university or anywhere else? The slightest excuse for postponing that terrible day when they will finally have to get down to earning a living is joyfully seized upon.

However, the question to which I was hoping for some kind of answer was this: in a profession in which, at the best of times, more of its members are out of work than in; upon which it is impossible to fix any generally acceptable professional standards; and to succeed in which depends, to a very large extent, upon luck, looks an innate talent, is there any place for organised training and, if so, what should be its form and function?

With two notable exceptions, all the schools I visited were agreed that the training they offer is a vocational one; that what they are trying to do is prepare students to enter the professional theatre, which, in the cheery words of the Central prospectus, 'could mean a spell in Coronation Street, a season at the National Theatre, an experimental play at the Roundhouse, playing tried favourites in commercial rep., or appearing in *Hair*'.

In other words, assuming that anyone who is capable of running the hard and ruthless gauntlet of the auditions and surviving both has the necessary talent, desire and determination to be an actor, it is then up to the drama school to teach him how to use and discipline his talent and make it last; how to adapt to different types of directors and different types of media; how to be aware of the people with whom he is working; how to be observant; how to cope with personal problems of all sorts – physical, emotional and financial; how in fact to be a professional actor.

To this end the student is taught how to use his voice, how to move, how to fight, how to sing, how to dance, how to improvise and so on. The only problem as Hugh Crutwell, RADA's Principal, sees it is that, since there never comes a point at which training can be generally agreed to have been completed, it cannot be geared towards a concept of perfection. The most he can hope to do, he believes, is to try and establish from the word go, and continue all the way through training, a balance between perfecting the actor's technique and developing his creativity. In this way, at the end of his seven terms (most other schools offer three-year courses; Mr Crutwell is wedded to the shorter length which he believes to be perfect), the student should be like a highly tuned instrument, ready to burst upon the profession in every way – ideally, realistically and, most important of all, psychologically.

At RADA then, the art and craft of acting are carefully dovetailed and co-related.

Norman Ayrton, one time principal of LAMDA, calls it 'forging the link between imagination and intelligence'.

Others see their job more in terms of adaptability and variety. 'Actors must be as various as the theatre,' says George Hall, Drama Director of Central. 'Our job is to let them try everything, and that way fill the theatre with people who dare in all sorts of terms. The worst crime an actor can commit is to bore the audience, and it's the boring bits in an actor that need treating most.'

All the schools offer courses in stage management; most have a teachers' course; one or two have begun to give courses for directors.

However, the course that all the drama school principals talk about most is the acting course. Understandably so, since of all of them, it's the most imprecise, the most open to question and, to most people, the most fascinating.

Jean-Norman Benedetti at Rose Bruford is no exception. And yet his school is the only one from which every student emerges with a teaching diploma as well. For this reason my impression, particularly after talking with some of the students, is that people choose Bru's when they're not quite certain what it is they want to do. 'If I decide after all that I don't want to act,' the attitude seems to be, 'I can always teach.' But if, as a result, the acting course receives less full-hearted attention than at other schools, it doesn't show. Benedetti steers a well-reasoned middle course.

'Firstly we prepare the students to earn a living (something for which, at the age of eighteen, they're usually singularly ill-equipped) and secondly try and prod them into doing the sort of theatre we older ones can no longer do. The trouble is, they're more conservative than the staff!' Raphael Jago at Webber-Douglas is another principal who lays stress on adaptability. 'People talk about it being necessary for an actor to have a vocation. The fact is, some have this terrible need to act, others don't, but act equally well, and sometimes better. And since the entertainment business does not put all that great an emphasis on excellence, and often all that's required is a number of actors who can do their job well and be easily cast, we feel it's our job here to help an actor examine his emotional and physical range and find those elements he can use to his advantage.'

Drama schools are frequently accused by their students of being too remote from the professional theatre; of cotton-woolling them to such a degree they are totally unprepared for the rude shock that waits in the cold world beyond the green baize notice board. My impression is that the fault, if fault is the right word here, lies not so much with the schools as with the students themselves. After all, one of the great joys – and great dangers – of being a student is that one does not need to concern oneself with the dreary problems of making a living. The student is perfectly well aware that one day the dream he inhabits will fade away, leaving him naked and stranded in the harsh light of common day, but he's blowed if he's going to bother himself with that until the day it happens. The drama schools do appear to make a great effort to forewarn their students of what they can expect in the professional theatre.

'Once upon a time,' remembers Peter Bucknell of the Guildhall, 'the drama student started with the disciplines and was only later allowed to search for freedom. Today it's the other way round. Our job now is, over the three years, to bring to a point idealism and reality. It's a fragile psychological act, I can tell you. The third-year student must, when he leaves, be in a position to adapt himself to any type of play, any type of director, any type of company; and to re-scale his work according to the media in which he's working – TV, radio, films, theatre or whatever. In other words, he must have his sights way up here, but also be able to do two weeks in rep. at the drop of a hat.'

Both E.15 and the Drama Centre seem less interested in the future of their students than in the future of the theatre.

'I believe the job of the theatre,' says Margaret Bury at E.15, 'is to raise the standards of the community, to show them there is something else to life than the pub and the telly. Really, this should not be a drama school so much as a school of life, or, if that sounds a bit pompous, a school of awareness. Really, that's where a student's training should be,' she pointed towards the council houses, 'out there.' I think she may have something there.

'The actor,' said Tony Dinner, Drama Centre's stage director, 'must be allowed to use his own creative time to create the inner life of the character he's playing. Otherwise that character cannot be real, cannot express emotions and the audience can never feel involved. If the theatre were the emotional experience it should be, people would feel more emotional and get more out of it.' (Mr Dinner had not seen any of the three London productions I mentioned that were at that time receiving a good deal of attention; had not seen a single production done in any of the other drama schools; and, as far as I could make out, had never witnessed a single production of a play anywhere that he had found in any degree satisfactory.)

However, Penelope Wilton, who was trained at the Drama Centre, believes that while Yat Malmgren and John Blatchley, the joint principals, are chiefly concerned with the craft of acting in general, it did not mean that her work at the Centre was irrelevant to the profession as she found it. 'From a personal point it taught me to draw on a central strength which has been a great help when I've got stuck over something; and more important than that, I learned that it isn't the individual who counts, but the production, and that everything you do should contribute towards the whole effect. You can't act on your own.' However, she admits she has had the luck to be working always at places like the Nottingham Playhouse and the Royal Court where high standards of work and experiment are not unknown.

On the other hand, [Timothy Block, an ex-E.15er,] who had spent two years playing in *The Man Most Likely To . . .* wondered whether Margaret Bury might not be training students for a theatre that doesn't actually exist.

It seems clear then that, at the very worst, drama schools can teach some people something about the craft of acting, and, at best, are actually playing a role in improving the standards of the theatre as a whole.

Every year more and more young people hear the call of the theatre; few, however, are chosen. LAMDA, for instance, picks twenty-five a year from 400–500 applications; Central thirty from the same number; RADA takes fourteen men and seven girls every other term.

'Once in,' say Hugh Crutwell, 'a student never again has to face such a terrible challenge as that first audition. Not, that is, until the next one.'

Norman Ayrton says he could always smell a good actor. 'It's an indefinable thing. The moment you meet one, you sit up and say yes. It's nothing to do with looks, some are really quite ugly. It's just that you want to know more, see him work, you know?'

George Hall says most people who audition are interesting. 'But we know at once if we want to teach them.'

'I warn them that the theatre is an overcrowded and underpaid profession,' says Peter Bucknell. 'But it's no good, they're all romantics.'

Margaret Bury at E.15 told me she'd noticed how many more of the people who come to auditions these days are stoned. 'It's awful. They stand there thinking they're giving something out, and in fact they're completely contained within themselves.'

Most schools are prepared to say goodbye to a handful of students every year, though the number who for one reason or another decide to throw in the towel, is surprisingly small. The Drama Centre makes a point of weeding out those whom they do not wish to 'stretch . . . to the fullest extent, and far beyond the point that would be expected of them on entering the profession', to quote the prospectus.

Hugh Crutwell is horrified at this attitude and deplores the whole idea of students competing for survival. 'How can students get on if they have the threat of dismissal hanging over them all the time? Once accepted, they're committed and we're committed. I never lose faith in my initial judgement. I will back my intuition up to the hilt.' Most students who are eligible are able to obtain government grants of some sort; though, since the awarding of them is still discretionary, it does sometimes happen that a student with the possibility of a grant will be admitted in preference to one without.

Hugh Crutwell is convinced that the day government grants become available to students saw a turning point in the history of drama schools. 'Not only did it mean that a training for the theatre was no longer a privilege for the children of the rich, but it also relieved students from the pressure of worrying whether or not they were getting value for their own money.'

It was the Old Vic School under Michel Saint-Denis in the early fifties that revolutionised drama teaching. Up till then students had attended a conglomeration of classes – speech, movement, mime, fencing and so on – none of which had the slightest connection one with another. Saint-Denis was the first to plan a training that deals with the actors in the round. In other words, everything that is taught is interrelated; the way you move has a relevance to the way you speak and so on.

In Room 5 at RADA I saw a little of this theory being put into practice during one of Mr McCallion's Diction classes. While two of the students went next door to warm up, the third was made to walk round and round the little room, relaxing every muscle, bouncing easily on the balls of his feet, at the same time trying to say the lines 'We are glad the Dauphin is so pleasant with us: His present and your pains we thank you for' as though he were carrying on a perfectly normal conversation. His efforts were punctuated on the one hand by the warblings and piano tinklings of the two warmer-uppers in the next room, and on the other by Mr McCallion's deep, soft, persuasive tones: '. . . feel your weight . . . nice and easily . . . that's right . . . use the same breath for speaking as you do in walking . . . we are glad the Dauphin is so pleasant with us . . . and again . . . open joints . . . that's it'.

Although unable to note a marked improvement myself, Mr McCallion seemed well satisfied with the young man's progress and finally despatched him to extend his thanks to the Dauphin in the solitude of the next room. The remainder of the class was taken up with Standard English in which, their voices by now well and truly warmed, a South African girl and a young man with a marked Berkshire accent read aloud passages of Shakespeare and attempted to correct each other's pronunciation, an interesting case of the blind leading the deaf. Fortunately there was always Mr McCallion at hand to urge them along with useful facts and hints. (Did you know, for example, that there were just the ninety-three ways of pronouncing the letter L in English?) I was particularly reassured by his comments on the tapped R. It seems a survey has been done at Eton College, where only one boy was found with tapped Rs and he was suffering from a speech impediment. 'And if you don't find the tapped R at Eton,' said Mr McCallion, 'I doubt you'll find it anywhere, except perhaps amongst people who've been taking elocution lessons.'

In another room a Polish lady named Miss Fedro teaches Period Movement in broken stentorian tones before which even the strongest students quake visibly. 'If you are supposed to be a servant, young man, you do not move while you are speaking. Servants always stand still when they are speaking. If we had had a butler at home like you who moved as he spoke he would have been in-stantly dismissed.'

I should dearly have liked to attend some classes at the Drama Centre, since although a great deal of what Mr Dinner handed out to me were so frequently clichés of the 'theatre should be a deeply emotional, deeply felt experience' type, some of their work sounded interesting. It is based on the theories of Rudolph Laban, the dancer. His idea was that everyone has a predominate inner state and that all movements are based on and reflect that inner state. Thus, feeling/thinking people (viz. images of mediaeval saints) move from their joints, not from their muscles; sensuous people stand with both feet firmly on the ground. The actor is an interpretive instrument upon which the character plays different notes. Therefore he must first free himself of all tension and idiosyncrasies before he can begin to draw on different ingredients of himself to create a character . . . and so on and so forth.

I'm sure it's all good stuff; unfortunately, the only way one is ever going to find out for certain is by taking the three-year course. However, even as Mr Dinner was talking, the thought did strike me: all this language is fine while one is at school, but what happens on the outside? What chance is there of finding others in the profession who can speak it too? Not much according to Penelope Wilton.

'If you used Drama Centre expressions like 'slashing point' and 'free flow' at a rehearsal, people would think you were completely mad.' And it is not only Drama Centre students who must suffer this language problem. George Hall's movement classes are couched in the faintly hippie language of dancing: '. . . everyone yawning . . . stretching to the invisible places . . . feeling where it all is . . . and now let the spine blob . . . and up . . . and blob . . . really give your spine an outing . . . cha-da-da-da-da-da-da . . . now just lift one shoulder . . . nothing else happens . . . it's an event . . . cha-da-da-da-da-da-da . . .'

The next moment he is splendidly down to earth: '. . . just moving one hip . . . as though you were auditioning for a strip show, which you may very well be sooner than you think . . . okay, you've all got the job . . . now on your back . . . now if you can imagine, for reasons that are best not gone into, that there's a rope tied to your crutch . . .'

The most colourful language of all I encountered in Mr Marshall's Stage Fights class at RADA, where the terminology reflects the pretend nature of the swordplay: for sext and quart, read twiddle bang plink. But nowhere do the students have more fun than in Tumbling, in which Mr Barry, a hefty, joking Cockney lad in vest and jeans, his hands forever trying to push back his long, unruly hair, teaches the students how to be circus clowns, fight with knives, kick each other in the crutch (very realistic that, particularly so if the victim happens to move at the wrong moment) and making pyramids.

Ah well, it's all much more fun than working.

However, the suggestion that the students might merely be enjoying themselves was instantly squashed by every drama school principal to whom I put it. Partly it is simply that, thanks to centuries of prejudice, anything to do with the theatre must necessarily be of questionable validity, and therefore the position they hold in the ranks of further education establishments is precarious; thus it is in their interests to present their schools as hard working, no mucking about, not like the universities, vocational training establishments. Also they don't consider drama training a laughing matter themselves.

Norman Ayrton thinks that for a start the word student needs eliminating altogether, since it has all the overtones of young people with no fixed aims, looking for the secret of life; whereas the drama student is really an apprentice with a very fixed aim, looking for work.

He admits though that they are bound to spend a lot of their time in self-examination, which is in many cases very necessary. 'A lot of students lose their self-confidence halfway through the course. They arrive here fresh from their latest triumph as Hamlet at school, or in the local drama group, and no one has ever questioned their success. And then suddenly it all goes and they're in the tunnel, as Saint-Denis called it. Nearly everyone goes through it sooner or later. The only answer is to build a whole new confidence based on the strong foundation of technique. It's better they should get over all that here rather than in the working situation.'

Although at RADA Hugh Crutwell feels the need to crack the whip from time to time, he sees in his students a far greater sense of responsibility than ever before. 'In the old days people thought of the stage in terms of glamour, having their photographs in *Vogue* and so on. Today they're none the less stage struck, but they no longer admire brilliant façades and tricks. What they respect most of all in a performance are truth and honesty and integrity.'

'The students who leave here know their jobs and are disciplined to cope with any pressures in any medium,' says Mr Benedetti. 'The fact is, when a director asks you to cry, you've jolly well got to cry. If you're Gielgud, you can do it just like that. Others have to know how to put themselves in a situation where it's possible to cry. It's like being able to speak a language fluently.'

George Hall sees the students' problem as even more fundamental. 'From kindergarten onwards, education in this country is dreadfully fragmented. The children are completely starved of any imagery of sound or movement. They nearly all arrive here in a cage of purely verbal and conceptual thinking, with no sensational vocabulary of any sort. So we have to take them right back to the kindergarten and teach them once again to *feel* like a dwarf, *feel* like a giant . . .'

Robert Morley was offered four jobs on the day he left RADA, which is not, he claims, saying a lot.

'We were paid labourers' wages; and besides, one was not expected to be able to act in the provinces in those days. Indeed, until the arrival of the talkies, very few actors did. Then, of course, they discovered just how terrible their acting had been.'

Today, the standards of acting have improved everywhere, and there are many more actors jostling for work. And although the Equity minimum has now risen to £18 a week, the turnover of actors in rep. has, as a result, diminished.

Even so, it is encouraging to hear that, of the 250 or so who emerge annually from the major schools, nearly all find employment within a few months. The difficulty, as Mr Jago of Webber-Douglas pointed out, sets in two or three years later; the best the drama schools can hope for is that the central strength with which they have attempted to endow their students over the three years will serve them to some good purpose.

And yet, when all's said and done, does it honestly make the slightest scrap of difference whether an actor has been to a drama school or not? There's no evidence to show that jobs are given to those who have in preference to those who haven't. Are ex-drama school actors more successful in the profession than those who have not attended drama schools? And what does success mean anyway?

Can any of us, by looking at a number of actors on stage, tell which have been to drama school and which haven't? And if we could, would we care?

As long as entry into the theatre does not depend upon a compulsory vocational training, the answers are bound to be inconclusive. On the one hand you have a well-known agent who firmly believes that drama schools are a complete waste of time and that the only way to learn the craft is by going into the provinces for the forty compulsory weeks and getting on with it; on the other, you have actresses like Annabel Leventon, who, despite a distinguished career with OUDS, says she knew damn all about acting, had no basis for working on, felt totally limited by her ignorance of her craft, and had she not been to LAMDA, would never have dared try anything with which she was not completely familiar.

John Challis began his acting life in a children's theatre by answering an ad. in the paper ('Strong character actor wanted to tour. Ability to drive desirable but not essential') and believes every actor gets by on his own techniques anyway, and that in the end it all comes down to personality; Timothy Block, on the other hand, says that his experiences at E.15 are like a Bible on which he can draw in times of need. It's all very well Peter Plouviez of Equity saying 'We believe that just because the theatre's art, it need not necessarily be chaos.' The fact is that it is, and arguably the better for it.

In the end it comes down to why people go into the theatre in the first place. If it's to make a living at something they like doing more than anything else, then drama school will give them all the equipment they are likely to need. If they believe it's their duty in life to provide the public with a better theatre than that to which they are at present being treated, then drama school will fire them with all the idealistic zeal a crusader could want. If they want to be film stars they'd probably do better to take up modelling. At

14 *Traverse Theatre, Edinburgh: Traverse Tattoo 1972*

15A–I DESIGNS BY CECIL BEATON

15a The School for Scandal (*1952*) *New Theatre, London*

15b Marguerite and Armand (*1962*) *Royal Ballet, London*

15c La Traviata (*1966*) *Metropolitan, New York*

15d Lady Windermere's Fan (*1966*) *Phoenix Theatre, London*

15e (*left*) Lady Windermere's Fan (*1966*) *Design for Coral Browne*
15f (*right*) Gigi (*1958*) *Hollywood: Designs for Leslie Caron & Louis Jourdan*

15g My Fair Lady (*1964*) *Hollywood*

15h (*left*) My Fair Lady (*1958*) *Drury Lane: Design for Zena Dare*
15i (*right*) Coco (*1969*) *Hellinger Theatre: Design for Katharine Hepburn*

16A–D RADA ALUMNAE

16a *Flora Robson*

16b *Charles Laughton*

16c *Joan Greenwood*

16d *Kathleen Harrison*

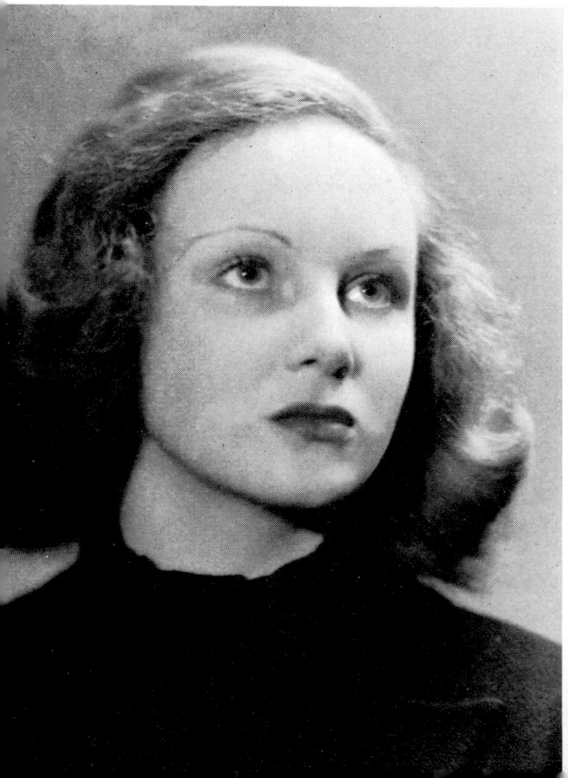

17a *Michael York, Tennessee Williams preparing* Out Cry

17b *In rehearsal: Cara Duff MacCormick, Peter Glenville* (*director*), *Michael York*

17c *Tennessee Williams*

present a drama school's usefulness probably lies somewhere in the middle.

Soon after leaving LAMDA, Annabel Leventon went back to see Michael McOwan, the then principal, with the news that in her experience she had been trained up to a standard of theatre that did not exist. He accepted her charges calmly. He told her he was perfectly well aware that students meet with hostility when they first enter the profession and that they get laughed at for practising their voice exercises before rehearsals in the morning. He also realised that a large number let their standards drop along with the rest. However, every year the profession is being infiltrated with actors who are determined to maintain the high standards they have been taught. It may take a long time, he told her, but in the end, we shall have a better theatre.

Perhaps in the meantime we could hurry things along a bit by starting schools for audiences.

Tennessee Williams in Rehearsal

'Out Cry', *originally called* 'The Two Character Play', *was Tennessee Williams's contribution to Broadway 1973; here one of the two actors concerned reports on its development during rehearsal.*

PROLOGUE – April 1972 – I meet Tennessee Williams in California where I am filming *Lost Horizon.* He has come over to present an Oscar. We discuss the possibility of my making a record of his hauntingly beautiful poetry. Later he sends me his new script, *The Two Character Play.* I am fascinated and intrigued by this work which is the combination and metamorphosis of two previous plays, one of which had previously been shown successfully in London.

We meet up again in Venice at the Film Festival where, out of the blue, he asks me to play the part of Felice in a proposed production of the play. I accept with alacrity and excitement, mixed with trepidation and a measure of awe. In October I fly to New York to meet the director, Peter Glenville, and the producers David Merrick and Roger Stevens. I also meet Cara Duff-MacCormick, a young actress who had attracted attention and awards in a play called *Moonchildren* presented the previous season. Peter had been persuaded that she was ideal for the role of Clare after requesting two actors to read the play for him and hearing her instinctive interpretation. Contracts are drawn up and I agree to mine over a crackling intercontinental telephone line in a hotel room in Delhi. This sense of unreality is translated into hard fact when on Monday, the 18th of December I find myself in New York City for the beginning of rehearsals of the play which is now retitled *Out Cry.*

First rehearsal, Longacre Theatre, 48th Street, West of Broadway. First introduction, before all others, to the Equity executive who demands dues. Fully paid up I proceed with meeting with company, and the rest of the cast – Cara! Peter Glenville prefaces the rehearsal with a talk. He stresses that with this play, there is no point in just putting on a performance, a show – it has to be a deeply felt personalised experience. The play is the exploration of the inner crisis of an artist – a 'cri-du-coeur' in a moment of despair. Above all he sees the play as a poetic allegory. It is the study of fear developing into panic. The play is broken down arbitrarily into four scenes: Prologue, two scenes of the play-within-the-play and an Epilogue. We rehearse from 10:00 a.m. to 5:00 p.m. without a major break. After the first few days I am totally exhausted and remember ruefully Olivier's dictum about talent being an adjunct to stamina. The dark and disused Longacre Theatre provides a perfect setting for rehearsals: it is gloomy, echoing and cold – totally appropriate for 'the mausoleum of a theatre' in which Tennessee places his drama.

24th of December, Christmas Eve – reunion with Tennessee who has come to New York to be with us during the crucial post-plotting period. He has shaved his beard off yet, paradoxically, approves of mine which I've grown for the part. He gives me a Christmas present of two beautiful theatrical prints.

28th of December – Tennessee to rehearsal with a cold. Peter had warned us not to let our performances reflect sub-consciously the presence of the author. But neither of us are prepared for T's stentorian and unpredictable laugh. I am amazed and humbled to learn that T is nervous – indeed I realise over the weeks just how vulnerable and how sensitive a man he is. T. gives Cara a present of a painting of roses – she is a picture of overwhelmment (I use this word unashamedly, having come to love such Williams' coinings as 'inhumanlessness'!) We play Messaien records during tea breaks – very strange and appropriate. Peter eventually chooses a piece for play's theme. There are costume fittings and a photo call. The first week's work centres on the discovery of the nature of the play. However, like Peer Gynt's onion, 'The more you peel, the more you reveal'. Peter isolates and emphasises our respective weaknesses When Cara is uncertain, she becomes lachrymose; I become noble and grandiloquent. Peter concerned about my hair which, together with the beard, is obscuring any facial expressions. So, ——

Monday, Jan. 1st – Haircut!

We concentrate now on getting a sense of reality back to the prologue and epilogue – our characters more familiar and theatrical types – bitchy and irritable. Peter gives me the image of Felice as a caged tiger which I cherish.

Friday, 5th Jan. – First run-through of entire play for the designer, Joe Mielziner. He encouragingly impressed – likewise myself with the try-out, on the back wall of the theatre, of the beautiful projections that he has designed. Images melt into images. Tennessee brings along some textural emendations that are forthwith incorporated. He is somewhat shocked that Cara and I touch each other so much in the play. He insists that his relationship with his own sister was not such a physical one – I have an immediate insight into the intense biographical nature of the play (by the end of the rehearsal period, T. has come to accept my kissing Cara – an image of poetic, not sexual, intensity).

6th Jan. – Second run-through. Not so energetic. Peter relieved to discover that the running time is one hour and fifty minutes – a substantial evening's theatre. He gives us Sunday off, on the proviso we meet sometime Monday to check the text. This we do and discover several consistent misquotations.

Afternoon – costume fitting. Cara very becoming in rosebud dress and velvet coat. T insists that we should look and feel right. Peter anxious that I look too dapper.

Wed., 10th Jan. – Run-through. Feel like a dervish – mad, fevered and unrestrained. Dash and over-lap lines and illuminate with an astonishing new-found insight the 'mad' elements of the play. That evening collapse with 'flu. Q.E.D.!

Thurs., 11th – Bed. Peter very solicitous as is Tennessee who telephones repeatedly and sends books. I study script.

Sun., 14th – Return to rehearsal for effortful run-through.

Mon., 15th – Run-through – feel horribly depressed, both physically and at inadequacies of performance. Nadir.

Tues., 16th – Drive to New Haven. Spend evening in Shubert Theatre familiarising self with new stage and acoustics. Feel weak and anxious for impending first night. T., in contrast, fighting fit from his daily swim – here at the Yale pool. I trim my beard down to a strange, slightly narcissistic goatee.

Wed., 17th – Dress rehearsal – well received.

Thurs., 18th – In afternoon change positions and pacing of opening monologue. In evening, World Première of play!

Friday, 19th – Post-mortem. Review sympathetic and encouraging, but finds play too opaque and obscure. T. immediately goes off to write emendations – these telephoned to me an hour before the curtain. I find Cara and we rehearse and incorporate them successfully in the evening's performance.

Sun. morning, 21st – T. phones with an idea for new lines that explain the significance of the sun-flower image that pervades the play (c.f. Van Gogh and his images of deranged nature). I suggest that T. writes a program note so that the audience does not come to play completely cold and uninformed. He agrees and later, over a lunch of Boston scrod, shows me a draft of both ideas which are admirable.

Afternoon – by train to Philadelphia. Barcley Hotel. Discover that I am staying in the suite previously occupied by Sir John Gielgud. A good omen? Feel exhausted and decline T's offer to accompany him to a Japanese restaurant. (T. is a Japanese food freak and lauds the cerebral stimulation provided by raw fish.)

Monday, 22nd – Awake after 12 hours' sleep. Rehearsal 5:00 p.m. Rehearse some new lines. Second first night – good performance. Peter informs us during the interval that it is our best so far. At a party afterwards, T. stresses to me that the relationship between Clare and Felice should be as if linked by a taut wire. Later, philosophises to my wife about the play's prospects 'While there's doubt, there's hope'.

Tues., 23rd – Reviews interesting but not over-favorable. 'We know that work comes from the depths of Williams' torment. But it has not come far enough yet to meet us even half way.' T. phones to say that he will postpone going to England today for the London premiere of 'Small Craft Warnings' in order to devote more time to the play.

Wed., 24th – Rehearse new ending. T. to England. Variety review good. Encouraging for play and positive for performances. 'Unquestionably this script is the groundwork for some rich dialogue and some top-flight acting. It presents a challenge to the play-goer who wants something more than just cream-puffs on his theatrical menu.'

Thurs., 25th – Two girls apologise to me in the street for the lack of response from the audience (notorious here).

Sat. – My friend Hugh Wheeler to the matinée performance. He claims to hear young couple next to him exclaim, 'How interesting his employment of syllogistic rifts'!! Evening performance – Cara and I discuss beforehand some bits of business that are not working and suggest remedies to try out that evening. Peter is back in New York – while the cat's away! At this performance a woman applauds the line 'Perhaps the audience demanded their money back'. This draws attention to the inherent danger of T's lines that anticipate and thereby defuse the audiences' potential hostility. Already Peter has cut several similar references, leaving a telling few, i.e. 'It sounds like a house of furious unfed apes' is retained, 'Do they seem human . . . No' is excised.

Wed., 31st Jan. – T. returns from England. I try a new costume that is both more becoming and appropriate – a chiffon shirt that is properly 'mystic'. At matinée cut ruthlessly much of the opening dialogue. Its logic is too abstruse and close packed for an audience that is quite literally just settling down (however, this opening dialogue is still not satisfactory. T. goes on to revise it in several versions, only arriving at a satisfactory re-write just before the opening night in N.Y.).

Thurs., 1st Feb. – At the end of the evening performance, T. remarks to man who is exclaiming that he must be mad himself to have come to see the play: 'Yes, you are; go look at yourself in the mirror'. However, audiences, if mystified, are generally good and especially those on subscription-based matinées. After the performance there is a symposium where students are invited to question the author and cast about the play. T. explains that it was written at time when he literally didn't know where he was. This traumatic experience he considers to be a legitimate subject-matter for a drama – it represents his expressed intention to write in a less representational style. He agrees that the characters of Felice and Clare can be considered as alter-egos: the masculine/feminine, positive/negative, active/passive aspects of one character.

Fri., 2nd Feb. – Hot, humid rainstorm. T.'s summer day in the South becomes a reality. A Negro lady laughs wildly at all the wrong places, a good test for the reflexes. We incorporate new lines.

The relationship now climaxes with a kiss: what was implicit made explicit.

Sun., 4th Feb. – To Washington.

Mon., 5th Feb. – To the Eisenhower Theatre at the Kennedy Center. A gem of a theatre. Acoustics good and the size of the auditorium inevitably changes the nature of the performance. No more straining to stretch the delicate fabric of the play to the back of a corridor theatre as in Philadelphia. Comfortable cell-block dressing rooms, reached by an elevator, below.

Opening night – good audience and performance despite a jinx that ensured that every prop was either dropped or came to pieces. We decide to wait up for the reviews, alleviating anxiety and a monstrous thirst with champagne. T. refers to the impending critical reception as 'The firing squad that waits in every city.' Bill Barnes, T.'s and my agent, enters beaming and flourishing newspapers. It is as if the review had been written to order. '*Out Cry* is a beautiful haunting personal elegy to life. Immensely tender visions of maturity not unlike the mellow wisdom of *The Tempest.* Williams is clearly writing autobiographically. He is daring to be himself, to go back to the poetic images of his youthful works. Using youth to express himself he shows indirectly what he has learned of living.' And, 'Next to Tennessee's *Camino Real, Out Cry* is the most personal inventive and deeply felt play he has written and it may be his most controversial play to date. It would be a long time before we see such perfectly blended performances.' T.'s relief at this positive reception is deeply moving – he interprets it as an authorisation to continue writing for the theatre.

Tues., 6th Feb. Box-office active, despite negative T.V. reviews. Business continues to build over our week stay, averaging an astonishing $45,000 a week. This demonstrates how radically the Kennedy Center has transformed the cultural face of Washington. The majestic building has focused and fired enthusiasm for the Arts, and we reaped the benefit.

Thurs., 8th Feb. – After the performance, T. discusses more new lines for the beginning of the play. He contemplates the introduction of a character called Roberto with explicit over-tones of homosexuality. I suggest that this might endanger the androgynous quality of the protagonists – their innocence and attractiveness. T. off for a week at home in Key West and promises to re-think this troublesome introductory scene. Projected rehearsal for scene cancelled.

Fri., 9th Feb. – Photo call for New York press. In afternoon listen to more Messaien record in search for more appropriate theme music. Find interesting movement and try it that evening: it works.

Sat., 10th Feb. – Before curtain rehearse new ending for First Act. Remove and replace Cara's speech about the sun-flower so that scene is arrested with her fixedly mesmerised by the man in the audience pointing a gun at her. Cara has burned her hand badly but her concentration is so extraordinary that both pain and blisters disappear in the course of the performance.

Tues. – Morning meeting with T. and Peter to resolve the beginning of the play. Peter says that the previous day's rehearsals had convinced him that the new re-write in which I addressed the audience, is wrong: it defuses the tension of the play too soon and also distracts from my later nervous speech to the audience where I announce that the company has left us and that my sister and I have to perform alone. Also Peter claims that the audience will resent being lectured by a young man at the outset of the play. T. and I agree. Peter shows us the ad that has just appeared in the New York Times. It is bold and attractive and dominates the page.

Thurs., 23rd Feb. – Rehearse new staging at the half in front of an audience of ushers. The opening speech feels good and after the performance Peter telephones his approval. He says the play must now be frozen – I agree!

Now feeling constantly exhausted, especially on matinée days. This is not a play that can be performed at half-cock: it demands the complete quivering involvement of every fiber. Cara confides that she is forced to spend every spare moment resting. We are both mocked by Washington's monuments, and wonderful galleries and museums; however, I manage to slip out to pay homage to the Bard at the Folger Shakespeare Library and catch Debbie Reynolds in a matinée of *Irene*. The latter, though entertaining, renews one's faith in T.'s uncompromising daring, and the sense of privilege at being allowed to interpret his mighty line.

Fri., 24th – Introduce real noises off-stage when Felice attempts to break out of the locked and barred theatre. I bang on a garbage can filled with metal pipes which is alarmingly effective.

Sun., 25th – To New York on the Metroliner. I meet Debbie Reynolds on the train and we commiserate over the agonies of touring shows. She has been on the road for four months with *Irene.* One compensation, however, was that President Nixon had been to see the show that week and had enthused publicly – thereby boosting ticket sales and company morale. Why couldn't he have seen our show, too? Debbie sleeps and I gaze at the New York papers. Predominate on the arts page is a photo of us both, thereby confirming the dreadful inevitability and reality of the impending première. Throw suitcases into new digs and rush off to première of Hal Prince's new musical *A Little Night Music.* However, cannot reconcile myself with being a member of an audience. My heart beats with sympathy for those about to be exposed on the other side of the curtain. It suddenly seems an extraordinary, cruel profession: why does one do it? All that work, dedication, energy held in balance of Fate – to be granted life or death by the events of a single evening and the caprices of a handful of critics. The enchantment of the production lulls and quells all further soul-searching, and masochistic torment.

Mon., 26th Feb. – To the Lyceum Theatre to watch the set-up but feel redundant amidst welter of organised chaos. Cannot resist temptation to look at the billing on the marquee – One's name up in lights on Broadway! All further swellings of pride punctured by stabbing anxiety. I go to see my doctor. He pronounces me totally exhausted and promises to charge up my batteries, cautioning me that three days is inadequate time to make for three months' losses.

Tues., 27th Feb. – Dress rehearsal. After the performance discuss several changes of detail. Scale down performance even more for intimate size of theatre. Restore and emphasise moments of peace and quiet we had at beginning of rehearsal and we lost en route. My dressing room is, as Clare remarks of hers in the play, 'a travesty of a dressing room.' However, I discover it has a noble lineage of occupancy. I hope the ghosts are benign.

Wed. 28th Feb. – First and only preview performance which is good and immediate reaction, enthusiastic. I am perversely depressed, believing, totally irrationally, that a bad dress rehearsal is a precursor of a good first night.

Thurs. 1st March – The Night! Awake late and shave off my beard entirely. Unlike Samson I feel invigorated. Then meet

Franco Zeffirelli's associate producer who tells me that F/Z. wants me to play in his new film of *Camille.* An auspicious beginning to the day? Go early to theatre and sooth nerves by mechanically opening telegrams and finding places to put the plants and presents that threaten to crowd me out of my narrow confine. Make up and dress ritualistically as if for a 'corrida'. All of Felice's neurosis and paranoia as an actor become reality for me. I remember, heart-sinkingly, a line that was cut but which now becomes invested with a horrid truth: 'A performance seems an impossible nightmare, but we've got to give one and it's got to be good.' My dressing room is two steps from the stage – the distance from cell to execution chamber? House-lights out, curtain up. You're on . . . Feel super-charged during the performance, which is well received. Relief, exultation. There is even an ovation when we retire to Sardi's restaurant for a drink. Stay up for morning papers and the press reaction which – thank God – is good. And so to Broadway, and so to bed.

To The Playhouse in an Omnibus

The actor and author leafs through his Edwardian theatre magazines.

As I am practically a hermit these days and rarely venture abroad after dark, a visit to the theatre is something of an occasion, and when my Auntie Emm asked me to accompany her to an entertainment with the strange title of *Hair*, I accepted with alacrity, though a trifle apprehensive about the outcome of my daring.

She suggested that we should approach the playhouse in an omnibus, a mode of transport I have not patronised for many years. But to refresh my memory and give me confidence I have been consulting my well-thumbed copy of *Manners for Men* by Mrs Humphry (better-known to you, perhaps as *Madge* of *Truth*). Although the book was published at the turn of the century, I am sure that the general trend of human behaviour cannot have changed all that much in seventy years.

Ah, here we are! 'In or on an omnibus.' Mrs Humphry reassures me at once of the propriety of Auntie Emm travelling in the vehicle. 'The humble omnibus may be thought by some readers too democratic a kind of conveyance to be considered in a book of manners. Not at all! During the last ten years or so the omnibus has been largely used by women of the educated, cultured and well-dressed classes, and, if a member of the opposite sex can behave like a gentleman in a carriage, he is almost certain to do so in an omnibus and vice versa. It is even more difficult in the humbler vehicle though.

'True courtesy, for instance, will prevent a man from infringing the rights of his neighbours on either side by occupying more than his own allotted space. Very stout gentlemen' (Here we go. I knew there would be a snag) 'are obliged to do so, but at least they need not spread out their knees in a way that is calculated to aggravate the evil. Nor need they arrange themselves in a comfortable oblique position at an angle of forty-five degrees, with the result of enhancing the inconvenience they must necessarily cause to those near them.

'Now let me deal' (says Madge) 'with the Umbrella. A gentleman must not let his wet umbrella lean up against a vacant part of the cushioned seat, rendering it damp for the next comer. His social conscience cannot be up to its work if he permits himself to ignore the rights of the absent, merely because they ARE absent. Carrying a stick or an umbrella under the arm, with the ferrule protruding at the back, is always a reprehensible practice and is even more dangerous when the proprietor is ascending or descending the omnibus. At such moments passengers are liable to sudden checks from various causes and the resultant backward jerk can be quite annoying enough to those behind, its numerous securing pins making havoc in her coiffure and eliciting lively expressions of pain.

'In escorting a lady a man hands her into the omnibus before entering it himself: and if she prefers the top, he lets her mount the staircase in front of him. There seems to be an idea in the lowly classes that it is correct to precede a lady in ascending steps or stairs. This is not in accordance with the practice of good society. If circumstances do not admit of the two walking abreast, then the lady goes first.

'Incidentally it is by no means necessary that any man should resign his seat in an omnibus, simply because a woman wishes for it. The conductor has no right to ask "if any gentleman will go outside to oblige a lady", and no gentlewoman would allow him to ask such a favour on her behalf. The inside passengers have selected inside seats, thereby testifying to their preference for them and they should be allowed to retain them without interference. I have seen a delicate-looking boy' (writes Mrs Humphry) 'racked with a hacking cough' (the boy, not Mrs Humphry) 'induced to ride outside on a cold and rainy night, in order that a fat, rosy, healthy woman might have his inside seat.'

Thank you, Madge. You have made everything crystal-clear and I think we might manage to arrive at the playhouse without my committing any major social gaffe. But supposing, dear lady, I decide to be recklessly extravagant and treat my Auntie Emm to the luxury of a brougham? I find there is an entire section in your esteemed volume appertaining to this method of conveyance.

But, on closer scrutiny, I see that some of the contingencies which might arise from such a gesture are almost as hazardous as those from travelling in the humbler vehicle. For instance, I would have to give instructions to the coachman as to where he is to be 'Found' and at what hour precisely he is to pick up 'my party' (I imagine that means Auntie Emm and me).

'It is an excellent plan' (you say, Mrs Humphry) 'to give the coachman a bright-coloured handkerchief (scarlet and orange perhaps) that he may wear it conspicuously displayed and in this way at once be recognised.'

But, dear Mrs H. or may I call you Madge? do you not think that even in this so-called permissive age, the waving of a scarlet and orange handkerchief in a crowded thoroughfare might lead to a misunderstanding and the fellow might well finish up in some sinister Soho 'stew' or a disorderly house, instead of driving my Auntie Emm and me to our destination?

Natheless I do realise, as you point out so graphically, that it's a miserable business on a wet night to hunt for a carriage when in evening dress and patent leather boots and no lady enjoys waiting in a draughty vestibule, while a short-sighted cavalier is groping about the ill-lighted streets.

But, dear Mrs Humphry, I shall not be wearing patent leather boots because I don't possess any and I am long-sighted, which should minimise the chances, to say nothing of the consequences, of 'groping about'. No, I think, on the whole, a number 19 or 22 omnibus would serve our purpose just as satisfactorily and these vehicles stop just outside the Shaftesbury Playhouse, or so a cousin (on my mother's side) has advised me by telephonic communication. She saw *The Mikado* (or, as it sometimes entitled *The Town of Titipu*) there some years ago.

And now we come to the crux of the entire expedition. How to behave in the building itself. Here, according to Mrs Humphry, fresh dilemmas seem to face us at every turn. It is apparently 'uncivil to betray inattention, once the curtain has risen. An actor told me' (well, not actually me but Mrs Humphry) 'that a little appreciation goes a long way with members of the professions of music and the drama. He told me that, after having made a certain speech two or three times without any sign of amusement from the audience, on the fourth night of the play a single silvery note of musical mirth was heard from the stalls. It was but one note, say E Flat on the treble clef, but the audience immediately joined in, perceiving the point of the speech, as though it had been illuminated for them by this one little laugh.'

Oh, Madge dear, what ARE we to do? Both Auntie Emm and myself are tone deaf. So how can we tell if the sound we make will be, say in E flat? I fear it is more likely to be B Flat, which may annoy one of the artistes in the entertainment *Hair*, who will tend to think that there is an 'underbred' person in evidence. I read in your book that this type is 'often in evidence, not only in the low-priced seats but ALL OVER THE HOUSE. He has been seen and heard even in private boxes. A well-known music-hall celebrity administered a scathing reproof to one of there, who persisted in talking loudly while she was singing. Stopping short, she looked up at the box in which he sat and cried "One fool at a time please" after which he was as quiet as a mouse.'

Even the purchase of a programme appears to present difficulties. I am sure Auntie Emm will want to get into the atmosphere of the piece by finding out where the action is laid. I suspect that the setting will have something to do with a hairdressing establishment but one never knows. Madge tells me that it is up to the gentleman of the party to pay for the programme at the 'Few Theatres' where a charge is made. She adds (in her firm inimitable way) that it is not considered 'very good form' to pay for programmes at places of entertainment where managements make no charge. Instances have been known where attendants have been discharged for accepting such fees, though many of them are superior to accepting it.

So I must wait and see what happens. If I get caught in a seemingly hopeless dilemma, we can always fall back on a copy of *The Play Pictorial* which I shall take with me. This features a delightful musical play called *The Duchess of Dantzig* which has Napoleon and Madame Sans-Gêne as its principal characters. Two of the most popular musical numbers were entitled 'My dear Wife and I' and 'Me and my old man'.

It was presented at the Lyric Theatre in 1903 and both the advertising and editorial sections of the illustrated magazine are full of the most interesting and fascinating information, although clearly orientated principally for feminine perusal

The most impressive advertisement in the journal is that for Edwards' *Harlene for the Hair* which is not only a hair restorer but a hair-producer Among the ladies who use it are H.M. the Queen of Greece, H.R.H. the Grand Duchess George of Russia, the Grand Duchess of Mechlenbergh-Scherin and H.R.H. the Duchess of Sparta (and her husband the Duke of the same place).

It says nothing about the Duchess of Dantzig using it on herself but it is reassuring to read that Mrs Langtry ('the charming actress-manager') writes 'Previous to my using Harlene, my hair had become brittle and was falling off. I have used your preparation daily for eighteen months and my hair is quite restored'.

Doubtless she took some bottles of the concoction to America where she was to appear in a play called *The Cross-Ways*. In the *Theatre Magazine* of February 1903 there is some rather caustic comment on what should have been a most auspicious occasion. 'There must be something in heredity after all. It was often declared that Marie Corelli was the favourite novelist of the late Queen Victoria; now her son, Edward VII has put himself on record as well pleased with Mrs Langtry's new piece, which goes to further prove that His Gracious Majesty is to be better praised for loyalty to old favourites than for literary acumen. It was a generous act on his part to try and give Mrs Langtry the benefit of his approval before her departure for America, but it is doubtful whether it has done her much good in this land of independent thought and conclusion: for, after all, the piece in which she made her American reappearance at the Garrick is a feeble effort, hardly destined to stand up under the various rebuffs it was certain to receive. In the quieter scenes Mrs Langtry acted with refinement and taste, Her various poses were beautiful pictures and she wore some stunning gowns, but there was little conviction in the movements where doubt, fear and suspense were demanded.'

Another legendary lady of the theatre of the period, Mrs Brown Potter, obviously felt the same about *Harlene* for she wrote a fulsome recommendation. But it strikes my unsophisticated mind that all these distinguished ladies were taking a bit of a chance with a product which declared itself 'unequalled for promoting the growth of the Beard and Moustache'.

Perhaps this problem could however be solved by the application of 'JOY', the new and wonderful Vanishing Cream. 'Ladies generally, but particularly Golfers, Motorists, Yachtswomen and all who are exposed to sun and wind, owe it to themselves to test its marvellous effect.' Miss Zena Dare asserts that 'it has improved my complexion very much' while her sister Phyllis really 'cannot speak too highly of it'. Miss Isabel Jay asks Valerie Joy to send her two more jars while Miss Gertie Millar wants four.

Another beauty-aid is 'Lotion de la Reine' (Lotion of the Queen) which is apparently used by three European Crowned Heads and the World's Greatest Actress (all alas un-named). The nearest specific information we can derive from the advertisment is that 'Lotion de la Reine has made me look at least ten years younger', from the Duchess de S . . . a statement which does not quite convince me, even though the liquid is said to be prepared from an 18th century recipe, which has been a closely guarded secret for the last 150 years.

Crowned heads appear frequently to promote goods and Schweitzers 'Cocoatina' was apparently used by Queen Victoria, her children, her grandchildren and her great grandchildren. It was also reported to be in daily use at the Imperial and Royal Courts of Great Britain, Germany, Russia, Denmark, Greece etc.

Apart from advertisements of special feminine appeal, the magazine is full of news about modern inventions, some of which may tempt Auntie Emm or myself into a flurry of extravagance. There is, for instance, the intriguing 'Pianotist' which claims to be the only Piano Player which can be operated without physical exertion. It can also be fitted to any piano without ultimate injury though it doesn't say whether to the instrument or oneself. But 'it has no clumsy cabinet, no perishable rubber pneumatics and can emphasise a melody in any desired part of the keyboard but does not at any time interfere with the use of the piano in the ordinary manner'. Which means, I imagine, that Auntie Emm and I could play duets together on our separate instruments.

'The Pianotist' is unequivocally endorsed and recommended as the best of all by Mark Hambourg, Henry J. Wood, Adelina Patti (Baroness Cadestrom) Landon Ronald, Leslie Stuart, Sousa and 500 other prominent and discriminating patrons.

Then there is 'The Kinora', the latest and greatest Achievement in Animated Photography Produced by the Biograph Studio, who are now prepared to take photographs of persons whilst MOVING for reproduction. This is the only method by which the actual gesture, expression, smile, and other characteristics can be reproduced. Animated portraits of your own family can be reproduced, with perfect steadiness and clearness, showing every motion as exactly in life and can be viewed day or night without any special illuminating apparatus.

I may be able to persuade Auntie Emm to pose with me for 'The Kinora' though I doubt if she will go half shares in the purchase of 'The Monarch' Gramophone, even though it has a New Tapered Arm with handsome oak pedestal. The Gramophone and Typewriter Ltd are offering it for fifteen pounds.

Mr Dan Leno has apparently made twenty-four records and the Great Coquelin himself wrote to the Gramophone and Typewriter Ltd. to say 'Your wonderful gramophone has at last given me what I have so much desired. And that is the surprise and (shall I confess it?) the pleasure of hearing myself. I have heard the recitation of "Les Limaçons" which I recite in the role of M. de la Motte in the "Mèrcure Galant" of Boursault and my word. . . . I did what I have seen the public do for a long time. I laughed. Thank you for having made me amuse myself. That doesn't often happen to me and I congratulate you.'

But of course in spite of these diversions in print and the opportunity for Auntie Emm and me to discuss current affairs with élan, there are still problems of deportment for me to face. For instance, during the first act of *Hair* I will be wondering what steps to take in the interval.

'Between the acts,' asserts Mrs Humphry, 'the modern man thinks it is his duty to himself to go out and have a drink, perhaps smoke a cigarette. There was a time when a gentleman, who had committed himself to escort a lady, could have asked, though perhaps not in Milton's words:

"And leave thy fair side unescorted, lady?"

'But nowadays the majority of men visit the bar or the foyer. Yet who shall say what golden opinions are won by those who do not follow the custom, who refrain from acquiring the company of ladies in the heated atmosphere of a theatre? A lady sometimes says to the men of her party:

' "I see that there is a general stampede going on. Don't mind me if you would like to go out."

'If they go, she thinks:

"Oh they are just like the others."

'If they stay, she says to her heart:

"How delightful it is to find a man who can do without a B and S, or a smoke for two or three hours."

'And up he goes many pegs in her estimation.'

That's all very well, Mrs Humphry, but what am I to do when Auntie Emm says:

'I'm off to have a B and S, Cuthbert. Coming?'

You see, I happen to know that she is much addicted to the beverage in question. I fear I will go down a great many pegs in her estimation if I do not accompany her. And yet how much happier I would be sitting quietly in my seat, trying to solve the major problem of the entire evening.

Did I hear you ask me, dear Madge, what that could possibly be? How kind and considerate of you. But alas I fear your excellent book of advice can offer me no solution to this particular dilemma. It is quite simply this. Supposing I can, after the playhouse outing, ensnare a brougham or one of those new taximeter cabriolets, how am I going to persuade the driver of the vehicle to take my Auntie Emm to the Egyptian Gardens Café, where she has just informed me on the telephone she is appearing as a belly-dancer in an entertainment called *Belles, Baubles and Balls*?

Reference Section

The first checklist gives brief details of all commercial theatre productions in central London over a period of twelve months; it does not include lunchtime, Sunday-night or club productions, nor does it take account of vaudeville seasons, ice shows or fringe ventures. Transfers are only noted when they were inter-London, and principal cast changes are in the footnotes. Separate checklists for the subsidised companies and certain seasonal theatres as well as for opera and ballet companies will be found on subsequent pages.

CHECKLISTS

London First Night Diary 172
Longest London Runs 179
The National Theatre 180
Royal Shakespeare Company 181
World Theatre Season 183
Chichester Festival Theatre 184
Opera 185
Ballet 187
Honours and Awards 191
Obituary 192

London First Night Diary

DATE	THEATRE	PLAY	AUTHOR
April 5	New	*London Assurance*	Dion Boucicault
April 6	Shaw	*Come When You Like*	Joyce Rayburn
April 10	Sadler's Wells	*All My Sons*	Arthur Miller
April 10	Jeannetta Cochrane	*Lying Figures*	Francis Warner
April 12	Court Upstairs	*Within Two Shadows*	Wilson John Haire
April 18	Royal Court	*Big Wolf*	Harold Mueller
April 29	Palace	*Maid of the Mountains*	Frederick Lonsdale/ Harold Fraser-Simson
May 1	Sadler's Wells	*The Rivals*	Richard Brinsley Sheridan
May 3	Drury Lane	*Gone With The Wind*	Mitchell/Rome/Foote
May 4	Westminster	*Cross Road*	Henry Cass, etc.
May 9	Cambridge	*Tom Brown's Schooldays*	Maitland/Andrews
May 16	Shaw	*Twelfth Night*	William Shakespeare
May 18	Mermaid	*Journey's End*	R. C. Sherriff
May 24	Royal Court	*Crete & Sergeant Pepper*	John Antrobus
May 29	Queens	*Marlene Dietrich*	
May 30	Open Air	*The Tempest*	William Shakespeare
May 30	Stratford East	*The Hostage*	Brendan Behan
June 6	Aldwych	*Love's Labour's Lost* (Prospect Guest Season)	William Shakespeare
June 7	Aldwych	*King Lear* (Prospect Guest Season)	William Shakespeare
June 14	Apollo	*The Mating Game*	Robin Hawdon
June 18	Royal Court	*Hedda Gabler*	Ibsen/John Osborne
June 27	Sadler's Wells	*Trelawny*	Pinero/Woods/Rowell/ Slade
July 4	Savoy	*Lloyd George Knew My Father*	William Douglas Home
July 5	Prince of Wales	*Smilin' Through*	John Hanson/ Constance Cox
July 7	Court Upstairs	*Was He Anyone?*	N. F. Simpson
July 10	Mermaid	*Cowardy Custard*	Noël Coward
July 11	Queens	*I, Claudius*	John Mortimer
July 12	Globe	*Parents' Day*	Ronald Millar
July 13	Shaw	*Mary Rose*	J. M. Barrie
July 13	Open Air	*Twelfth Night*	William Shakespeare
July 13	Roundhouse	*Rock Carmen*	Hendler/Hughes

DIRECTOR	LEADING PLAYERS
Ronald Eyre	Donald Sinden, Judi Dench,[1] Elizabeth Spriggs
Alexander Doré	Amanda Barrie, Raymond Francis, Bill Maynard
Caroline Smith	Evie Garratt, Malcolm Hayes, Jeremy Treglown
Francis Warner	Maxine Audley, Ken Wayne, Philip Bond
Alfred Lynch	Garfield Morgan, Peggy Marshall, Frances Tomelty
William Gaskill/ Pam Brighton	Nigel Terry, Leon Vitali, Michael Kitchen
Emile Littler	Lynn Kennington, Jimmy Edwards, Jimmy Thompson
Malcolm Taylor	Maxine Audley, Anthony Sharp, Philip Bond
Joe Layton	June Ritchie, Harve Presnell, Patricia Michael
Henry Cass	Garard Green, Paul Campbell
Peter Coe	Roy Dotrice, Judith Bruce, Adam Walton
Michael Bakewell	Vanessa Redgrave, Nyree Dawn Porter, Peter Jeffrey
Eric Thompson	Peter Egan, James Maxwell, Harry Landis
Peter Gill	Bill Maynard, James Hazeldine, Bernard Gallagher
Richard Digby Day	Michael Denison, Celia Bannerman, Wayne Sleep
Joan Littlewood	James Booth, Patience Collier, Maxwell Shaw
Toby Robertson	Prunella Scales, Timothy Dalton, John Bailey
Toby Robertson	Timothy West, Timothy Dalton, Sheila Ballantine
Ray Cooney	Terry Scott, Julia Lockwood, Aimi Macdonald
Anthony Page	Jill Bennett, Denholm Elliot, Ronald Hines
Val May	Max Adrian, Ian Richardson, Gemma Craven
Robin Midgley	Ralph Richardson[2], Peggy Ashcroft[3], David Stoll
David Gardiner	John Hanson, Tony Adams, Laverne Gray
Nicholas Wright	Yvonne Antrobus, Carol Gillies, Geoffrey Chater
Wendy Toye	Patricia Routledge, John Moffatt, Una Stubbs
Tony Richardson	David Warner, Sara Kestleman, Freda Jackson
Robert Chetwyn	Gwen Watford, Robin Bailey, Elspeth March
Braham Murray	Mia Farrow, Ralph Bates, Oliver Ford Davies
David Conville	Michael Denison, Celia Bannerman, Hugh Manning
Irving Davies	Terri Stevens, Robert Coleby, Davy Clinton

[1] Later replaced by Sinead Cusack.
[2] Later replaced by Andrew Cruickshank.
[3] Later replaced first by Celia Johnson then by Avice Landone.

DATE	THEATRE	PLAY	AUTHOR
July 18	Piccadilly	*Pull Both Ends*	John Schroeder
July 20	Cambridge (from Mermaid)	*Journey's End*	R. C. Sherriff
July 24	Victoria Palace	*The Rupert Show*	Ken Martyne
July 27	Stratford East	*Finest Family In The Land*	Henry Livings
Aug. 3	Prince of Wales (from Sadler's Wells)	*Trelawny*	Pinero/Woods/Rowell/Slade
Aug. 8	Royal Court	*The Old Ones*	Arnold Wesker
Aug. 9	Palace	*Jesus Christ Superstar*	Tim Rice/Andrew Lloyd Webber
Aug. 10	Bankside Globe	*Hamlet*	William Shakespeare
Aug. 16	Jeannetta Cochrane	*The Apprentices*	Peter Terson
Aug. 16	Comedy	*Time and Time Again*	Alan Ayckbourn
Aug. 16	Shaw	*Zigger Zagger*	Peter Terson
Aug. 22	Globe	*Popkiss*	Ashton/Addison/Heneker
Sept. 5	Jeannetta Cochrane	*Good Lads At Heart*	Peter Terson
Sept. 6	Shaw	*Measure for Measure*	William Shakespeare
Sept. 19	Royal Court	*Richard's Cork Leg*	Brendan Behan
Sept. 20	Roundhouse	*Mother Earth*	Ron Thronson/Toni Shearer
Sept. 21	Queens	*Private Lives*	Noël Coward
Oct. 2	Shaw	*Bakke's Night of Fame*	John McGrath
Oct. 4	Lyric	*The Day After The Fair*	Frank Harvey
Oct. 5	Stratford East	*Costa Packet*	Norman/Bart/Klein
Oct. 16	Court Upstairs	*Eye Winker Tom Tinker*	Tom MacIntyre
Oct. 18	Globe	*A Touch of Purple*	Elleston Trevor
Oct. 19	Haymarket	*Crown Matrimonial*	Royce Ryton
Oct. 24	Roundhouse	*Stand and Deliver!*	Mankowitz/Norman
Oct. 31	Criterion	*Hullabaloo*	Rice/Lloyd Webber, etc.
Nov. 2	Royal Court	*A Pagan Place*	Edna O'Brien
Nov. 6	Piccadilly	*I and Albert*	Allen/Strouse/Adams
Nov. 7	Shaw	*After Magritte/The Real Inspector Hound*	Tom Stoppard
Nov. 8	Roundhouse	*Joseph and the Amazing Technicolor Dreamcoat*	Tim Rice/Andrew Lloyd Webber

DIRECTOR	LEADING PLAYERS
Leslie Lawton	Christine Holmes, Gerry Marsden, Miles Greenwood
Eric Thompson	Peter Egan, James Maxwell, Bruce Robinson
Ken Martyne/David Cullen	Diane Robillard, Kalman Glass, Godfrey Charles
Henry Livings	Griffith Davies, Maxwell Shaw, Brian Murdoch
Val May	Max Adrian,[4] Ian Richardson, Gemma Craven
John Dexter	Max Wall, Wanda Rotha, George Pravda
Jim Sharman	Paul Nicholas, Stephen Tate, Dana Gillespie
Peter Coe	Keith Michell, Donald Houston, Carolyn Seymour
Michael Croft	Members of the National Youth Theatre
Eric Thompson	Tom Courtenay, Cheryl Kennedy, Michael Robbins
Michael Croft	Members of the National Youth Theatre
Richard Cottrell	Daniel Massey, John Standing, Isla Blair
Michael Croft	Members of the National Youth Theatre
Paul Hill	Members of the National Youth Theatre
Alan Simpson	Joan O'Hara, Angela Newman, Ronnie Drew
Terry Palmer	Peter Straker, Helen Chappel, Linda Kendrick
John Gielgud	Maggie Smith, Robert Stephens,[5] James Villiers
Peter James	Hywel Bennett, Nikolas Simmonds, David Healy
Frith Banbury	Deborah Kerr, Julia Foster, Duncan Lamont
Joan Littlewood	Avis Bunnage, Maxwell Shaw, Valerie Walsh
Robert Kidd	Donal McCann, Harry Webster, Frances Tomelty
Philip Grout	Ray Barrett, Maxine Audley, Bernard Horsfall
Peter Dews	Wendy Hiller, Peter Barkworth, Amanda Reiss
Wendy Toye	Nicky Henson, Derek Godfrey, Paul Hardwick
Frank Dunlop	Jimmy Edwards, Chelsea Brown, Rogers & Starr
Ronald Eyre	David Burke, Colette O'Neil, Veronica Quilligan
John Schlesinger	Polly James, Sven-Bertil Taube, Lewis Fiander
Paul Hill/Nigel Gordon	John Bluthal, Lynda Baron, Jenny Laird
Frank Dunlop	Gary Bond, Joan Heal, Paul Brooke

[4] Later replaced by Roland Culver.
[5] Later replaced by John Standing.

DATE	THEATRE	PLAY	AUTHOR
Nov. 16	Her Majesty's	*Applause*	Comden/Green/Strouse/Adams
Nov. 21	Cambridge	*Behind the Fridge*	Peter Cook/Dudley Moore
Dec. 4	Royal Court	*A Sense of Detachment*	John Osborne
Dec. 6	Globe	*My Fat Friend*	Charles Laurence
Dec. 6	Shaw	*The Plotters of Cabbage Patch Corner*	David Wood
Dec. 7	Westminster	*Give A Dog A Bone*	Peter Howard
Dec. 13	Court Upstairs	*Owners*	Caryl Churchill
Dec. 16	Jeannetta Cochrane	*Toad of Toad Hall*	A. A. Milne
Dec. 18	Criterion	*Bunny*	Norman Krasna
Dec. 18	Phoenix	*Winnie The Pooh*	A. A. Milne/Julian Slade
Dec. 18	Shaw	*Between the Bars*	Donald Swann
Dec. 18	Royalty	*Rupert and the Paperfall*	A. E. Bestall
Dec. 19	Mermaid	*Treasure Island*	Miles/Coe/Wilson
Dec. 19	Palladium	*Babes In The Wood*	Park/Morrison/Steele
Dec. 20	Prince of Wales'	*The Good Old, Bad Old Days*	Anthony Newley/Leslie Bricusse
Dec. 20	Coliseum	*Peter Pan*	J. M. Barrie
Dec. 21	Duke of York's	*Once Upon A Time*	Newell/Webb
Dec. 26	Stratford East	*Big Rock Candy Mountain*	Alan Lomax/Yola Miller
Jan. 2	Roundhouse	*The Littlest Clown*	Christopher Cable
Jan. 11	New London	*The Unknown Soldier & His Wife*	Peter Ustinov
Jan. 16	Royal Court	*Not I/Krapp's Last Tape*	Samuel Beckett
Jan. 17	Shaw	*Willie Rough*	Bill Bryden
Feb. 1	Shaw	*After Magritte/ The Real Inspector Hound*	Tom Stoppard
Feb. 14	Stratford East	*Is Your Doctor Really Necessary?*	Ken Hill/Tony Macaulay
Feb. 15	Piccadilly	*Mistress of Novices*	John Kerr
Feb. 17	Albery (from Roundhouse)	*Joseph and the Amazing Technicolor Dreamcoat*	Tim Rice/Andrew Lloyd Webber
Feb. 20	Criterion	*A Doll's House*	Henrik Ibsen
Feb. 21	Vaudeville	*A Private Matter*	Ronald Mavor
Feb. 27	Royal Court	*The Freedom of the City*	Brian Friel
Mar. 6	Westminster	*G.B.*	Henry Cass, etc.
Mar. 6	Garrick (from St. Martin's)	*Sleuth*	Anthony Shaffer

DIRECTOR	LEADING PLAYERS
Ron Field	Lauren Bacall, Angela Richards, Basil Hoskins
Joseph McGrath/Peter Cook/ Dudley Moore	Peter Cook, Dudley Moore
Frank Dunlop	John Standing, Rachel Kempson, Denise Coffey
Eric Thompson	Kenneth Williams, Jennie Linden, John Harding
Jonathan Lynn	Myvanwy Jenn, Ben Aris, Timothy Davies
Henry Cass/Bridget Espinosa	Donald Scott, Liz Edmiston, Richard Warner
Nicholas Wright	Stephanie Bidmead, David Swift, Richard O'Callaghan
David Conville	Ian Talbot, Nikolas Simmonds, Richard Wilson
Alexander Doré	Eartha Kitt, David Kossoff, Robert Beatty
Malcolm Farquhar	Ronald Radd, Frank Thornton, Maria Charles
Donald Swann	Donald Swann, Catherine Martin, Richard Day Lewis
Ken Martyne	Diane Robillard, Clive Bennett, Laurie Webb
Sally Miles	Christopher Benjamin, Laurie Payne, James Warwick
Albert J. Knight	Edward Woodward, Derek Nimmo, Adrienne Posta
Anthony Newley	Anthony Newley, Paul Bacon, Bill Kerr
Robert Helpmann	Dorothy Tutin, Ron Moody, Ian Trigger
Gillian Lynne	Patsy Rowlands, Joyce Grant, Kerry Gardner
Avis Bunnage	Long John Baldry, Maxwell Shaw, Toni Palmer
Riggs O'Hara	Kim Braden, David Morton, Doreen Keogh
Peter Ustinov	Peter Ustinov, Brian Bedford, Jeffrey Wickham
Anthony Page	Albert Finney, Billie Whitelaw, Brian Miller
Bill Bryden	James Grant, Roddy McMillan, Fulton Mackay
Paul Hill/Nigel Gordon	Lorna Heilbron, David Healy, Jenny Laird
Ken Hill	Maxwell Shaw, Avis Bunnage, Brian Murphy
Charles Hickman	Rita Tushingham, Geoffrey Keen, Barbara Jefford
Frank Dunlop	Gary Bond, Joan Heal, Paul Brooke
Patrick Garland	Claire Bloom, Colin Blakely, Anton Rodgers
Ian McKellen	Alastair Sim, Dorothy Reynolds, Derek Fowlds
Albert Finney	Carmel McSharry, Basil Dignam, Stephen Rea
Henry Cass	Penny Croft, Gladstone Adderley, Mike Fields
Clifford Williams	Michael Allinson, Del Mooney

DATE	THEATRE	PLAY	AUTHOR
Mar. 7	**Aldwych**	***Suzanna Andler***	**Marguerite Duras**
Mar. 8	**St. Martin's**	***Lover***	**Brian Clemens**
Mar. 13	**Comedy**	***Small Craft Warnings***	**Tennessee Williams**
Mar. 19	**Jeannetta Cochrane**	***Sarah B. Divine***	**Tom Eyen**
Mar. 20	**Shaw**	***Only A Game***	**Barrie Keeffe**
Mar. 29	**St. Martin's**	***Say Goodnight To Your Grandma***	**Colin Welland**

DIRECTOR	LEADING PLAYERS
Howard Sackler	Eileen Atkins, Dinsdale Landen, Lynn Farleigh
Philip Grout	Sally Ann Howes, Jeremy Hawk, Max Wall
Vivian Matalon	Elaine Stritch, Edward Judd, Frances de la Tour
Rogers & Starr	Rogers & Starr
Michael Croft	Peter Gilmore, Jan Waters, Basil Lord
Patrick Dromgoole	Madge Ryan, Colin Welland, Stephanie Turner

The ten London productions with longest runs as at June 1st 1973, were:

The Mousetrap	8529
Hair	1948
Pyjama Tops	1524
Sleuth	1369
Oh! Calcutta!	1173
The Philanthropist	992
No Sex Please—We're British	840
Show Boat	776
Suddenly At Home	702
Godspell	637

The National Theatre 1972–73

Old Vic
Directors: Sir Laurence Olivier, Peter Hall (73 only)

THE FRONT PAGE
by Ben Hecht and Charles MacArthur
Prod: Michael Blakemore

'TIS PITY SHE'S A WHORE
by John Ford
Prod: Roland Joffé (Mobile)

JUMPERS
by Tom Stoppard
Prod: Peter Wood

MACBETH
by William Shakespeare
Prod: Michael Blakemore

THE MISANTHROPE
by Molière, ad. Tony Harrison
Prod: John Dexter

EQUUS
by Peter Shaffer
Prod: John Dexter

THE SCHOOL FOR SCANDAL
by Richard Brinsley Sheridan
Prod: Jonathan Miller

RICHARD II
by William Shakespeare
Prod: David William

LONG DAY'S JOURNEY INTO NIGHT
by Eugene O'Neill
Prod: Michael Blakemore

TWELFTH NIGHT
by William Shakespeare
Prod: Peter James (Mobile)

THE CHERRY ORCHARD
by Chekhov, ad. Ronald Hingley
Prod: Michael Blakemore

The Company included: Gillian Barge, David Bauer, David Bradley, Shelia Burrell, Anna Carteret, Nicholas Clay, Jeremy Clyde, Graham Crowden, Constance Cummings, Paul Curran, Gawn Grainger, Paul Gregory, Mary Griffiths, David Healy, Anthony Hopkins, Michael Hordern, Barry James, David Kincaid, Maureen Lipman, Harry Lomax, Kenneth Mackintosh, Alan MacNaughtan, Christopher Martin, Jo Maxwell-Muller, Alec McCowen, Desmond McNamara, Laurence Olivier, Lousie Purnell, Denis Quilley, Louie Ramsay, Malcom Reid, Diana Rigg, Maggie Riley, David Ryall, John Shrapnel, Jeanne Watts, David Whitman, Benjamin Whitrow.

Royal Shakespeare Company 1972–73

Artistic Director: Trevor Nunn

Stratford 1973:
(*Company Director:* John Barton)

ROMEO AND JULIET
Prod: Terry Hands

AS YOU LIKE IT
Prod: Buzz Goodbody

THE TAMING OF THE SHREW
Prod: Clifford Williams

RICHARD II
Prod: John Barton

LOVE'S LABOUR'S LOST
Prod: David Jones

The Company included: John Abbot, Ray Armstrong, Robert Ashby, Eilen Atkins, Annette Badland, Alan Bates, Sydney Bromley, Brenda Bruce, Gavin Campbell, Janet Chappell, Tony Church, Timothy Dalton, Jeffery Dench, Michael Ensign, Susan Fleetwood, Brian Glover, Nickolas Grace, Wilfred Grove, Denis Holmes, Louise Jameson, Charles Keating, Estelle Kohler, Beatrix Lehmann, Bernard Lloyd, Clement McCallin, Lloyd McGuire, Peter Machin, Colin Mayes, Richard Mayes, Richard Pasco, Anthony Pedley, Ian Richardson, Sebastian Shaw, Derek Smith, David Suchet, Janet Whiteside.

Aldwych 1972–73
(*Company Director:* David Jones)

THE MERCHANT OF VENICE
by William Shakespeare
Prod: Terry Hands

OTHELLO
by William Shakespeare
Prod: John Barton

THE ISLAND OF THE MIGHTY
by John Arden and Margaretta D'Arcy
Prod: David Jones

THE LOWER DEPTHS
by Maxim Gorky (ad. Blair/Brooks)
Prod: David Jones

MURDER IN THE CATHEDRAL
by T. S. Eliot
Prod: Terry Hands

A MIDSUMMER NIGHT'S DREAM
by William Shakespeare
Prod: Peter Brook

The Company included: Patrick Allen, Robert Ashby, Julia Blalock, Hugh Keays Byrne, David Calder, Heather Canning, Tony Church, Valerie Colgan, Jane Cussons, Lynn Dearth, Alison Fiske, Susan Fleetwood, Peter Geddis, Gordon Gostelow, Nickolas Grace, Lisa Harrow, Denis Holmes, Alan Howard, John Hug, Emrys James, Gemma Jones, Lila Kaye, Kwesi Kay, Estelle Kohler, Beatrix Lehmann, Marion Lines, Bernard Lloyd, Robert Lloyd, Philip Locke, Lloyd McGuire, Peter Machin, Brewster Mason, Colin Mayes, Richard Mayes,

Richard Moore, Richard Pasco, Anthony Pedley, Mike Pratt, Roger Rees, Malcom Rennie, Matthew Robertson, Zhivila Roche, Philip Sayer, Michael Shannon, Morgan Sheppard, Jennie Stoller, George Sweeney, Ted Valentine, Gillian Webb, Michael Walker, Peter Woodthorpe.

World Theatre Season

Aldwych Theatre
Artistic Director: Sir Peter Daubeny

1973 (Tenth and Closing Season)

WEST GERMANY:	*Bochum Schauspielhaus:* Dorst: LITTLE MAN-WHAT NOW?
SPAIN:	*Nuria Espert Company:* Lorca: YERMA
AUSTRIA:	*Vienna Burgtheater:* Schnitzler: LIEBELEI
FRANCE:	*Comédie Française:* Molière: LE MALADE IMAGINAIRE Shakespeare: RICHARD III
ITALY:	*Peppino De Filippo Company:* Filippo: METAMORPHOSES OF A WANDERING MINSTREL
BELGIUM:	*Rideau de Bruxelles:* Apollinaire: L'ENCHANTEUR POURRISSANT
POLAND:	*Cracow Stary Theatre:* Wajda/Dostoyevsky: THE POSSESSED
SWEDEN:	*Royal Dramatic Theatre:* Ibsen: THE WILD DUCK
JAPAN:	*Umewaka Noh Troupe:* Three Programmes
SOUTH AFRICA:	*Natal Theatre Workshop Zulu Company:* Msomi: UMABATHA

Chichester Festival Theatre

Artistic Director: Sir John Clements

1973

THE DIRECTOR OF THE OPERA
by Jean Anouilh
Prod: Peter Dews

R LOVES J
by Ustinov/Faris/More
Prod: Wendy Toye

THE SEAGULL
by Anton Chekhov
Prod: Jonathan Miller

DANDY DICK
by Arthur Pinero
Prod: John Clements

The Company included: Cristina Avery, Derek Beard, Antony Brown, Michael Burgess, John Clements, Robert Colman, Primula Cotton, Gemma Craven, Anna Dawson, Richard Denning, Peter Eyre, Lucinda Gane, Mercia Glossop, John Grillo, Pip Hinton, Lee Hudson, June Jago, Reginald Jessop, Charles Lloyd Pack, Philip Lowrie, Ciaran Madden, Ralph Michael, Ian Milton, Cynthia Morey, Andy Mulligan, Maureen O'Brian, Richard Pearson, Patricia Routledge, Alastair Sim, Robert Stephens, Dudley Stevens, Topol, David Watson, Eileen Way, Penelope Wilton, Irene Worth.

Opera 1972—73

Royal Opera House, Covent Garden:

TOSCA: Puccini/Downes, Atherton
BILLY BUDD: Britten/Mackerras
PELLÉAS ET MÉLISANDE: Debussy/Boulez
COSÌ FAN TUTTE: Mozart/Leppard, Klee
EUGENE ONEGIN: Tchaikovsky/Atherton
SIMONE BOCCANEGRA: Verdi/Ceccato
DER FLIEGENDE HOLLÄNDER: Wagner/Schmidt-Isserstedt
NABUCCO: Verdi/Davis/Kašlik
AIDA: Verdi/Matheson
FALSTAFF: Verdi/Ceccato
JENŮFA: Jánaček/Mackerras
DON CARLOS: Verdi/Pritchard
VICTORY: Bennett/Downes
MADAME BUTTERFLY: Puccini/Matheson
KING PRIAM: Tippett/Atherton
ORFEO ED EURIDICE: Gluck/Mackerras
OTELLO: Verdi/Davis
ELEKTRA: Strauss/Solti
LA TRAVIATA: Verdi/Cillario
TAVERNER: Maxwell Davies/Downes/Geliot
LES TROYENS: Berlioz/Davis
LE NOZZE DI FIGARO: Mozart/Leppard
KHOVANSHCHINA: Mussorgsky-Shostakovich/Downes
RIGOLETTO: Verdi/Atherton
THE KNOT GARDEN: Tippett/Davis

Sadler's Wells Company, Coliseum:

ORPHEUS IN THE UNDERWORLD: Offenbach/Barker, Davies
THE BARBER OF SEVILLE: Rossini/Lloyd-Jones
DIE FLEDERMAUS: J. Strauss/Wilks
LA BOHÈME: Puccini/Braithwaite
THE MAKROPULOS CASE: Jánaček/Mackerras
THE MARRIAGE OF FIGARO: Mozart/Mackerras
THE RHINEGOLD: Wagner/Mackerras/Byam Shaw-Blatchley
TWILIGHT OF THE GODS: Wagner/Barker
DUKE BLUEBEARD'S CASTLE: Bartók/Mackerras/Byam Shaw
OEDIPUS REX: Stravinsky/Mackerras
CARMEN: Bizet/Braithwaite, Mackerras
THE SERAGLIO: Mozart/Davies
THE CORONATION OF POPPEA: Monteverdi/Vivienne
COUNT ORY: Rossini/Balkwill
IL TROVATORE: Verdi/Mackerras/Copley
GLORIANA: Britten/Mackerras
COSÌ FAN TUTTE: Mozart/Balkwill

THE TALES OF HOFFMANN: Offenbach/Balkwill
MADAM BUTTERFLY: Puccini/Mackerras
WAR AND PEACE: Prokofiev/Lloyd-Jones/Graham
CAVALLERIA RUSTICANA: Mascagni/Brydon
PAGLIACCI: Leoncavallo/Barker
PATIENCE: Sullivan/Vivienne
THE MERRY WIDOW: Lehár/Krips/Cox

Glyndebourne Festival:
ARIADNE AUF NAXOS: Strauss/Fredman, Ceccato/Cox
IL RITORNO D'ULISSE IN PATRIA: Monteverdi/Leppard/Hall
DIE ENTFÜHRUNG AUS DEM SERAIL: Mozart/Haitink, Pritchard/Cox
MACBETH: Verdi/Pritchard, Fredman/Hadjimischev

Welsh National Company:
RIGOLETTO: Verdi/Lockhart, Suttie/Moody
THE MARRIAGE OF FIGARO: Mozart/Hose
TURANDOT: Puccini/Armstrong/Geliot
AIDA: Verdi/Lockhart
FALSTAFF: Verdi/Lockhart
THE MAGIC FLUTE: Mozart/Hose
DON GIOVANNI: Mozart/Lockhart
BILLY BUDD: Britten/Lockhart, Armstrong/Geliot
NABUCCO: Verdi/Armstrong
LULU: Berg/Lockhart, Armstrong

Scottish Opera Company:
OTELLO: Verdi/Erede/Besch
A MIDSUMMER NIGHT'S DREAM: Britten/Brydon/Robertson
THE BARBER OF SEVILLE: Rossini/Brydon, Dodd/Watt-Smith
COSÌ FAN TUTTE: Mozart/Gibson/Besch
PELLÉAS ET MÉLISANDE: Debussy/Gibson/Graham
LES TROYENS: Berlioz/Gibson/Ebert
THE MARRIAGE OF FIGARO: Mozart/Betini/Besch
DON PASQUALE: Donizetti/Gibson/Ebert

Ballet 1972–73

The Royal Ballet (*large company*)
New Productions:
TRIAD (Kenneth MacMillan/Prokofiev/Peter Unsworth)
POÈME DE L'EXTASE (John Cranko/Scriabin/Jürgen Rose)
LABORINTUS (Glen Tetley/Luciano Berio/Rouben Ter-Arutunian)
REQUIEM CANTICLES (Jerome Robbins/Stravinsky)
THE WALK TO THE PARADISE GARDENS (Ashton/Delius/William Chapell)
Also in repertory during the year:
THE DREAM (Ashton/Mendelssohn), DANCES AT A GATHERING (Robbins, Chopin), SERENADE (Balanchine/Tchaikovsky), FIELD FIGURES (Tetley/Stockhausen), ENIGMA VARIATIONS (Ashton/Elgar), SONG OF THE EARTH (MacMillan/Mahler), LES NOCES (Nijinska/Stravinsky), CHECKMATE (de Valois/Bliss), AFTERNOON OF A FAUN (Robbins/Debussy), MARGUERITE AND ARMAND (Ashton/Liszt), LA FILLE MA GARDÉE (Ashton/Hérold arr. Lanchberry), SWAN LAKE (Petipa, Ivanov/Tchaikovsky) GISELLE (Petipa prod. Wright/Adam), ROMEO AND JULIET (MacMillan/Prokofiev), THE SLEEPING BEAUTY (Petipa, Ashton, Wright/Tchaikovsky), LA BAYADÈRE (Petipa, prod. Nureyev/Minkus), SYMPHONIC VARIATIONS (Ashton/Franck), ANASTASIA (MacMillan/Tchaikovsky & Martinu), MONOTONES 1 and 2 (Ashton/Satie), THE FIREBIRD (Fokine/Stravinsky), THE RITE OF SPRING (MacMillan/Stravinsky), JOB (de Valois/Vaughan Williams), RAYMONDA Act 3 (Nureyev after Petipa/Glazunov), CINDERELLA (Ashton/Prokofiev)

The Royal Ballet (*new group*)
New productions:
O.W. (Joe Layton/William Walton/John Conklin)
GROSSE FUGE (Hans van Manen/Beethoven/Jean-Paul Vroom)
LAURENCIA Pas de Six (Nureyev after Chaboukiani/Krein/Phillip Prowse)
BALLADE (MacMillan, Fauré)
SIESTA (Ashton/Walton)
THE POLTROON (MacMillan/Rudolf Maros/Thomas O'Neil)
IN A SUMMER GARDEN (Ronald Hynd/Delius/Peter Docherty)
Also in repertory during the year:
SOLITAIRE (MacMillan/Arnold), LES RENDEZVOUS (Ashton/Auber), FACADE (Ashton/Walton), THE MAIDS (Ross/Milhaud), CAPRICHOS (Ross/Bartok), THE LADY AND THE FOOL (Cranko/Verdi arr. Mackerras), THE GRAND TOUR (Layton/Coward arr. Hershy Kay), LES PATINEURS (Ashton/Meyerbeer arr. Lambert), PINEAPPLE POLL (Cranko/Sullivan arr. Mackerras), LAS HERMANAS (MacMillan/Martin), DANSES CONCERTANTES (MacMillan/Stravinsky), MONOTONES No 2 (Ashton/Satie), TRIAD (MacMillan/Prokofiev), MIRROR WALKERS duet (Wright/Tchaikovsky)

Ballet Rambert

New productions:

FOR THESE WHO DIE AS CATTLE . . . (Christopher Bruce/no music/ Nadine Baylis)
LADIES, LADIES! (Norman Morrice/Anthony Hymas/Baylis)
STOP-OVER (Joseph Scoglio/Takemitsu/Baylis)
4 PIECES FOR 4 DANCERS (Pietje Law/various/Baylis)
THEME AND VARIATIONS (Graham Jones/Villa-Lobos/Baylis)
AD HOC (John Chesworth/various/Baylis)
PATTERN FOR AN ESCALATOR (Chesworth/Jonathan Harvey & George Newson)
CONSIDERING THE LILIES (Lar Lubovitch/Bach)
LISTEN TO THE MUSIC (Jonathan Taylor/Anthony Hymas/Jenny Beavan)
TOTEMS (Graham Jones/Michael Gibbs/Robin Don)

Also in repertory during the year:

FOUR ACCORDING (Chesworth/Bacewicz), GEORGE FRIDERIC (Bruce/ Handel), THE ACT (Hodes/Page & Johnson), THAT IS THE SHOW (Morrice/Berio), 'TIS GOODLY SPORT (J. Taylor/16th century court music), RAG DANCES (Tetley/Hymas), WINGS (Bruce/Downes), SOLO (Morrice/Downes), PIERROT LUNAIRE (Tetley/Schoenberg), RICERCARE (Tetley/Seter), THE EMPTY SUIT (Morrice/Salzedo), OPUS '65 (Sokolow/ Macero), ZIGGURAT (Tetley/Stockhausen), TIC-TACK (Chesworth/ Kreisler), BLIND-SIGHT (Tetley/Downes), Bertram Batell's Sideshow

Festival Ballet

New productions:

SWAN LAKE (Petipa/Ivanov prod. Beryl Grey/Tchaikovsky/John Truscott)
EBB AND FLOW (Ulf Gadd/Teleman/Gadd)
MENDELSSOHN SYMPHONY (Denis Nahat/Mendelssohn/Peter Farmer)
DANSSCAPE (Walter Gore/Hindemith/Gore)
SUMMER SOLSTICE (Barry Moreland/John Field/Charles Dunlop)

Also in the repertory during the year:

THE NUTCRACKER (J. Carter/Tchaikovsky), LES SYLPHIDES (Fokine/ Chopin), PETRUSHKA (Fokine/Stravinsky), SCHEHERAZADE (Fokine/ Rimsky-Korsakoff), GISELLE (Petipa prod. Mary Skeaping/Adam), PRINCE IGOR (Fokine/Borodin), THE SLEEPING BEAUTY (Petipa prod. Stevenson/Tchaikovsky), PIÈGE DE LUMIERE (Taras/Damase), BOURRÉE FANTASQUE (Balanchine/Chabrier), NIGHT SHADOW (Balanchine/Rieti after Bellini), ETUDES (Lander/Riisager), GRADUATION BALL (Lichine/Strauss), COPPÉLIA (J. Carter/Delibes), Dances from NAPOLI (Bournonville prod. Vangsaa/Paulli, Helsted & Gade), NOIR ET BLANC (Lifar/Lalo)

London Contemporary Dance Theatre
New productions:
COLD (Richard Alston/Adolphe Adam)
KONTAKION (Barry Moreland/Renaissance Festival & Spanish Medieval/Moreland)
. . . ONE WAS THE OTHER (Noemi Lapzeson & Robert North/Michael Finnissy/ Norberto Chiesa)
SCENES FROM THE MUSIC OF CHARLES IVES (Anna Sokolow/Charles Ives/ Sokolow)
DANCE (Remy Charlip/improvisations)
COMBINES (Richard Alston/Schubert, Bach, Chopin, jazz/Sally Potter film)
SCALENE SEQUENCE (Flora Cushman/Luciano Berio)
PEOPLE ALONE (Robert Cohan/Bob Downes/Norberto Chiesa)
TIGER BALM (Richard Alston/Anna Lockwood)
DANCE ENERGIES (May O'Donnell/Ray Green)
BRIAN (Robert North/Michael Finnissy/Peter Owen)
ENDS AND ODDS (Lotte Gosler/various)
RELAY (Siobhan Davies/Colin Wood & Bernard Watson)
TREEO (Xenia Hribar/Alastair Leonard)
GAMMA GARDEN (Flora Cushman/Shusha & Ignatius Temba)
Also in repertory during the year:
STAGES (Cohan/Downes), CANTIBLE (Lapzeson Finnissy), RAGA SHANKARA (Cushman/Alford & Sathe), THE ROAD OF THE PHOEBE SHOW (Beatty/ Ellington & Strayhorn), ECLIPSE (Cohan/Lester), 3 EPITAPHS (P. Taylor/early American folk music), CONSOLATION OF THE RISING MOON (Cohan/John Williams), HUNTER OF ANGELS (Cohan/Maderna), CELL (Cohan/Lloyd), NOWHERE SLOWLY (Alston/Stockhausen)

Scottish Theatre Ballet
New productions:
AN CLÒ MOR (Stuart Hopps/Trad. Gaelic Songs/Audrey Gie)
TALES OF HOFFMANN (Peter Darrell/Offenbach/Alistair Livingstone)
SOME BRIGHT STAR (Peter Cazalet/Pink Floyd, Ivo Malec and Tonto's Expanding Headband/Cazalet)
VARIATIONS ON A DOOR AND A SIGH (Peter Darrell/Pierre Henry/ Amanda Colin)
BALKAN SOBRANIE (Richard Alston/Stravinsky, Jean Françaix, Fukushima/Myra Visser)
POSITIVELY THE LAST FINAL FAREWELL PERFORMANCE (Stuart Hopps/ Glen Miller Favourites/Alan Alexander)
THE NUTCRACKER Act 2 (Ivanov prod. Peter Darrell/Tchaikovsky/ Philip Prowse)
Also in the repertory during the year:
STREET GAMES (Gore/Ibert), Dances from WILLIAM TELL (Bournonville

prod. Hans Brenaa/Rossini), THE LESSON (Flindt/Delerue) LA FÊTE ETRANGE (Howard/Fauré), JOURNEY (Killar/Janaček), LIGHT FANTASTIC (Gore/Chabrier), CAGE OF GOD (J. Carter/Rawsthorne), SONATE À TROIS (Béjart/Bartók),

Northern Dance Theatre
New productions:
VALSE TRISTE (Laverne Meyer/Sibelius)
THREE QUARTER PROFILE (Suzanne Hywel/Frank Martin/Glynn Kelly)
SCHUBERT VARIATIONS (Laverne Meyer/Schubert)
TCHAIKOVSKY SUITE (Simon Mottram/Tchaikovsky)
THE WANDERER AND HIS SHADOW (Jonathan Thorpe/Brahms/Michael Holt)
THE NIGHT AND SILENCE (Walter Gore/Bach arr. Mackerras)
THE PIG AND THE PANTHER (Fergus Early/soundtrack/Michael Holt)
WITHIN WALLS (John Haynes/Fernando Soler/Michael Holt)
HOOPS (Walter Gore/Poulenc/Kenneth Rowell)
Also in the repertory during the year:
BRAHMS SONATA (Meyer/Brahms), DEATH AND THE MAIDEN (Howard/Schubert), TANCREDI AND CLORINDA (Thorpe/Monteverdi), SILENT EPISODE (Meyer/Webern), TOWARDS NIGHT (Haynes/Schumann), INTRODUCTION PIECE (Meyer/Poulenc), GAMES FOR 5 PLAYERS (Chesworth/Takemitsu), PAS DE CINQ (Meyer/Suppé), PETER AND THE WOLF (Staff/Prokofiev), DANCE PICTURES (Gore/Maros), THE PRISONERS (Darrell/Bartók), QUARTET (Thorpe/Beethoven), NUTCRACKER PAS DE DEUX (Ivanov prod. Mottram/Tchaikovsky), THE PREDATORS (Roope/Lloyd)

Visiting companies:
Ballet of the Twentieth Century (Brussels) in NIJINSKY, CLOWN OF GOD; *Chuha Dancers of Bengal* (West Bengal); *Dan Wagoner Dance Company* (New York); *Black Theatre of Prague; Jean Babilée and company* (Paris) in Stravinsky's THE SOLDIER'S TALE; *Kabuki Theatre* (Tokyo); *Kathakali Dance Theatre* (India); *Korean National Dance Company; Little Angels* (Korea); *Mahalli Dancers of Iran* (Teheran); *Mazowsze Dance Company* (Poland); *Marcel Marceau* (Paris); *Merce Cunningham Dance Company* (New York); *Murray Louis Dance Company* (New York); *National Ballet of Canada* (Toronto); *National Dance Theatre of Jamica; Paco Pena Flamenco Puro* (Spain); *Royal Swedish Ballet Sololists* (Stockholm); *Toronto Dance Theatre; Trinidad Folk Company.*

Theatre Honours and Awards 1972–73

Birthday Honours 1972:
C.H.: Lord Goodman
C.B.E.: Robert Bolt, L. du Garde Peach, Charles Randolph Taylor

New Year Honours 1973:
C.B.E.: Evelyn Laye, Beryl Grey

Plays & Players *1972 London Drama Critics' Awards:*
Best Play: JUMPERS; *Best Musical:* COMPANY; *Best Performance by an Actor:* Laurence Olivier in LONG DAY'S JOURNEY INTO NIGHT; *Best Performance by an Actress:* Constance Cummings in LONG DAY'S JOURNEY INTO NIGHT; *Best Supporting Actor:* Denis Quilley for work at the National Theatre; *Best Supporting Actress:* Yvonne Antrobus for THE EFFECT OF GAMMA RAYS ON MAN-IN-THE-MOON MARIGOLDS; *Most Promising Actor:* Peter Egan for JOURNEY'S END; *Most Promising Actress:* Veronica Quilligan for A PAGAN PLACE; *Best Production (Director):* Michael Blakemore for THE FRONT PAGE; *Best Production (Designer):* Victor Garcia for YERMA.

Plays & Players also gave the following (editorial) Special Awards: *Most Overrated Play:* JUMPERS; *Most Underrated Play:* ALL OVER; *Most Underrated Performance:* Angela Lansbury for ALL OVER; *Worst Productions:* ROCK CARMEN, TITUS ANDRONICUS.

Evening Standard *1972 Drama Awards:*
Actor: Laurence Olivier (LONG DAY'S JOURNEY INTO NIGHT); *Actress:* Rachel Roberts (ALPHA BETA); *Best Play:* JUMPERS; *Best Comedy:* VETERANS; *Best Musical:* APPLAUSE; *Most Promising Playwright:* Wilson John Haire (WITHIN TWO SHADOWS); *Special Award:* Peter Daubeny (WORLD THEATRE SEASONS).

1972 Shakespeare Prize: Paul Scofield.

Clarence Derwent Awards: Heather Canning (MISS JULIE); Richard O'Callaghan (BUTLEY)

Variety Club Stage Awards: Actor: Tom Courtenay (TIME AND TIME AGAIN); *Actress:* Maggie Smith (PRIVATE LIVES)

USA:
Time Magazine's Best Productions of 1972: SMALL CRAFT WARNINGS; THE REAL INSPECTOR HOUND; THAT CHAMPIONSHIP SEASON; MUCH ADO ABOUT NOTHING; OH, COWARD!; PIPPIN; BUTLEY; THE SUNSHINE BOYS.

Theatrical Obituary

Mab Ackland, *Playwright*
Max Adrian, *Actor* (69)
Jean-Pierre Alban, *Dancer* (38)
Bob Bahl, *Designer* (34)
Seoghan Barlow, *Abbey Theatre Designer*
André Barsacq, *Designer* (64)
David Bauer, *Actor* (55)
Hugh Beaumont, *Impresario* (65)
Henry Beckett, *Actor* (83)
John Beresford Fowler, *Actor* (80)
Esmé Beringer, *Actress* (96)
Eugene Berman, *Designer* (73)
Max Berman, *Costumier* (88)
Carl Bernard, *Actor* (66)
Jean-Jacques Bernard, *Playwright* (84)
Mary Bloomfield, *Actress*
Buddy Bradley, *Choreographer*
Pierre Brasseur, *Actor* (67)
Judith Bretherton (Lady Guthrie) (57)
Frederick Bromwich, *Manager*
Lawrence Brown, *Accompanist* (79)
John Burrell, *Director* (62)
Leo G. Carroll, *Actor* (80)
Robert Chesselet, *Critic* (70)
Esmé Church, *Actress/Teacher* (79)
Sir Noël Coward (73)
Richard Crooks, *Singer* (72)
Fanny Dango, *Actress* (94)
R. F. Delderfield, *Playwright* (60)
Jacques Deval, *Playwright* (82)
George Dudley Smith, *Actor* (91)
Chris Durham, *Theatrical landlady* (72)
Sophie Ellis, *Actress*
Maurice Escarde, *Actor* (80)
Arthur Fear, *Singer* (70)
George Fearon, *Press Representative* (71)
Alexandra Fedorova, *Ballerina* (83)
Catherine Ferguson, *Soubrette* (77)
Felix Felton, *Actor* (60)
Dudley Foster, *Actor* (48)
Teresa Franchini, *Actress* (95)
Margaret Fraser, *Actress* (96)
Rudolph Friml, *Composer* (92)
Roger Furse, *Designer* (68)
Marine de Gabarain, *Soprano* (46)
Archie Gardner, *Critic*
Jack Gatti, *Theatre Proprietor* (73)
Goyan Gertele, *General Manager, N.Y. Metropolitan Opera*
John Gillies, *Stoll General Manager*
Colin Gordon, *Actor* (61)
Reginald Green, *Actor* (70)
Bernard Grun, *Composer* (71)
Nicholas Hannen, *Actor* (91)
Harry Hansen, *Actor-Manager* (77)
Gerard Heinz, *Actor* (68)
Elsie Hilton, *Box Office Manager, Globe Theatre* (77)
W. H. Holden, *Musical Director* (93)
Miriam Hopkins, *Actress* (70)
Bobby Howes, *Actor* (76)
David Hughes, *Singer* (44)
Sidney Jarvis, *Designer* (62)
Caryl Jenner, *Director* (55)
Frank Jerram, *Company Manager* (49)
Roy Jessen, *Conductor* (46)
Rosemary Johnson, *Actress* (59)
Walter Johnstone Douglas, *Singer* (85)
Emrys Jones, *Actor* (56)
Kay Jones, *Actress*
Cecil Kellaway, *Actor* (79)
Hetty King, *Male Impersonator* (89)
Gabrielle Laye, *Actress*
Charles Leno, *Actor* (64)
Jack Leopold, *Acrobat* (88)

David Levine, *Pianist* (72)
David Lichine, *Choreographer* (61)
Jose Limen, *Dancer* (64)
Boris Livanov, *Actor* (68)
John G. Lloyd, *Agent* (42)
Fyodor Lopokhov, *Choreographer* (86)
James Lovell, *Artistic Director* (59)
Viola Lyall, *Actress* (71)
Jack MacGowran, *Actor* (54)
Sir Compton Mackenzie, *Screenwriter* (89)
Jean Madeira, *Soprano* (47)
John McPhillips, *Catholic Theatre Chaplain*
Lauritz Melchior, *Singer* (82)
Jack Melford, *Actor* (73)
Rita Meoney, *Actress* (69)
Robert Mitchell, *Director*
Henry de Montherlant, *Playwright* (76)
Edna Morris, *Actress*
Janet Munro, *Actress* (38)
Bill Nagy, *Actor* (51)
Rina Nikeve, *Ballerina* (75)
Geoffrey Ost, *Director*
Reginald Owen, *Actor* (85)
Val Parnell, *Impresario* (78)
A. D. Peters, *Critic and Agent* (80)
Bert Postlethwaite, *Linkman* (62)
Klaus Prigheim, *Director* (89)
Peggy Rae, *Actress* (77)
Clarence Raybould, *Conductor* (85)
Josif Rayevski, *Actor* (71)
Cyril Raymond, *Actor*
Matthew Ricketts, *Theatrical Lawyer* (91)
John Roberts, *Impresario* (56)
Harry Robinson, *Stage Carpenter* (67)
Peggy Rowan, *Actress*
Lucy Rowlands, *Actress* (97)
Dame Margaret Rutherford, *Actress* (80)
Anthony Sagar, *Actor* (52)
J. Rowland Sales, *Theatre Valuer* (82)
Alfred Sangster, *Actor* (92)
Elizabeth Scott, *Designer* (74)
Anthony Selby, *Theatre Manager*
Raymond Somerville, *Actor* (75)
John Sullivan, *Technical Director*
Russell Thorndike, *Actor* (87)
Ben Toff, *Technical Director*
Helen Traubel, *Opera Singer* (69)
Bruce Walker, *Actor* (66)
Margaret Webster, *Director* (67)
Michael Weight, *Designer* (66)
Frank Weil, *Band Manager*

Index

Compiled by F. D. Buck

Numbers and letters in italics refer to illustrations

Ad Hoc, 102
Adrian, Max, 10, 44
Aeschylus, 106
After Magritte, 119
Agate, James, 136
Ah, Wilderness, 106
Ain't Supposed to Die a Natural Death, 120
Albee, Edward, 38
Albert, Lewis M., 44
Albery, Donald, 44, 45
Alchemist, The, 81, 83
Aldridge, Michael, 33, 35
Alferoff, Tamara, 125
Alice in Wonderland, 121, 129
Allen, Patrick, 66, *6d*
All Over, 38
Alpha Alpha, 52
Alpha Beta, 38
Alston, Richard, 103
Amaya, Carmen, 22
Ambrose, David, 38
An Clò Mor, 98
An Italian Straw Hat, *3c*
An Othello, *5b*
Anderson, Lindsay, 35
Animal Farm, 67
Annals, Michael, 32, 70, 74, 76
Anouilh, Jean, 35, 107, 111, 112
Antony and Cleopatra, 55, 58, 59, *6b*
Antrobus, John, 42
Apparitions, 134
Applause, 44, *4a*
Arden, John, 10, 33, 34, 38, 65, 66
Aristophanes, 113
Armstrong's Last Goodnight, 33
Arrabal, Fernando, 119
Art of Coarse Acting, The, 85
Arturo Ui, 45
Ashcroft, Dame Peggy, 39, 55, 112, *4f*
Asherton, Ernée, 35
Ashton, Frederick, 134
As You Like It, 54
Atkins, Eileen, 33, *3e*, *3g*
Ayrton, Norman, 144, 147, 150

Bacall, Lauren, *1a*
Baddeley, Hermione, 22
Bailey, Robin, 82,
Baker, Sophie, 11
Baker, the Baker's Wife and the Baker's Boy, The, 111
Bakst, Leon, 133
Ballade, 101
Ballygonbeen Bequest, The, 51
Banana Box, The, 108
Banbury, Frith, 43
Barber and the Cow, The, 12
Barker, Howard, 52
Barnes, Bill, 159
Barnes, Kenneth, 140
Barrault, Jean-Louis, 20, 25
Barrie, Barbara, *13a*
Barry, Mr., 150
Bart, Lionel, 124
Barton, John, 58, 63
Batell, Bertram, 103
Baxter, Jane, 35
Baxter, Keith, 112,
Beaton, Sir Cecil, 11, 132–9
Beaumarchais, Pierre Augustin, 91
Beaumont, Hugh, 10
Beauty and the Beast, 98
Beckett, Samuel, 38, 42
Beethoven, Ludwig von, 101

Beggar's Opera, The, 121
Beheading, The, 38
Béjart, Maurice, 104
Bell, Marie, 23, 24
Belles, Baubles and Balls, 170
Bellow, Saul, 121
Benedetti, Jean-Norman, 144, 151
Bennett, Hywel, 82
Bennett, Jill, 41
Berberian, Cathy, 99
Bérénice, 23
Bergman, Ingmar, 24
Bergner, Elizabeth, 22
Bergstrom, Beata, 11
Berio, Luciano, 99
Bickerstaff's Establishment, 52
Big Wolf, 42
Black Comedy, 34
Blaikie, Julia, *11b*
Blakeley, Colin, 60, *6c*
Blakemore, Michael, 9, 70, 74, 75, 76
Blatchley, John, 146
Block, Timothy, 152
Blood Wedding, 107
Blow Job, 40
Bodywork, 108
Bolt, Robert, 33, 34, 199
Bond, C. G., 111
Bond, Edward, 35, 42, 121
Book of Proverbs, 65
Boulez, Pierre, 90
Bragg, Melvyn, 67
Brand, 107
Brasseur, Pierre, 20
Break at Noon (*see Partage de Midi*)
Breath, 42
Brecht, Bertolt, 33
Brenton, Howard, 50, 52, 127
Brett, Jeremy, 112
Briers, Richard, 113, *12a*
Britannicus, 23
Britten, Benjamin, 90
Brook, Peter, 55, 139
Brown, John Russell, 9
Bruce, Christopher, 102
Brustein, Robert, 60
Bryden, Bill, 106, 130
Bryden, Ronald, 11
Buchner, Georg, 49, 50
Bucknell, Peter, 145, 147
Bugiarda, La, 25
Buhs, Jise, 11
Bullins, Ed, 121
Burge, Stuart, 108
Bury, John, 79, 130
Bury, Margaret, 145, 146, 147
But for the Grace of God, 22
Butler Did It And Judging By The Smile On His Face He's Been Doing It For Years, The, 86

CADESTROM, BARONESS (*see* Patti, Adelina)
Caesar and Cleopatra, *3h*
Calder, David, 64
Calder-Marshall, Anna, *3h*
Callas, Maria, 93
Camen, Art, *13a*
Camile, 162
Camino Real, 159
Canning, Heather, 64
Captain of Kopenick, The, 24
Caretaker, The, 40
Carmen, 94
Carmen, Art, *13a*
Carravaggio Buddy, 130
Casson, Lewis, 92
Castlerose, Lord, 16, 17
Cato Street, 83
Caucasian Chalk Circle, The, 33, *3k*
Cazenove, Christopher, 142
Chairs, The, 81
Challis, John, 152
Chalk Garden, The, 136
Chances, The, 27, 29, 30
Chappell, Eric, 108
Charley's Aunt, 37
Charlip, Remy, 98, 103
Charon, Jaques, 24, *2e*
Chat en Poche (*see Pig in a Poke*)
Cheeseman, Peter, 105, 110
Chekhov, Anton Pavlovich, 31, 35, 52, 107, 128, 139
Chesworth, John, 102
Chopin, Frédéric François, 92
Church, Tony, 63
Cinderella, *11a*
Clandestine Marriage, The, 36, *3j*
Claudel, Paul, 21, 106
Clements, John, 9, 27, 30, 34, 35, 112, *3a*
Clifford, Roger, 11
Clyde, Jeremy, 74
Cochran, C. B., 134
Cocktail Party, The, 29, 30, *3g*
Coco, *15i*
Codran, Michael, 38, 42, 43, 45
Coe, Peter, 33
Coffey, Denise, 81, 83
Cohan, Robert, 103
Cohen, Alexander, 44
Cold, 103
Collyer, Hester, 112
Colvin, Sheila, 126
Comdon, Michael, 9

Comedy of Errors, 59, 82
Company, 44
Considering the Lilies, 103
Cooper, Ewan, 105
Corelli, Marie, 167
Coriolanus, 55, 56, 57, 58
Cosi Fan Tutti, 91
Cottesloe, Lord, 10
Country Wife, The, 36
Courtenay, Tom, 43
Coward, Noël, 10, 21, 22, 41, 43, 100, 109, 136, *frontispiece*
Cowardy Custard, 41
Cranko, John, 98, 100
Crete and Sergeant Pepper, 42
Crickmay, Anthony, 11
Cries from Casement, 67
Crisis in Heaven, 136
Crisis of Conscience, 113
Critic, The, 113
Cross-Ways, The, 167
Crown Matrimonial, 43
Crucible, The, 121
Crutwell, Hugh, 143, 146, 147, 151
Cummings, Constance, 70
Cunliffe, Alan, 11
Cunningham, Merce, 104
Curtains, 130
Cymbeline, 54

DACQMINE, JACQUES, 23
Dale, Jim, 80, 81, *8c*
Daly, Joxer, 105
Dame aux Camelias, La, 23, 135
Dance, 103
Dance Energies, 103
Dances at a Gathering, 92
Dankworth, John, 82
Dante, Alighieri, 99
D'Arcy, Margaretta, 10
Dare, Phyllis, 168
Dare, Zena, 168
Darrell, Peter, 97
Daubeny, Sir Peter, 11, 20–6
David, Michael, 121
Day After the Fair, The, 43
Dean, Isabel, 112
Dear Antoine, 35
Deathwatch, 81
Debden, Hilary, 97
Deep Blue Sea, The, 112
Delfont, Bernard, 43, 44, 45
Delius, Frederick, 101
Demarco, Ricky, 125, 126, 127, 129
Devil Is An Ass, The, 108
Devine, George, 42
Dexter, John, 31, 78
Dignam, Mark, 57, *6a*
Dinner, Tony, 145, 146, 149
Dirtiest Show, 45
Divine Comedy, The, 99
Docherty, Peter, 101
Doctor's Dilemma, The, 137
Doll's House, A, 106
Dominic, 11
Donat, Robert, 64
Donizetti, Gaetano, 91
Donn, Jorge, 104
Don Pasquale, 94
Don't Bother Me I Can't Cope, 120
Don't Pinch the Teaspoons, 108
Don't Play Us Cheap, 120
Dossor, Alan, 110
Dostoievsky, Fydor Mihailovich, 62
Downright Hooligan, 111
Drake, Gabrielle, *4e*
Duchess of Danzig, The, 166
Duff-MacCormick, Cara, 154–60 *passim*
Dumas, Alexandre (fils), 23, 135
Dunham, Katherine, 22
Dunlop, Frank, 44, 81, 82, 84, 130
Duplex, The, 121
Dusart, Richard, *13b*
Dwarfs, The, 82

Ecoutez Bien, Messieurs, 23
Edgar, David, 51, 113
Edmond, Terence, 108
Edward VII, 167
Egan, Peter, 40
Eliot, T. S., 29, 34, 64
Elliot, Andrew, 127
Elliott, Denholm, 41
Enemies, 65
Enfants du Paradis, Les, 20
Enghien, Bois d', *2e*
England's Ireland, 50
Espert, Nuria, *2f*
Etherege, Sir George, 106
Euripides, 106
Evans, Edith, 35
Eveling, Stanley, 127
Evershed-Martin, Leslie, 28
Eyre, Ronald, 41

FAIRWEATHER, DAVID, 11
Faixat, Estudo, 11
Fallen Angels, 22
Farmer's Wife, 30
Farrow, Mia, 107, 114
Fasken, David, 39
Fedo, Miss, 148
Ferris, Barbara, 41
Feuillère, Edwige, 21, 23, 24

Feydeau, Georges, 107, 109
Fidelio, 91
Field Figures, 99, 101
Fielding Harold, 44
Fil à la patte, Un, 24, *2e*
Filippo, Peppino de, Company, 25, *2a*
Finlay, Frank, 33
Finney, Albert, 33, 38, 41
First Shoot, The, 134
Fiske, Alison, 65
Fleetwood, Susan, 63
Fletcher, John, *11a*
Follow The Sun, 134
Fonteyn, Margot, 100, 134, *11c*
Ford, John, 109
For Sylvia, 52
For those who die as cattle, 102
Foster, Julia, 39, 43
Foursome, The, 38
Fraser, Bill, 33
Fraser, Lovat, 133
Fridh, Gertrud, *2b*
Friend, Philip, 121
Front Page, The, 75, 76, 77, *7c*
Furse, George, 119

GABLER, HEDDA, 24, 41, *2b*
Gainsborough Girls, The, 139
Gale, John, 39
Gaskill, William, 41, 42
Gautier, Jean-Jaques, 21
Gay Invalid, The, 22
Gay Pavillion, The, 22
Geddes, Peter, 63
Genet, Jean, 83, 121
George, Colin, 109
George Jackson and the Black and White Minstrel Show, 47
Gide, André, 21
Gielgud, John, 41, 42, 136, 157, *3k*
Gigi, 137, *15f*
Gingold, Hermione, 22
Ginsberg, Allen, 121
Giselle, 103
Glenville, Peter, 154, 155, 156, 158, 160, *17b*
Godspell, 119, 120
Going Home, 52
Goldby, Derek, 112
Goldoni, Carlo, 33
Goldsmith, Oliver, 83
Gone With the Wind, 44
Good Humoured Ladies, The, 133
Goodman, Lord, 96
Good Old Bad Old Days, The, 44
Gordon, Richard, 86, 87
Gore, Walter, 98
Gorky, Maxim, 65, 108
Gostelow, Gordon, 65, *6f*
Grab (*see Plutus*)
Graham, Martha, 22, 104
Grainger, Gawn, *7d*
Grand Magic Circus, 47, 48
Grand Tour, 100
Grant, Micki, 120
Granville-Barker, Harley, 61
Grease, 119
Great Coquelin, 169
Great Exhibition, The, 40
Great Northern Welly Boot Show, The, 129
Greenwood, Joan, *16c*
Greer, Herb, 40
Gregg, Hubert, 33, 35
Gregory, André, 116, 121, 129
Grey, Beryl, 102
Grey, Simon, 119
Griffith, Hugh, 113, *12c*
Griffiths, Trevor, 62
Grillo, John, 52
Grosse Fuge, 101
Grotowski, 121
Grout, James, *4f*
Groves-Raines, Nick, 130
Guare, John, 120
Gudgeon, Mark, 11
Guilbert, Yvette, 92
Guinness, Alec, *3g*
Guitry, Sacha, 23
Gullachsen, Willoughby, 11
Guthrie, Tyrone, 30

Hair, 120, 143, 163, 166, 169
Hall, George, 144, 147, 149, 151
Hall, Peter, 9, 61, 79, 84, *7b*
Hambourg, Mark, 169
Hamlet, 18, 54, 121
Hammond, Kay, 112
Hampshire, Susan, 106
Hampton, Christopher, 42
Handke, Peter, 121
Handman, Wyn, 121
Hands, Terry, 64, 130
Harborth, Sheila, 130
Hare, David, 40, 50
Harlock, Peter, 11
Harris, Rosemary, 118, *13c*
Harrison, John, 9
Harrison, Kathleen, *16d*
Harrison, Tony, 77, 78, 79
Harrow, Lisa, 64
Hauptmann von Köpenick, Der, *2c*
Hauser, Frank, 10
Haynes, Jim, 123, 124, 125, 127, 129
Haynes, John, 11, 99

Heartbreak House, 36
Hecht, Ben, 75, 77
Heine, Heinrich, 92
Henry IV, 133
Henry V, 138
Henson, Nicky, 83, *8a*
Hewitt, Muriel, 13
Hilary, Jennifer, 108, 112
Hirst, Joan, 11
Hitler Dances, 52
Hobson, Harold, 66, 124, 129
Hochhuth, Rolf, 117
Holloway, Stanley, 38
Home, William Douglas, 39
Hopkins, Anthony, 73, *3f*, *7d*
Hopps, Stuart, 98
Hordern, Michael, 71, 72, *7e*
House of Bernarda Alba, The, 107
How Beautiful with Badges, 52
Hughes, Ted, 82
Huis Clos, 21
Hume, David, 123*n*
Humphrey, Mrs., 163, 164, 165
Hunter, Ian, 44
Hurst, Allan, 11
Hynd, Ronald, 101
Hywell, Suzanne, 99

I and Albert, 44
Ibsen, Henrik, 33, 107, 139
I, Claudius, 39
Ideal Husband, An, 137
Impossible Theatre, The, 28
In a Summer Garden, 101
Inferno, 99
Ingram, Philip, 11
In the Heart of the British Museum, 130
Ionesco, Eugene, 81
Irene, 160, 161
Irving, Jules, 120
Island of the Mighty, The, 61, *6d*
Italian Straw Hat, An, 33

JACOBI, DEREK, 113, *12a*
Jago, Raphael, 144, 151
James, Emrys, 63, 64, 66
James, Henry, 91
James, Peter, 81, 84
Jay, Isabel, 168
Jeffrey, Douglas, 11
Jesus Christ Superstar, 44, 119, *4c*
Johnson, Richard, 58, 59, *6b*
Jones, David, 60–7
Jones, Freddie, 111
Jones, Henry Arthur, 106, 112
Jonson, Ben, 108
Joseph and the Amazing Technicolor Dreamcoat, 44, 82
Journey's End, 40, *4b*
Joyeux Chagrins (*Present Laughter*), 21
Joy, Valerie, 168
Julius Caesar, 55, 56, 57, 58, 84, 87, *6a*
Jumpers, 38, 70, 71, 72, *7e*

Kaddish, 121
Kane, Jack, 124
Karenina, 137
Kay, Richard, 81
Kaye, Danny, 33
Keach, Stacy, 121
Kean, 45
Keeler, Ruby, 119
Kemp, Jeremy, 40
Kemp, Lindsay, 129
Ken Campbell Road Show, The, 129
Kerr, Deborah, 43
Kestelman, Sara, 112
Kidd, Robert, 127
Kilbrandon, Lord, 126
Kipps, 137
Kohler, Estelle, 66, *6d*
Kohlhaas, 107
Kontakion, 103
Korda, Sir Alexander, 137
Kulukundis, Eddie, 40, 43, 45

La Traviata, *15c*
Laban, Rudolph, 149
Laborintus, 99
Ladies Ladies! 102,
Lady Windermere's Fan, 136, *15d*, *15e*
Laine, Cleo, 82
Lakmé, 95
Lambert, Constant, 134
Land, David, 45
Lane, Terry, 126, 127
Langtry, Lily, 167
Lapotaire, Jane, 81
Last Analysis, The, 121
Late Sir Christopher Bean, The, 107
Laughton, Charles, *16b*
Laurence, Charles, 43
Lawrence, Gertrude, 43
Lawson, Wilfred, 65
Lay-By, 40, 130
Layton, Joe, 100
Leary, Timothy, 124
Leigh, Vivien, 21
Lemmon, Jack, 119
Leno, Dan, 169
Leventon, Annabel, 81, 142, 152, 153
Lewenstein, Oscar, 41, 42
Lewin, John, 109

Liars, The, 106, 112
Liebman, Marvin, 39
Life of the General, A, 106
Linklater, Eric, 136
Linklater, Kristen, 56
Lipman, Maureen, 77
Lipscomb, William, 22
Listen to the Music, 103
Lister, Laurier, 105
Liszt, Franz, 134
Little Black Dress, 139
Little Night Music, A, 161
Lloyd, Bernard, 63, 65, 66, *6f*
Lloyd George Knew my Father, 39, *4f*
London Assurance, 43
Long Day's Journey into Night, 70, 76
Long, Mark, 130
Lonsdale, Frederick, 22
Look Back in Anger, 83, *8a*
Lopez, Pilar, 22
Lorca, Federico Garcia, 26, 107
Lorrayne, Vyvyan, 101
Lost Horizon, 154
Louis, Murray, 104
Lower Depths, The, 61, 65, *6f*
Low Moan Spectacular, 129
Lubovitch, Lar, 103
Lucia di Lammermoor, 91
Luisillo, 22
Lunt, Alfred, 136

MACARTHUR, CHARLES, 75, 77
McCallion, Mr., 148
Macbeth (Shakespeare), 73, 74, 75, 86, 112, 113, 139, *7d*, *12b*
Macbeth (Verdi), 89
MacCormick, Cara Duff, *17b*
McCoy Real, The, 113
MacDermott, Galt, 120
MacDonald, Craig, 11
McDonald, Elaine, 97
McDougall, Gordon, 127
McEnery, Peter, 82
McFuzz, Hamish, 128
McGinn, Peter, 125
McGinn, Walter, *13b*
McGrath, Barry, 101
McGrath, John, 51, 52, 110
McKellen, Ian, 10, 109, *12d*
Mackler, Nancy, 130
MacMillan, Kenneth, 100, 101
MacNamara, Desmond, *8b*
MacNaughtan, Alan, 74, 76
McOwan, Michael, 153
Mabinogian, The, 66
Madge of Truth (*see Manners for Men*)
Magdalany, Philip, 67
Magic Flute, The, 94
Maids, The, 83
Malade Imaginaire, Le, 22
Malbrook s'en va-t-en guerre, 92
Malcontent, The, 108
Malmgren, Yat, 146
Man and Superman, 112
Mander, Ray, 11
Manen, Hans van, 101
Man for all Seasons, 33
Man Most Likely To . . ., The, 146
Manners for Men, 163
Mantle, Doreen, 52
Marcus, Frank, 39
Marguerite and Armand, 134, *15b*
Marowitz, Charles, 49, *5b*
Marriage of Figaro, 91, 94
Marshall, Mr., 150
Marston, John, 108
Martin, John, 126, 127
Martin, Mel, *8a*
Martin, Millicent, 33
Mary Stuart, 121
Mason, Brewster, 64
Massey, Daniel, 44
Master Builder, 122
Mating Game, The, 39
Matthews, A. E., 22
Mavor, Ronald, 106
Maxwell, James, 40
May, Val, 105
Medea, 106
Mendelssohn Symphony, 102
Menuhin, Yehudi, 129
Mercer, David, 35, 40, 72
Merchant of Venice, The, 61, 63, 87
Merrick, David, 116, 154
Messel, Oliver, 136
Metamorphosis of a Wandering Minstrel, 25
Meyer, Laverne, 98, 99
Michell, Keith, 27, 28, 29, 34, 36, *3b*
Midgley, Robin, 108
Midsummer Night's Dream, A, 82, 139
Mielziner, Joe, 156
Mikado, The, 165
Miles, Sarah, *3d*
Miles, Sir, Bernard, 40
Millar, Gertie, 168
Miller, Arthur, 121
Miller, Jason, 121
Miller, Jonathan, 9, 75
Mills, John, 41
Misanthrope, The, 77, 78
Missen, David, 126
Miss Julie, 62
Mitchell, Tom, 125

Mitchell, Yvonne, 111
Mitchenson, Joe, 11
Moffat, John, 38
Moiseiwitsch, Tanya, 78, 109
Molière, 22, 77, 78, 79, 80
Montgomery, Robert, 62
Moonchildren, 118, 154
Moreland, Barry, 103
Moreno, Juan, *12d*
Morgan, Gareth, 111
Morike, 92
Morin, Patrick, 11
Morley, Christopher, 59
Morrice, Norman, 102
Morse, Bobby, 119
Mortimer, John, 24
Mottram, Simon, 99
Mower, Patrick, 112
Mozart, Wolfgang Amadeus, 90, 91
Mueller, Harald, 42
Murder in the Cathedral, 61, 64, *6e*
Murdoch, Iris, 109, 110
Muschamp, Thomas, 38
My Fair Lady, 137, 138, *15h*
My Fat Friend, 43

NAHAT, DENIS, 102
Naples by Day, 26
Naples by Night, 26
Narrow Road to the Deep North, 121
Neville, John, 129
Newley, Anthony, 44
Newman, Ernest, 91
Nicholas, Peter, 72
Night Watch, 119
Nijinsky, Clown of God, 104
Nilsson, Birgit, 93
Nixon, President Richard, 161
Noh Theatre, *2d*
No, No, Nanette, 119
Notes on a Love Affair, 39
Not I, 38, 42, *4d*
Noye's Fludde, 90
Nuits de la Colère, Les, 21
Nunn, Trevor, 54–60, 61, 63
Nureyev, Rudolf, 99

O'CASEY, SEAN, 108
Occupations, 62
O'Donnell, May, 103
O'Donovan, Desmond, 32
Oedipe, 21
Oedipus, 81, 113, *8b*
Oedipus Now, 50
Offenbach, Jaques, 97
Oh! Calcutta! 45
Oh Les Beaux Jours, 25
Old Ones, The, 42
Old Times, 118, *13c*
Olivier, Sir Laurence, 9, 11, 12–9, 20, 21, 23, 27, 30, 31, 32, 34, 36, 68, 70, 79, 81, 82, 84, 138 *1*, *7a*
O'Neill, Colette, 126
O'Neill, Eugene Gladstone, 76, 106
On the Road, 52
Open House, 111
Oresteia, 91
Orton, Joe, 72
Osborne, John, 35, 38, 41, 42, 110
Othello, 61, 63
Othello, An, 49
Out Cry, 154, 159, *17a*
Out of Sight, 52
O.W., 101

PAGE, ANTHONY, 38, 41
Pantanglieze, 130
Papp, Joseph, 116, 120, 121
Parent's Day, 39
Partage de Midi, 21, 39, 106
Pasco, Richard, 64, *6e*
Pattern for an Escalator, 102
Patti, Adelina (Baroness Cadestrom), 169
Pavillons, Les, 136
Peace In Our Time, 109
Pedley, Anthony, 86, 87
Peebles, Melvin van, 120
Peepshow, 98
Peer Gynt, 33
Pelléas et Mélisandre, 90
Peppino de Filippo Company, *2a*
Persian Wars, The, 109
Persians, The, 106
Petit, Roland, 22
Phèdre, 23, 39
Phillips, Jennifer, 108
Phillips, Robin, 9, 35, 62, 107
Pickup, Ronald, 73, 81, *8b*
Pig in a Poke, 107
Pilbrow, Richard, 40, 44
Pinero, Sir William Wing, 35, 106
Pinter, Harold, 9, 35, 40, 79, 82, 118
Pirandello, Luigi, 133
Plaisir de rompre, Le, 24
Play Pictorial, The, 166
Plays and Players, 24
Pleasance, Donald, 119
Plough and the Stars, The, 108
Plouviez, Peter, 141, 152
Plowright, Joan, 32, 36, *3f*
Plugged In, 51
Plutus, 113
Poème de l'Extase, 100, *11c*
Poltroon, The, 101

Po' Miss Julie, 40, *4e*
Popkiss, 39, 44, 106
Portrait of a Lady, 136
Potter, Mrs. Brown, 167
Pourchot, Jacques, 11
Present Laughter (*see Joyeaux Chagrins*)
Priestley, J. B., 111
Prince, Hal, 161
Prince, Harold, 44
Prisoner of Second Avenue, The, 118, *13a*
Private Lives, 43, *4g*
Private Matter, A, 106
Prodigal Daughter, The, 114
Prods, Julie Daugherty, 38
Prokofiev, Serge, 100
Provoked Wife, The, 107
Puccini, Giacomo, 135
Puce à l'orielle, Une, 24
Purnell, Louis, 81
Pygmalion, 138
Python, Monty, 72

Q Planes, *1*
Quadrille, 136, 137
Quartet, 98
Quigley, Jane, 125
Quilley, Denis, 70, 73, 75, 76, *7c*

RABB, ELLIS, 121
Rabe, David, 118, 120
Rattigan, Terence, 40, 112
Real Inspector Hound, The, 119
Redgrave, Michael, 32, 55
Redgrave, Vanessa, 83
Redman, Joyce, 35
Reed Gavin, 81
Rees, Roger, 64, 86, 87
Renard, Jules, 24
Restoration of Arnold Middleton, The, 127
Revenger's Tragedy, 63
Reynolds, Debbie, 160, 161
Richard II, 73, 74
Richard III, 20, *12a*
Richardson, Penny, 130
Richardson, Sir Ralph, 12, 13, 17, 39, *1*, *4f*
Richardson, Tony, 39
Ride Across Lake Constance, The, 121
Rigg, Diana, 72, 74, 79, *7e*
Ring of the Nibelung, The, 91, 94
Rivals, The, 35
Robbins, Jerome, 92
Roberts, Rachel, 38
Robertson, Andrew, 83
Robertson, Patrick, 75
Robson, Flora, *16a*
Romeo and Juliet, 81, 113
Ronald, Landon, 169
Roose-Evans, James, 50
Rose, Jurgen, 100
Rossini, Gioachino Antonio, 90
Rossiter, Leonard, 40, 108
Royal Hunt of the Sun, The, 32, 36
Rudkin, David, 67
Rudman, Michael, 9
Ruling Class, The, 108
Ruling the Roost, 109
Rutherford, Margaret, 36, *3j*
Ryton, Royce, 43

ST. CLAIRE, MARIAN, 97
Saint-Denis, Michel, 147, 148, 150
St. George and the Dragon, 51
St. Joan, 31, 36
Salacrou, Armand, 21
Sands, Leslie, 111
Sanguinetti, Edoardo, 99
Satre, Jean-Paul, 21
Satton, Lon, *4e*
Saunders, James, 107
Savary, Jerome, 47, 49
Scapino, 80, 81, 83, *8c*
Scenes from the Music of Charles Ives, 103
Schiller, Johann, 92, 121
Schlesinger, John, 9, 79
School for Scandal, The, 15, 75, 133, *15a*
Schubert Variations, 99
Schumann, Robert Alexander, 92
Schweigsame Frau, Die, 94
Scofield, Paul, 24
Scoglio, Joseph, 102
Scott, Terry, 39
Scoulor, Angela, *12c*
Screens, The, 121
Second Mrs. Tanqueray, The, 136
Secretary Bird, The, 37
Section Nine, 67
Semi-Detached, 114
Sense of Detachment, A, 42
Serguéef, Nicolai, 100
Servant of Two Masters, A, 33
Seymour, Lynn, 99
Shaffer, Peter, 32, 34
Shaft, 120
Shakespeare, William, 18, 28, 30, 49, 54, 55, 61, 63, 64, 72, 79, 81, 92, 113
Shaw, Robert, 118, *13c*
Shepherd, Jack, 129, *12d*
Shepherd, Sam, 52
Sheppard, Morgan, 65
Sheridan, Richard Brinsley, 75, 113, 133
She Would If She Could, 106
Sibelius, Jean Christian, 99
Siege, 38

Sim, Alastair, 38, *3i*
Simmons, Pip, 128
Simon, Neil, 118
Simpson, Michael, 9
Sirènes, Les, 136
Sitwell, Edith, 133
Sitwell, Osbert, 134
Skin of our Teeth, The, 33
Slade, Julian, 44
Slag, 40
Sleuth, 45
Sly, Christopher, 81
Small Craft Warnings, 119
Smith, Maggie, 24, 30, 43, 76, *4g*
Smith, Olivier, 137
Soirée Musicale, 98
Sokolow, Anna, 103
Some Like It Hot, 119
Sondheim, Stephen, 44
Sophocles, 113
Sousa, John Philip, 169
Spencer, Colin, 51
Sphinx, The, 126
Spurling, John, 109
Stafford-Clark, Max, 127
Stages, 103
Standing, John, 44
Stephens, Robert, 36, 43, *4g*
Stevens, Roger, 154
Stewart, Ellen, 116
Stewart, Patrick, 58
Sticks and Bones, 118, 120, 121
Stigwood, Robert, 44, 45
Stockhausen, Karl-Heinz, 99
Stop-Over, 102
Stoppard, Tom, 38, 71, 72, 83, 119
Storey, David, 127
Stravinsky, Igor, 124
Strindberg, August, 40
Stuart, Leslie, 169
Sty of the Blind Pig, The, 121
Subject to Fits, 62
Sugar, 119
Superfly, 120
Suzman, Janet, 59, *6b*
Swan Lake, 100, 102, 136
Swift, Clive, 35

TAGG, ALAN, 32
Tailleur pour Dames (*see Taylor for Ladies, A*)
Tailor for Ladies, A, 107
Tales of Hoffmann, 97
Taming of the Shrew, The, *3f*
Tammes, Diane, 11
Taylor, Cecil, 127
Taylor, Jonathan, 103
Tchaikovsky, Peter Ilyich, 98
Tchaikovsky Suite, 99
Tchekhov, Anton, 65
Tederella, 51
Tempest, The, 113, 139, 159, *12c*
Ter-Arutunian, Rouben, 100
Teresa, 22
Terson, Peter, 111
Tetley, Glen, 99, 100, 101
That Championship Season, 121, *13b*
Theatre Magazine, 167
There's a Girl in my Soup, 37, 107
There was a Time, 102, *11b*
They Put Handcuffs on the Flowers, 119
Thompson, Eric, 40, 112
Thorpe, Jonathan, 98, 99
Thoughts of Chairman Mao, 65
Three Arrows, The, 109, *12d*
Threequarter Profile, 99
Three Sisters, 25, 26, 107
Timbers, John, 11
Time and Time Again, 43
Time Out, 41
Timon, 54
Tintagel, 136
'Tis Pity She's A Whore, 109
Titus Andronicus, 55, 59, 60, *6c*
Tooth of the Crime, The, 52
Topol, 33, 36, *3k*
Town of Titipu, The (*see Mikado, The*)
Traveller Without Luggage, 107, 112
Travers, Ben, 44, 106
Traverse Tattoo, *14*
Traviata, La, 136
Trelawny, 44, 106
Trelawny of the 'Wells', 32
Trevor, William, 52
Triad, 100, 101
Tristan and Islode, 89
Troilus and Cressida, 63
Tudor, Anthony, 98, 99
Turandot, 135
Turner, David, 114
Twelfth Night, 86, 121
Twigs, 119
Two Character Play, The (*see Out Cry*)
Two Gentlemen of Verona, 120
Tynan, Kenneth, 24, 79

Un Fil à la Patte, *2e*
Uncle Vanya, 17, 31, 36
Unknown Soldier and his Wife, The, 34, 43, *3i*
Ure, Mary, 118, *13c*
Ustinov, Peter, 34, 35, 36, 43, *3i*

VALOIS, NINETTE DE, 96
Valse Triste, 99
Vanburgh, Sir John, 107
Vanessa, 136
Verdi, Guiseppe, 89
Veterans, 41
Vicious Circle, 21
Victoria, Queen, 167, 168
Vivat! Vivat! Regina, 33, 119, *3d*, *3e*
Voltaire, 92

WALKER, JIMMY, 126
Walton, William, 134
Wagner, Richard, 91
Wagoner, Dan, 104
Wanderer and his Shadow, The, 98
War and Peace, 86
Warner, David, 39, 52
Warren, Leigh, *11b*
Warwick, Richard, 82
Weller, Michael, 118
Welles, Orson, 124
Wesker, Arnold, 35, 42
Wheeler, Hugh, 158
Whistler, Rex, 136
White, Michael, 39, 45
Whitehead, E. A., 38
Whitelaw, Billie, 42
White Raven, The, 108
Wilde, Oscar, 112, 128, 136
Wilder, Billy, 119
Williams, Clifford, 59
Williams, David, 73
Williams, Emlyn, 107
Williams, Heathcote, 127
Williams, Kenneth, 43
Williams, Peter, 11
Williams, Red, 125
Williams, Tennessee, 40, 119, 154–62, *17a*, *17c*
Willie Rough, 106
Willis, Ted, 111
Wilson, Reg, 11
Wilson, Robert, 116, 121
Wilson, Snoo, 50
Wilton, Penelope, 142, 146, 149
Winckley, Rosemary, 11
Wise Child, 119
Within Walls, 99
Wolf, Hugo, 92
Wood, Charles, 41
Wood, Henry J., 169
Wood, John, 58, 59, *6a*
Wood, Peter, 71
Woodthorpe, Peter, 65
Workhouse Donkey, The, 33
Worth, Irene, 35
Wound, The, 82
Woyzeck, 50

YAMASH'TA, STOMU, 48, *5a*
Yerma, 26, *2f*
York, Michael, *17a*, *17b*
York, Patricia, 11
Young Mr. Pitt, The, 137

ZEFFIRELLI, FRANCO, 162